ANTHROPOLOGISTS IN THE FIELD

ANTHROPOLOGISTS IN THE FIELD

Cases in Participant Observation

Edited by Lynne Hume and Jane Mulcock

Columbia University Press   New York

Columbia University Press
Publishers Since 1893
New York   Chichester, West Sussex
Copyright © 2004 Columbia University Press
All rights reserved

Library of Congress Cataloging-in-Publication Data

Anthropologists in the field : cases in participant observation /
edited by Lynne Hume and Jane Mulcock.
p. cm.
Includes bibliographical references and index.
ISBN 978–0–231–13004–2 (alk. paper)
ISBN 978–0–231–13005–9 (pbk. : alk. paper)
1. Participant observation. 2. Ethnology—Field work.
3. Ethnology—Methodology. 4. Anthropological ethics.
I. Hume, Lynne. II. Mulcock, Jane.

GN346.4.A68   2004
305.8'0072'3—dc22   2004052786

Columbia University Press books are printed on permanent and
durable acid-free paper.

Printed in the United States of America

We dedicate this volume to Jonathon Telfer, who passed away while it was still in preparation. An edited version of his paper appears as chapter 6.

CONTENTS

ACKNOWLEDGMENTS

The editors would like to thank the people who contributed to the production of this volume. Martin Forsey and Gillian Hutcherson provided constant discussion, support, and encouragement. Jill Rundle, Victoria Burbank, and Greg Accaioili shared important theoretical and methodological insights. David Trigger provided patience and advice. Thanks are also due to each of the contributors whose work is showcased here, who labored to meet our deadlines in the midst of their own busy schedules.

Lynne Hume and Jane Mulcock

INTRODUCTION: Awkward Spaces, Productive Places

Ethnographic research involves the use of a variety of techniques for collecting data on human beliefs, values, and practices. The ethnographer's core methodology, participant observation, requires that researchers simultaneously observe and participate (as much as possible) in the social action they are attempting to document. The rationale for this approach is that; by "being there" and actively taking part in the interactions at hand, the researcher can come closer to experiencing and understanding the "insider's" point of view.[1] At the same time, the practice of ethnography also assumes the importance of maintaining enough intellectual distance to ensure that researchers are able to undertake a critical analysis of the events in which they are participating. This means that they should be willing, and able, to take a step back from the relationships they form with the people they encounter in the field for long enough to identify and reflect upon some of the taken-for-granted rules and expectations of the social world they are studying. The ethnographer must be able to see with the eyes of an outsider as well as the eyes of an insider, although both views are, of course, only ever partial. Good participant observation thus requires a self-conscious balance between intimacy with, and distance from, the individuals we are seeking to better understand. By definition, participant observers deliberately place themselves in a series of very awkward social spaces, some of which are more difficult to inhabit than others.

The uncomfortable and contradictory nature of these fieldwork relationships has long been acknowledged in anthropological and sociological literature (e.g., Powdermaker 1966; Malinowksi 1967; Golde 1986 [1970]; Hammersley & Atkinson 1995 [1983]) through a discourse of reflexivity that has become increasingly "mainstream" over the last three decades. This collection of sixteen original papers, by anthropologists and one religious studies scholar (Harvey), differs from similar publications in that it highlights the potential productivity of such ethnographic discomfort and awkwardness. The contributors describe a range of fieldwork experiences that left them feeling, at different stages in their academic careers, as though they had at least partially failed to achieve their goals as professional researchers. Each author also shows how careful reflection on these same experiences eventually allowed them to gain important insights into the nature of the social settings they were documenting. Together their work contributes to the important ongoing project of developing a candid and intellectually rigorous "ethnography" of participant observation.

This volume is intended to help normalize the occasional (or frequent) feelings of personal inadequacy and social failure that are, perhaps, an inevitable part of successful participant observation; deliberately attempting to simultaneously position oneself as both insider and outsider is, after all, socially disruptive. By resisting total integration and commitment to the social domains we are researching, by attempting to maintain our intellectual distance while also indicating our desire to "belong," we choose a socially anomalous identity that is fraught with inconsistency and ambiguity, both for ourselves and for our research participants. The personal and emotional costs of inhabiting such a space are often high. They also tend to be undertheorized. The papers included here combine to reveal some of the reasons why participant observation remains a powerful and seductive research tool, and why many of us continue to be committed to it, despite its deeply personal challenges and its often unexpected costs. Participant observation is primarily an "advanced" exercise in forming and maintaining intimate relationships for professional purposes. And therein lie its greatest strengths and its greatest weaknesses—as the stories that fill these pages so clearly show.

Our own awkward fieldwork experiences provided the initial impetus for this book. We describe them briefly here in order to illustrate the sort of research processes that we want to unravel in the hope that our readers may be better able to bypass some of the methodological anxieties and self-doubts that shape so many fieldwork encounters.

Lynne

In the mid-1980s I did thirteen months of fieldwork at Yarrabah, an Aboriginal community in northeast Queensland, Australia. My year there was the most difficult of my life. Believing that I had "proven" myself as an anthropologist during earlier research in a small, remote village on the Melanesian island of Vanuatu (see Hume 1985), I thought I was ready for any fieldwork situation. I soon realized, however, that different situations require different personal resources in order to assist the researcher in overcoming feelings of frustration and even despair. I suffered extreme angst throughout this research, but having spent so much time and effort in the preparatory stages, I felt obliged to complete the fieldwork.

In Yarrabah I learned how very difficult ethnographic research can be. My study focused on Aboriginal Christianity and the influence of the Anglican missionaries who established the Yarrabah mission station in the late nineteenth century (see Hume 1988). Missionary influence had eliminated almost all traces of Aboriginal languages at Yarrabah. Apart from a smattering of "lingo,"[2] Aboriginal English was the mode of communication. While this made my work easier because I did not have to learn a new language, there were many other factors that made it more difficult, including Aboriginal distrust of whites based on decades of racism, and different ways of communicating[3] and of managing time.[4] I was—as the Yarrabah community saw it—yet another white researcher coming to probe into their lives, to ask questions, and then to leave. I was an unnecessary presence, and I felt this acutely. Additionally, there were many different factions within the community, which meant that becoming friendly with members of one faction made it difficult to approach another. Community problems with violence and alcohol also added to my discomfort and unease.

Direct experience of these factors did, however, give me deep insight into life at Yarrabah. I learned, for example, how difficult it is for people with strong kinship ties to police situations of conflict that involve their own close kin.[5] I also learned that it was far easier to get to know people in the community if I visited with an Aboriginal person from outside. My key informant was Tom, an old man who had been taken to the mission by white police from north Queensland when he was a young child[6] and who had since been living away from Yarrabah for many years. I would sit down and talk with him and other elders about the past and, slowly, people began to accept that I was documenting life in mission times. When this became my established role, I felt more comfortable, although nearly all attempts at communication on this topic relied on my initiative.

I never experienced the same rapport with Yarrabah people as I had with the people of Vanuatu. I felt like an interloper—and the more I learned about the history of the place, and the way some of the old people had been treated in Queensland in the past (see Kidd 1997), the more I began to feel that my own "mission" was a somewhat selfish one that would probably do little to enhance the current situation in the community. Entrenched racist beliefs held by a few people in the nearby towns began to depress me. The history of distrust on both sides exacerbated my feelings of inadequacy, and I continually questioned my own reasons for being there. I survived this fieldwork period by escaping to Cairns (a 45-minute drive away) to visit friends and frequent the Saturday cafés with their cappuccinos, newspapers, and markets.[7]

Once I had left the field, I looked back on my time there as a lesson: that some researchers are better suited to some types of research situations than to others (see also Prattis 1997:63) but that even in the most distressing situations one can still gain insights and valuable data. Through my embodied experience of attempting to participate and observe, I gained a better understanding of the difficulties of Aboriginal community life, of local white and black attitudes toward each other, and of how political decisions and well-meaning intentions can formulate and structure communities and lives well into future generations. Nonetheless, my own emotions, and those of my informants, influenced my sense of self and of the worthiness of my project. I could understand entirely why the people of Yarrabah did not welcome me with open arms, but this did not make my work easier, or negate the feelings of self-pity that at times overwhelmed me. I decided that my next project would be in a community of people with whom I could have more rapport and ease of movement.[8]

Jane

For almost three years after completing my first attempt at ethnographic fieldwork I avoided looking at my field notes or interviews. The thought of reliving many of the experiences and apparent failures of that time was simply too hard to face. Although there were a few select moments and conversations that I truly enjoyed, the two years (1996–1998) I spent doing fieldwork on the use of indigenous imagery in the Australian alternative health and spirituality (alias "New Age") movement were predominantly marked by feelings of discomfort, uncertainty, awkwardness, disappointment, and sometimes even anger (see Mulcock 2001, 2002). Several expectations arising from my anthropological training, especially in relation to the concepts of relativism and rapport, contributed significantly to the feelings of failure and inadequacy that I experienced during this time.

Although I did my research "at home" in the city where I had grown up (Perth, Western Australia), the alternative health and spirituality scene was almost completely unfamiliar to me. In the early stages of my fieldwork I felt a degree of disorientation, or "culture shock." In contrast to Ida Fadzillah's (chapter 3) surprise at finding similarity where she expected difference, I was constantly amazed and confronted by the degree of difference I encountered. I had (naively) expected that similar cultural and educational backgrounds would ensure that my research participants and I would share the same basic understandings of the world. The ground seemed to tilt beneath me as I tried to loosen my grip on life-long, taken-for-granted assumptions about physical and metaphysical "realities" in order to respectfully consider a range of "New Age" cosmologies / theologies. This sense of vertigo was intensified by the fact that I was doing research in my home town; I was moving between the strange and the familiar on a daily basis. Unlike those ethnographers who say farewell to their own cultural settings to temporarily immerse themselves in other ways of being, I was trying to maintain my balance across two, not always distinct but frequently competing cultural domains.

The stigma associated with the "New Age" in academic and everyday discourses[9] meant that I had to struggle hard to find and maintain an appropriately relativist position from which to approach my fieldwork. This struggle was further complicated by my focus on discourses of cultural appropriation and my anthropological tendencies to favor the "subaltern" (Marcus 1995:101). I initially sympathized so strongly with indigenous critiques of "appropriation" that I was unable to appreciate the agendas of the non-Indigenous, New Age "appropriators" who were at the center of my study.[10]

Fernandez (1990) writes about the confusion that often occurs between the concepts of cultural relativism and moral relativism. He argues that as ethnographers we should be able to "suspend" any disbelief we might feel when listening to our "informants'" narratives, at least long enough to gain an empathic understanding of their position. This kind of relativism is not the same as taking a moral position on the content of those cultural narratives. Learning to temporarily suspend my disbelief in New Age philosophies in order to listen respectfully helped me to overcome feelings of guilt and personal compromise associated with applying my critical researcher's gaze to the beliefs and practices of individuals who were generous enough to contribute to my study and who often displayed their own vulnerability and disempowerment.

A conversation with one of my supervisors, Greg Accaioili, provided important insights into the awkwardness of straddling multiple, conflicting perspectives—my own, those of my research participants, and those of the scholars and Indigenous activists who took anti-appropriationist stances.[11] Accaioili talked about the uncomfortable business of inhabiting interstitial social spaces, a fate he suggested was common to many anthropologists who became caught between "field" and "home," belonging to both and neither. His reflections contained the possibility that, as ethnographers and individuals, we are perhaps destined to live in-between, a condition exacerbated by our primary research methodology, which requires us to simultaneously participate in and observe social action, to seek intimacy while maintaining distance.[12] These ideas eventually reconciled me to the awkwardness I felt throughout my fieldwork. They also helped me to recognize the intellectual productiveness of such awkwardness, the diagnostic value of analyzing discomfort.

Expectations associated with the notion of "rapport"—its central importance to ethnographic endeavors and the forms that it should take—were foundational to the feelings of disappointment and failure that accompanied me throughout my "New Age" research. The rapport that developed between myself and my research participants was functional enough, but intrinsically, perhaps unavoidably, limited for a combination of reasons including: age differences (I was almost always a lot younger than the people I was working with); personal agendas (I was seeking academic, not spiritual knowledge and my sympathies lay with the so-called subaltern); the multi-sited nature and internal structure of my "fieldsite" (see Mulcock 2001; Muir, chapter 14), including the busy lifestyles of the people I was working with; and the conflicting demands of participant observation (I repeatedly felt caught between two counteractive forces, one of which pulled my focus inward—the intention of the workshops themselves—and the other of which pushed my attention outward—for the purposes of gathering information, making observations, remembering descriptive details). In most instances the intimacy I achieved was limited to single interviews and fleeting connections at New Age events. This was not what I expected, or hoped for, from my fieldwork, primarily because it did not reflect my understanding of what makes a successful ethnography. I was eventually able to recognize, however, that my "failure" to develop ongoing friendships or collaborations[13] with my research participants was symptomatic of the values and forms of interaction that characterized the field itself.

My first experience of ethnographic fieldwork thus pushed me to think much more critically about the purposes and challenges of doing participant observation and the kind of knowledge that it produced. At the end of 1999 I wrote a paper for the annual meeting of the American Anthropological Association entitled "When Fieldwork Isn't Fun: Personality and Positionality in Ethnographic Research; or, Ethnography in Awkward Spaces."[14] This was the beginning of an intellectual and emotional process that eventually allowed me to complete the "ethnographic cycle" (Spradley 1980).

The Ethnography of Participant Observation

This collection of papers reflects a growing recognition among ethnographers of the value of reflexive research practice.[15] All of our contributors bring their own experiences and insights to the ongoing project of uncovering, revealing, and exposing the complexity and value of participant observation as an extremely challenging (despite its deceptively simple title) but potentially rewarding methodology for social research. By openly deconstructing, analyzing, and interrogating our fieldwork experiences we are helping to enhance public understanding of our methodology. By drawing attention to the particular skills it demands of us and the personal tests that it subjects us to, we are able to advertise its intricacies and its rigor.

Other recent collections have undertaken similar tasks. Some have focused on particularly difficult aspects of fieldwork such as violence (e.g., Nordstrom & Robben 1995), sexual encounters (e.g., Kulick & Willson 1995), and experiences of alternative realities (e.g., Young & Goulet 1994) or on the challenges of implementing specific approaches to fieldwork (e.g., Wolf 1996). Others have simply sought to provide personal, or "realistic," accounts of doing fieldwork (e.g., Hobbs & May 1993; Lareau & Schultz 1996; Grills 1998a; Watson 1999; Amit 2000a) or to demystify the process through which fieldwork becomes academic knowledge (e.g., Okely & Callaway 1992; Hastrup & Hervik 1994; Emoff & Henderson 2002). We add our voices to these, acknowledging the difficult, often emotionally "dirty" work of participant observation, but simultaneously emphasizing the outcomes that have made it worthwhile for us.

Participant observation requires researchers to use their social selves as their primary research tool (e.g., Powdermaker 1966:19; Stacey 1988:22; Kaplan Daniels 1983; Krieger 1985; Ganguly-Scrase 1993). For many ethnographers, drawing boundaries between the private and preexisting selves that they bring with them to the field and the researcher selves that they must develop once they arrive is constantly confronting.[16] Ongoing internal conflict, between the desire to act upon deeply ingrained personal values and the need to maintain a professional and relativist position as a researcher, tends to characterize the participant observation experience—as many fieldworkers observe, the intellectual habits and philosophical shifts that often come of engaging a methodology that makes demands of this kind can be seriously life-changing. Such personal conflict differs radically in extent and intensity according to the nature of the research site and the research participants, the particular research topic, and the strengths and limitations of the individual ethnographer. We argue that sensitivity to, and serious reflection on, these internal conflicts can lead to powerful and unexpected insights, not only into the social worlds being studied, but also into the nature of the participant observation methodology itself, and from there into the epistemology of ethnographic knowledge. Within this framework, very good ethnography often emerges from very difficult fieldwork experiences.

Relating to the Field: Engaging the Self/Other

Building relationships with potential research participants, whether or not these reflect "traditional" anthropological notions of rapport, is one of the central requirements of participant observation (e.g., Stacey 1988; Okely 1992; Grills 1998b; Turner 2000). If we want to gather fine-grained information about the beliefs, values, and practices of others we need to be able to relate to those others on a one-to-one basis. And for that we rely heavily on our own interpersonal skills. Participant observation is thus an intensely humanistic methodology based almost entirely on the messy, complicated, and often emotionally fraught interactions between two or more human beings, one of whom is the researcher.[17]

The relationships that researchers build with participants vary enormously, depending on many factors, including the ethnographer, the people with whom she or he is working, the topic being researched, the time frame for the study, and the ways in which the fieldsite and the activities carried out there are structured. In some situations the researcher will need only to establish and maintain a relationship with a participant long enough to organize and carry out a productive and mutually satisfying (or at least acceptable) interview. In other instances a researcher will be living and/or working in a community for many months, sometimes years, and will therefore be required to build long-term relationships with participants, relationships that may continue throughout the lifespans of those involved.

There are a number of common threads associated with the idea of participant observation as relationship that bind the papers in this volume together. The most obvious of these, not surprisingly, is the experience of being both inside and outside of the social action being documented. Each of the contributors reflects in some way on the tensions of the insider–outsider dynamic, the awkward experiences of simultaneously belonging and not belonging. Most draw attention to the variable dichotomies between participant and observer, self and other, subjectivity and objectivity, dichotomies that move in and out of focus, sometimes painfully sharp, sometimes so blurry and indistinct that the divisions become extremely difficult to sustain. This issue is perhaps highlighted as a result of the fact that all but one of the papers addresses some aspect of doing fieldwork at "home," an experience that inevitably complicates traditional anthropological paradigms based on assumed distinctions between researcher and researched, insider and outsider, similarity and difference (e.g., Narayan 1993).

Fadzillah found that her Thai research participants were more familiar with some of the cultural rules of her Malaysian "home" than she was; Angrosino, Shuttleworth, Forsey, Coggeshall, and Muir had prior or ongoing experience of aspects of their "fieldsites" through their employment and/or through friendship and leisure networks; Telfer, Colic-Peisker, Kurotani, and Teaiwa were "insiders" to the extent that they shared key elements of their own identities and experience with their research participants; Birckhead, Tourigny, Beckerleg & Hundt, Robinson, and Harvey have all worked with communities in their own countries of origin or long-term residence even though their cultural and socioeconomic backgrounds are quite different from those of their "informants." Even Kelly, the single exception to this pattern, acknowledges that aspects of her personal history allowed her to feel "at home" with Mexican prostitutes and their coworkers during her study of urban Chiapas.

There are thus varying degrees of "home" at work (or work at home) in the ethnographic experiences of those researchers who chose to contribute to a volume on the awkwardness of doing participant observation. Perhaps this is simply a coincidence. Or maybe one of the things that these papers demonstrate is that undertaking fieldwork in familiar settings has a tendency to intensify some of the anxieties associated with doing participant observation. Perhaps this pattern speaks of the increasing difficulty of drawing intellectual distinctions between self and other in a rapidly globalizing world, and the ethical, methodological, and theoretical dilemmas and adjustments that ethnographers face as a result.

Closely related to the insider-outsider dilemma are the difficulties associated with juggling the simultaneous distance and intimacy of fieldwork, another unifying theme in this collection. When we apply the everyday learning strategy of participant observation to the business of doing research we become professional "relaters," developing, or expanding upon, connections with people for the purposes of gathering data, and repeatedly finding ourselves inextricably tangled or nestled in complicated emotional interdependencies, conflicts, or dilemmas. Each of the contributors to this volume reflects, directly or indirectly, on the emotional and intellectual complications of engaging intimately with others. Several refer to the messiness of fieldwork, the messiness of relationship. Most emphasize the importance of vulnerability and empathy, trust, dependency, emotional attachment,[18] reciprocity, and responsibility.[19]

The intimacy of long-term fieldwork relationships can be deeply enriching for both ethnographer and informant. The importance of "empathic witnessing" (Tourigny), the willingness to become emotionally, sometimes physically, vulnerable, to participate in processes of "self-disclosure" (Telfer), and to form strong attachments to individuals in the field, is highlighted by the contributors to this volume. As Robinson points out, the implications of such attachments for all involved are often hidden in academic discourse. Tourigny, Birckhead, Beckerleg & Hundt, and Robinson himself, for example, all had to deal with the premature deaths of people with whom they worked closely during their fieldwork. The emotional costs—for both researcher and research participant—of establishing research-based friendships, dependencies, and reciprocal relationships tend to be subsumed under the technical notion of "rapport," "the threshold level of relations . . . necessary for . . . subjects to act effectively as informants" (Marcus 1998:106). These costs, rarely acknowledged, are often an unavoidable and extremely significant part of the ethnographic endeavor.

As many of these authors show, good fieldwork relations can lead to much heartbreak as research participants in vulnerable situations suffer the injustices of the systems that contain them, or as researchers struggle to meet the obligations and commitments that accompany various degrees of intimacy. The very fact of trying to maintain some kind of emotional distance, or of leaving or staying away from the field for long periods of time (e.g., Birckhead), can also be painful for those involved. Tourigny and Beckerleg & Hundt also show how trust and dependency in the field can be a matter of personal safety, even of life or death. As a result, questions such as "What kind of knowledge does my emotional involvement generate?" are important and valid and can provide us with important information about ourselves and our informants (Corsino 1987; Kleinman & Copp 1993).

Ethnographic fieldwork has an intrinsically autobiographical quality (Okely & Callaway 1992; Behar 1994, 1995). Both researchers and research participants have to repeatedly negotiate their own feelings of trust and fear to maintain their relationships (e.g., Beckerleg & Hundt and Tourigny). Revealing parts of ourselves and our backgrounds often enhances our relationships with others and encourages the sharing of information that informants might otherwise be reluctant to disclose. As

Jon Telfer shows, for example, personal revelation is sometimes an essential step toward achieving a sense of "resonance," or "empathic understanding," in the field. Such understanding is the ground of social knowledge and the principal means we have of truly appreciating[20] the standpoint of others.

Another of the themes that emerges from some of these papers as presenting a particular challenge to the research relationship is linked to the shock of recognizing the self as other, that is, the "subjective" self in the role of supposedly "objective" researcher. For some of the contributors the researcher role carries connotations of the colonial or hegemonic gaze and raises questions about the ethics of "studying others." Shuttleworth and Harvey describe the awkwardness of working with communities who were highly critical of research practices that were not properly accountable to research participants. Colic-Peisker discusses the discomfort she experienced as an "insider" anthropologist when resisting expectations that she take on an advocatory role for some of her respondents. These and other contributors also show how the researcher's field identity is constructed in collaboration with research participants who have expectations of "their anthropologist" and are rarely passive in their involvement.

Siting the Field: Safety Nets and Danger Zones

The changing nature of "the field" is also a recurring theme in the papers collected here, although it features most clearly in those on multi-sited research (Muir, Kurotani, and Teaiwa). George Marcus (1995, 1998, 1999a, 1999b, 2002) has written extensively about the changing conditions of ethnographic fieldwork and the implications for anthropological praxis, his most significant contribution to this conversation being the notion of "multi-sited ethnography" itself. Ahkil Gupta and James Ferguson (1997a) have also furthered debates by probing and deconstructing long-standing anthropological ideas and assumptions about "the field" and asking how we might reconceptualize it to better reflect the diversity of ethnographic research now being undertaken (see also Fog Olwig & Hastrup 1997).[21]

The issue of anthropology at home has often been central to these disciplinary discussions. It has been a topic of interest to American (e.g., Messerschmidt 1981; Moffat 1992) and European (e.g., Jackson 1987; Okely 1996) anthropologists for some years and more recently to those working in Australia (e.g., Morton 1999). The methodological and theoretical implications of doing anthropology (and participant observation) at home, however, have not been widely addressed. As Marcus (1999a:10–11) notes, traditional anthropological "rhetoric and language for evaluating fieldwork and ethnography," the "old standards," are often not sufficiently "sensitive [to] or accommodating" of the conditions in which many contemporary research projects take place. For a combination of reasons, anthropology at home is on the rise. It is thus highly appropriate that many of the contributors to this volume offer interesting insights, often indirectly, into the business of doing fieldwork in, or near, their home territories.

The fieldwork injunction to go elsewhere construes "home" as a site of origin, of sameness. While a certain degree of "sameness" can prevail in a "home" situation, our contributors suggest that that sameness can highlight the nuances of difference that are invaluable in collecting data. Merely speaking the same language, having similar histories, and coming from the same socioeconomic group does not necessarily equate with sameness. In some cases it might cause more discomfort and dis-ease to the ethnographer. The notion that "home" is a place of safety, a comfortable, nonthreatening research environment, is repeatedly challenged by the contributors to this volume. Fieldwork is often inherently hazardous. The possibility of experiencing physical and emotional trauma is frequently unavoidable.[22] Some of the authors represented here were placed in dangerous and/or illegal situations while in the field. Several of the ethnographers in this collection write about the "ambient" danger they faced simply through doing research in a dangerous setting (Lee 1995:3–4). They show, however, that such incidents provided the opportunity for deeper insight into their research. As Tourigny points out, risk is a part of what we do and needs to be anticipated and accommodated, even if it cannot be eliminated.

The anthropological field is social and relational and calls on the intersections of relationships, actions, interests, and identity constructs (Gupta and Ferguson 1997b:35–37). Sawa Kurotani confirms this with her observation that the anthropological field exists in the collaborative building of relationships between an anthropologist and her informants even when the anthropologist is "one of them." It is important to recognize that such processes, and the emotional responses that accompany them, are a normal part of fieldwork. Participation needs continuous theorizing, and the way we can do this is through revealing and interrogating our emotional and personal experiences (Okely 1992; McCarthy Brown 1991; Dubisch 1995).

Perhaps by looking to other disciplines we will find frameworks of value in this process. The work of neuroscientists such as Antonio Damasio, for example, reveals that reason and emotion are inextricably interwoven. Damasio's findings show that, although emotional upheavals can lead to irrational decisions, neurological evidence suggests that selective absence of emotion is also a problem. Well-deployed emotion is a support system without which the edifice of reason cannot operate properly. Indeed, emotion is an integral component in reasoning and decision making (Damasio 1999:283). Emotional identification with informants and our extent of practical involvement influence the field and the fieldwork over time (Norman 2000:140). Further, such experiences can shape and change the direction of any project, either positively or negatively. As Ida Fadzillah writes below, "the fieldwork process is charged with the energy and emotions of its participants, and its participants include both the fieldworker and the subjects of her study."

Redefining Good Fieldwork

Fear, self-doubt, and feelings of failure can haunt us throughout our entire stay in the field. It is important to acknowledge these feelings, especially to novice ethnographers about to embark on lengthy (or short) sojourns in the field. Many of the contributors refer to the feelings of self-doubt that they experienced during their fieldwork, and several asked the self-probing question, "What am I doing here?" In his reflections on the impacts that our fieldwork can have on research participants, Robinson writes that "wisps of human shame inhabit the expert account"; Muir remarks on his feelings of voyeurism, given that much of his data was gleaned from casual conversations with people who regarded him as a friend; and Angrosino questions his own spiritual motives for doing research in a monastery.

Each of these situations and feelings creates a sense of awkwardness, a kind of social and personal uneasiness. They are, however, an unavoidable part of what we do as participant observers. One of the main intentions of this volume is to argue that uncomfortable fieldwork is often very good fieldwork. If we can accept this we might at least be able to overcome some of the anxieties about social, professional, or personal failure and/or inadequacy that plague many of us during and after difficult fieldwork encounters. The authors of the essays in this volume suggest a number of ways for dealing with the awkwardness and discomfort of fieldwork, the most important being a willingness to embrace a rigorous reflexive process as a necessary component of the participant observation methodology. They have also raised a number of points about the difficulties of doing fieldwork "at home," close to home, or as "insiders." Additionally,

Muir, Kurotani, and Teaiwa have productively added their voices to ongoing conversations about the realties of doing multi-sited research. All have helped to showcase participant observation as a highly demanding but very productive methodology.

Participant observation is hard work—even though lack of formal training (in some places) and general appearances tend to deny this. It requires constant awareness of multiple sensory input and often demands extensive personal compromise in order to "fit in"; it also calls for high levels of sensitivity and relativism. Individuals with these skills are also likely to be very self-critical and/or susceptible to criticism from others. The very personal nature of participant observation, along with the challenges of entering an unfamiliar social setting and/or taking on a new role as a researcher, can mean that many first-time ethnographers experience intense feelings of self-doubt, confusion, and anxiety. Such challenges, however, can be highly rewarding, self-revelatory, and productive.

This book emerges out of our belief in the importance of normalizing the self-doubt, confusion, and feelings of personal inadequacy that are, perhaps, an inevitable part of successful and sensitive participant observation. The papers in this volume remind us not simply that doing fieldwork is intensely personal and often difficult, but that painful fieldwork experiences can also be productive, especially when combined with a willingness for careful reflection. In early 2001 we circulated an international call for papers inviting ethnographers to reflect upon the difficulties they encountered while doing participant observation and the useful things that they learned from these difficulties. We received many expressions of interest and close to fifty abstracts, an indication that the issue we were exploring was significant to a wide range of ethnographers of varying seniority and experience based in different countries and working in diverse locations around the world, on a wide range of topics. The papers presented here are clearly part of a much broader, ongoing conversation in contemporary anthropology (and the social sciences more generally) about how we do what we do and how what we do allows us to know what we know.

Although the issues addressed by our authors frequently overlap, we have divided the papers into three categories according to their main foci: positioned engagements; ethical engagements; and multi-sited engagements. The papers included in the first section emphasize the significance both of how the participant observer is positioned by people encountered in the field, and of the position that she or he actually brings into the field. These papers directly consider some of the dilemmas associated with managing the dual statuses of insider and outsider that are intrinsic to the experience of participant observation. The papers in the second section focus on some of the ethical issues that arise in the course of undertaking participant observation, the questions that are asked, the personal risks that are endured, and the experiences of emotional and intellectual transformation that can occur as a result of building (sometimes very intimate) relationships with participants while also managing a particular research agenda. In the third section researchers explore challenges and insights associated with conducting ethnographic fieldwork across multiple geographic locations, where the relationships built and the roles of insider and outsider are further complicated by the scattered and disjunctive nature of the fieldsites themselves.

As the previously specialized methodology of participant observation (and ethnography more generally) gains wider popularity, it falls to those who are most familiar with it to offer up their insights and understandings on a complex, and often personally compromising, research strategy. This volume attempts to normalize the awkwardness and discomfort inherent in the paradoxical task formalized in the theory and practice of participant observation. It also makes the argument that such awkwardness is often itself the source of insight and revelation. By rigorously analyzing our own emotional responses to particular field encounters (i.e., by carefully monitoring and testing our primary research tool, especially after it has undergone some kind of trauma) we can usually learn something about the values of those around us and the social processes we have become part of during the research process. In doing so we might also find ourselves well positioned to identify new standards by which to judge "good" fieldwork, standards that address the unique conditions of our individual fieldsites, the people we work with, and our own personal circumstances and dispositions.

Notes

1. See Bradburd (1998) for further discussion of the importance of "being there."
2. Any Aboriginal language spoken in this area is known as "lingo."
3. It is considered rude to ask direct questions, and to look another person directly in the eye. Much information was gained by listening to people talking to each other in my car while I drove them long distances from one location to another, or by just sitting quietly listening.
4. Making appointments with people was rather futile. If I arranged to meet someone on a certain day at a certain time, other events almost always took over (for instance, they might have gone fishing or shopping, or to pick up a welfare check, or else just did not want to talk then).

5. The Yarrabah police were members of the community themselves and were expected to be just that. In a situation that had brought many different linguistic groups together decades earlier, when people from outlying communities came in (voluntarily and involuntarily) to join the mission, factional fighting occurred fairly frequently. In spite of the aversion to white police based on a history of maltreatment and colonial control, calling them in sometimes became the only way of dealing with escalating violence because the local community police were unable to arrest their own kin.

6. Many "half-castes" were taken from Aboriginal mothers because government policy at the time was to collect children with any "white blood" and rear them as whites rather than blacks. It was thought that the children would fare better and assimilate into the white community.

7. Beckerleg and Hundt (chapter 10) also describe the need for an "escape" from the field, for personal safety but also to avoid empathic overload. They were able to do this by creating a space in the field, an ethnographic field station that was strictly out of bounds to "informants."

8. My third fieldwork experience (in 1991) was multi-sited and involved traveling vast distances across Australia to conduct research on contemporary paganism and witchcraft (see Hume 1997). In this case the methodological difficulties I faced included tracking down potential research participants in a very dispersed, decentralized, and often stigmatized social domain; the challenges of making generalizations about a set of amorphous beliefs and practices that are continually under construction by geographically diverse groups; and the "discourses of disdain" promoted by my academic colleagues who saw this study as "lightweight" and too "New Age" (one even suggested that it was not "real anthropology," and despaired that the discipline had "come to this"). Nonetheless, I found that this fieldwork entirely suited my own personality and interests.

9. See Lynne's comment in the previous footnote about academic responses to her "New Age" study, for example. Mattley (1998:151–153) also writes revealingly about academic responses to stigmatized fieldsites.

10. My position shifted a number of times throughout my research and is now a lot more tempered for reasons similar to those outlined by Martin Forsey (chapter 5) in his discussion of critical ethnography. See also Mulcock (2002).

11. See Marcus (1999a:7–8) on the challenges of working in "disjunctive" fieldsites.

12. Hammersley and Atkinson (1995:113–117) suggest that the experience of "marginality" is one of the most stressful aspects of doing participant observation. They also argue that this is not necessarily something that should be avoided, and that becoming too comfortable, too much "at home" in the field, is also undesirable (114–115).

13. The feminist ideals that I carried into the field—of collaborating closely with research participants on written and intellectual outcomes—were also unachievable (see Stacey 1988, Wolf 1996, and Bloom 1997 for further discussion), partly because the people I worked with were simply not

interested enough in me or my research to devote time to additional levels of involvement. Most did not even want to check the transcripts of
their interviews.

14. See Mulcock (2001) for the published version of this paper.

15. In fact, Crick (1993:4) suggests that writing about fieldwork has become "a
    major anthropological growth industry" since the 1970s.

16. See, for examples and discussion, Rambo Ronai (1992), Fortier (1996),
    Reinharz (1997), and Mattley (1998). It is interesting, but perhaps not sur-
    prising, to note that all of these authors, along with Powdermaker, Stacey,
    Kaplan Daniels, Krieger, and Ganguly-Scrase, listed above in the text, are
    women.

17. Crick (1993:4) points out, however, that it is also important to recognize
    the more formalized strategies and tools, or "methodological routines,"
    that ethnographers use. There are many "handbooks" available that
    describe these research techniques (e.g., Agar 1980; Spradley 1980; Crick
    & Geddes 1993; Stewart 1998; Schensul & Le Compte 1999; Atkinson et
    al. 2001).

18. Gary Robinson (chapter 12) and Sylvie Tourigny (chapter 9) provide espe-
    cially powerful reflections on the implications of trust, dependency, and
    attachment in two very different fieldwork situations.

19. The theme of researcher responsibility to "informants" is particularly
    addressed in Graham Harvey's discussion (chapter 13) of "guesthood" as a
    way of thinking about the ethnographer's role in the community he or she
    is studying.

20. Forsey (2000) writes about the idea of "critical appreciation," a stance that
    encourages researchers to first acknowledge the value of other worldviews
    before leaping into critical analysis.

21. The influence of this work, along with that of James Clifford (e.g., 1988,
    1997) and others writing on related themes, is evident in many of the papers
    collected here.

22. Some ethnographers even risk being killed by their informants (see Howell
    1990 and Noone 1972).

PART I **POSITIONED ENGAGEMENTS**

CHAPTER 1

Awkward Intimacies

Prostitution, Politics, and Fieldwork in Urban Mexico*

In the early spring of 1999 the people of the *ejido*[1] Francisco I. Madero were seeking to reclaim their land—four hectares located at the end of a lonely dirt road, eight kilometers east of the bustling city center of Tuxtla Gutiérrez, the capital of Chiapas, Mexico. Since 1991, however, the once communally held agricultural lands had been occupied by nearly one hundred and fifty female prostitutes selling their services from within eighteen *módulos,* or barracks-style buildings, to men of the laboring classes. The land, now called the Zona Galáctica (Galactic Zone), is a "tolerance zone," a legal brothel zone administered by Tuxtla's municipal government. The *ejidatarios* (communal landholders) warned that if the city did not return their lands by April 2, they would "arrive well armed" and evict the inhabitants of the Zone, shedding blood if necessary. The Zona Galáctica was my fieldsite.

In this essay, I examine the trials of undertaking research in the Galactic Zone and explore the ways in which the personal and political challenges unique to this fieldsite enhanced my understanding of my informants and myself, ultimately providing me with new insights into anthropological theory and ethnographic practice. I suggest here that the process of fieldwork is as important as the final written product and that the "trials" of field research are as important as the "successes" (and sometimes even constitute the successes). In the struggle to write a cohesive and coherent account of field research, the moments of illumination that emerge from the challenges and awkward moments in the field can easily, but should not, be lost.

The Galactic Zone's awkwardness had many dimensions: it was a brothel—a highly sexualized environment occupied by a population labeled deviant and dangerous by hegemonic norms and cultural moral codes. It was also a highly conflictual environment with extreme factionalism and shifting loyalties among and between Zone workers and staff. As one worker said, "Our daily bread here is arguing and gossip." Fieldwork in the Zone required delicacy and a balance of neutrality and engagement. The awkwardness of the Galáctica was further compounded by its location within a city run by the right wing National Action Party (PAN), which placed itself in opposition to the entrenched ruling centrist Institutional Revolutionary Party (PRI), in a militarized state in the throes of severe political, economic, and social turmoil.[1] It was under these conditions, further enhanced by global political-economic trends, that the *ejido* conflict erupted. The many awkward moments I experienced, including this event and the subsequent threatened loss of the Galáctica, had a pivotal impact upon my understanding of my fieldsite.

The Setting

> Tuxtla is not a place for foreigners—the ugly new capital of Chiapas is without attractions. . . . It is like an unnecessary postscript to Chiapas, which should be all wild mountains and old churches and swallowed ruins and Indians plodding by.
>
> —Greene (1939:194)

On New Year's Eve 1994, a small army of Mayan peasants, calling themselves the Zapatista National Liberation Army (EZLN), emerged from the jungle lowlands of eastern Chiapas to declare war upon the corrupt government of Mexican president Carlos Salinas de Gortari and upon the existing and unjust order of things, which kept most of Chiapas' indigenous peoples living in serflike conditions. Following a few days of skirmishes, the EZLN retreated back to the jungle, where they remained. While this event propelled Chiapas, one of Mexico's poorest states, to the forefront of the global political scene, the region was already well known to anthropologists, who had been working with the indigenous populations of the Highlands for decades. The Chiapas constructed in anthropological texts was indigenous, rural, and agricultural. This image was reinforced by media coverage of events following the 1994 uprising, which also highlighted the desperate poverty of the indigenous farmers trying to survive in a rapidly changing economic system that favored agribusiness over small-scale and subsistence production.

As capital of the state and known since 1994 as the birthplace of the New Mexican Revolution, Tuxtla Gutiérrez is not what one may think it should be. Unlike the Chiapas portrayed by the social scientists, Tuxtla is .

urban, *ladino* (*mestizo*), and relatively prosperous.[2] The city has a population of nearly half a million, only two percent of whom speak an indigenous language (Instituto Nacional de Estadistica e Información 1993:60). Most *Tuxtlecos* (residents of Tuxtla) earn their living in the commercial and service sectors; the city's consumer culture is highly developed, with businesses such as McDonald's, Sam's Club (a Wal-Mart affiliated store), and the Plaza Cristal (an upscale shopping mall) dotting the urban landscape. While Chiapas is one of Mexico's most impoverished states, Tuxtla is one of the nation's least marginalized municipalities (Archivo Municipal de Tuxtla Gutiérrez [CIACH] 1997:7). The city attracts immigrants from Central America and southern Mexico who seek the economic prosperity they cannot find at home. Some seek this prosperity in the Galactic Zone. I arrived in Tuxtla to study something in the region that is not generally studied: urbanism, the nonindigenous population, and commercial sex. I settled in hot, lowland Tuxtla, the "ugly" city bypassed by researchers and tourists alike as they make their way to the temperate, pine-forested highlands or as close to the jungle as the military and migration authorities allow. In Tuxtla I thought I would escape the politics of land that so infused (and, in my mind, unbalanced) the anthropology of Chiapas. I would study sex and cities, not land and rebellion. And, in part, I did.

Into the Galactic Zone

Few social science researchers enter the contemporary brothel. Studies of sex work are often historical, the research done in the comparative safety of the past. There are, of course, reasons for this. As Ronald Weitzer (2000:13) notes, "This world [of commercial sex] does not offer easy access to the outsider, which helps to account for the paucity of research in many key areas; but gaining access should be viewed as a challenge rather than an insuperable barrier."

Surprisingly, gaining access to the Galactic Zone and its inhabitants proved to be perhaps the least challenging part of the fieldwork experience—it was once I was in that things became difficult. To gain access to the Zone, I only had to endure weeks of countless lunches with a dear platonic friend who had worked there in the past, and who promised me he would give me the phone number of the doctor currently in charge at the brothel's onsite health center, the Anti-Venereal Medical Service (SMAV). After many meals together, it slowly began to dawn on me that perhaps my dear friend was keeping the phone number from me so that we could continue to lunch together. Maybe he hoped for more than my company and chicken in pumpkin seed sauce. I grew agitated and finally kindly but firmly told him that I desperately needed to begin my fieldwork and that if he was not going to help me I would have to leave Tuxtla and work somewhere else. This was untrue but effective. By the next day I had an appointment with the Zone's head doctor.

I next secured permission from the municipal government, led by the National Action Party (PAN). I feared that my contrasting political views would make me an unwelcome presence to city officials. My views never came up. I met with Tuxtla's Director of Public Health, a *panista* (member of the PAN) and a gynecologist, who introduced me to the mayor, also a *panista* and a gynecologist. Young, charismatic, and handsome, the mayor extended a hand to me and modestly said in English, "Hello. I am the mayor." I liked him immediately. I would be studying regulated prostitution in a city run by young, handsome, right-wing gynecologists.

Inside the brothel, I was somewhat shy at first. During the first weeks, not a day passed when I did not ask myself questions such as: "How dare I bother these people for my own selfish interests?" "How the hell did I end up here?" "Wouldn't it be better if I just went home and took a nap?" In part, my concerns stemmed from the potential contradictions between feminism and field research and the ways in which the development of rapport in the field can ironically put research subjects at "greater risk of exploitation, betrayal, and abandonment by the researcher" (Stacey 1988:21). I did not want to approach the women, but found that I did not have to. Many of them came to me. I was first approached by Magda and Adriana, who sat me down and instructed me on how to go about my research. I must be friendly, they said, social. I must go out and drink with them. This was not a problem—I like to drink. But they also warned me that I must be careful, hinting at the divisiveness that I would later find permeated the Zone. Magda said that were I to associate with her too frequently, people might begin to talk, since she is a lesbian (one of many working the Galactic Zone). I shrugged and felt thankful for my upbringing—a childhood that included some brief but memorable times spent in bars chatting with diverse groups of people (my father was a bartender), and less than placid adolescent and college years. No amount of anthropological training or theory could have prepared me for the field as life had. As Watson (1999:4) suggests, while in the field "we use ourselves and our own personal experience as primary research tools."

While entering the world of the brothel went relatively smoothly, its awkwardness as a fieldsite manifested in other ways. First, the women who worked there sold sex. In this culture purchasing sex is acceptable, but selling it is not, and the women of the Zone are stigmatized for doing so. During my year in the Galactic Zone I came to understand the terrible power of stigma.

My introduction to stigma and shame came early. I had returned to Tuxtla to do fieldwork after my first and only visit to the Galactic Zone the previous year. The first time, I was driven there in a private car. The second time, I was on my own. To get to the Zone—located at the end of a long isolated road dubbed by local newspapers the "Highway of Death" due to the occasional murders and assaults that happen there—it is necessary to drive or take one of the microbuses or "pirate" taxis that depart from the city center carrying sex workers, staff, and clients. Not owning a car, I found myself wandering Tuxtla's busy downtown alone, searching for the rumored terminal from which the pirate taxis departed. I walked for a few hours, repeatedly passing the same butcher shop, flower sellers, and vendors. I thought myself a feminist, a woman able to endure and even shrug off the judgments of others, but I was unable to ask a stranger for directions to the Galactic Zone's taxi terminal. I was not ready to bear the raised eyebrows and stares I feared would accompany any answer I received. I was silenced and disempowered.

Though with time the stigma had less of a hold on me, throughout the year it impacted on my actions and words. In Chiapas, and throughout much of Mexico, the *gringa* (foreign woman) is believed by many to be a highly sexual creature, and, in Tuxtla, a *gringa* who also has chosen to do work in the Zone could be accused of *morbosidad*, morbid perversity. While close friends knew the nature of my research, I often lied to neighbors and casual acquaintances, replying to their inquiries about my work with vague references to public health and social science. When outside the Zone, I preferred not to be too closely associated with it.

Due to stigma, sex workers often keep their work a secret, especially from those closest to them. When outside the Zone, sex workers never refer to the place by name; rather they refer to it euphemistically as *allá,* or "there." As my relationships with the sex workers grew deeper and they invited me into their homes, I became responsible for maintaining their secrets, lying to their acquaintances and even to their children about how it was I came to know their mother or where I worked. Such lies produce a sense of alienation, create situations of inauthenticity in daily life, and are incredibly stressful to maintain.

When the false lives created by sex workers begin to crack and fissure, the results are sometimes painful. This became apparent at a birthday party I attended for Paula, the teenage daughter of Vivi, a prostitute who worked in a private house. The festivities began at La Palapa, a popular bar-restaurant. I was surprised and saddened to find that the people attending the party were largely affiliated with the Zone: taxi drivers, sex workers, a food vendor, and myself. The only other guests were Vivi's younger daughter, Mari, and a friend of Paula's. We ate *botanas*, small dishes of vegetables, meats, and cheeses, drank, and watched the show. I was impressed by Miguel, an elderly Zone food vendor, for drinking what appeared to be simply mineral water, and more impressed when I realized hours later that he had quietly been downing a large number of vodka tonics. Before we left the bar to head back to Vivi's house for cake, she approached me in the bathroom and lowered her voice, saying of her daughters, "They don't know what I do." I reassured her that I would keep her secret.

At Vivi's house we sat on the porch on rickety wooden chairs and continued to drink. More workers from the Zona arrived and we all, Vivi's daughters included, gathered in a circle, talking. Miguel sat in his chair, concentrating, it appeared, on not falling out of it. He then began to talk as drunk people often do. His big watery brown eyes tried to focus upon me as he said loudly, "I love you. I love you more than anyone. I love you more than anyone in Mexico. I love you more than anyone in the Galactic Zone!" The last two words cut through the warm night air and everyone fell silent—it seemed a long and sobering silence. Finally someone shouted, "Miguel!" and scolded him. Even in his drunken state, he appeared to know he had done something very, very wrong. And as silent as it had been only moments before, conversation suddenly erupted everywhere, as we attempted to cover up the awkward moment.

Stigma controls, disempowers, and divides. Throughout my time in Mexico I witnessed again and again the difficulties experienced by women in similar situations. I also learned that I, a foreigner, an anthropologist, a feminist, an outsider, was not immune to the powerful effects of stigma, and I recognized how potentially devastating those effects could be.

Many awkward but productive moments were generated by my identity as a young woman new to the brothel whose role there was unclear to many. In the Zone, there were four types of women: sex workers, food vendors, SMAV staff, and landlords of the workers' quarters. During my early days in the Zone, I was most often mistaken for a prostitute, which was not an unreasonable assumption. Propositions by clients and their reactions upon finding out I was not a sex worker were always illuminating. I learned about the distinction between a "decent" woman and a sex worker. When one potential client, an older gentleman, realized his error, he apologized profusely, paid my microbus fare back to the city center, and as we rode along proceeded to give me the standard tourist information on the sights of Tuxtla and Chiapas. He was embarrassed not simply for "insulting" me, but also for revealing himself to me as a purchaser of sexual services.[3]

Such awkward encounters offered me a glimpse into the strict boundaries of identity within the Zone and of the moral borders that are created and crossed there. The workers told me stories of "disrespectful" clients who would approach them while they were outside the brothel, in the city center, sometimes with their boyfriends or children. Outside the Zone, the women leave behind their identities as sex workers: they are mothers, daughters, girlfriends, and expect to be treated as such, even by clients. Yet these moral borders and categories of identity are often blurred, shifting, and subject to dispute. When exactly does Olivia, the mother of two, become Ximena, the sex worker who uses an alias? I recall one early morning ride in a pirate taxi to the Zone. It was a hot, humid day and the Volkswagen Beetle was crowded with workers and clients, our skin sticking to one another's in the heat. Clients never propositioned workers in the taxi; the taxi served as an in-between place, the literal and figurative connection between the boundaries of moral order and the Zone. As we approached a red traffic light, I gazed out the window into the eyes of a man on the sidewalk who mouthed to me the following simple, powerful word: *Cuanto?* How much? I looked away. Again, his assumption was reasonable, but because his actions were spatially wrong, I felt extremely uncomfortable. His simple one-word question and the feelings it triggered helped me to identify these invisible moral borders between the Galactic Zone and the city.

I soon grew tired of would-be clients and was urged by a secretary in the SMAV to purchase and wear a labcoat, as she and the other staff did. In the Zone, the four roles occupied by women were demarcated both spatially and through appearance. Female SMAV staff wore labcoats and rarely ventured into the areas where the prostitutes worked. Sex workers wore a variety of clothing—anything from sweatsuits to lingerie—and occupied their rooms, food stands, and the offices of the SMAV for medical visits. Female landlords and food vendors alike wore aprons and generally stayed among the workers whom they served and in their food stands. The role of anthropologist was new, undefined both spatially (I went everywhere) and in terms of dress. I had some reservations about purchasing the labcoat, fearing that it would so align me with the staff of the SMAV that it would alienate workers and clients, but I tired of fending off propositions and gave in. I learned to love the labcoat and to use it selectively. I wore it during travel from my home to the Zone, while meeting with Zone staff, and sometimes when moving among the buildings that housed the workers. The labcoat came off when I was with the workers in their rooms or elsewhere. It offered me some protection from unwanted attention, and freedom of movement among the diverse groups in the Zone. Yet I found that I needed more than a labcoat that I could take off and on in order to move peacefully among the various factions inhabiting the Zona.

In order to fully realize my project, a study of sexuality, morality, and modernity in contemporary Mexico through the examination of regulated prostitution, I needed the cooperation of various populations within the Zone who more often than not had competing and conflicting interests: workers, clients, SMAV and other staff, Zone landlords, and city officials. During my first weeks in the Galactic Zone, I naively believed that the brothel community was fairly harmonious and cohesive. I spent many mornings sitting at Miguel's food stand, located just outside the SMAV: sex workers stopped to chat on their way to their mandatory gynecological examinations; nurses and secretaries gathered at the window of the medical offices overlooking Miguel's stand to talk and buy breakfast; fresh papaya was picked from a nearby tree, to be sliced and shared, eaten with chile and lime. During these early days I failed to see the cracks and fissures, and even gaping chasms, that permeated many Zone relationships. I did not see that perhaps, as in the early stages of a romance, my informants were on their best behavior. I ignorantly moved happily and easily among and between groups for many months.

As time passed, I found that I had developed close professional and social relationships with both sex workers and officials in the city government. Staff members of the SMAV were bothered by my extracurricular activities: my social relationships with some sex workers caused them to question my moral character and good sense (one SMAV staffer warned me away from Zone workers, saying that among their ranks were criminals and lesbians). I also believe they felt slighted—I did indeed prefer the company of sex workers (who were often a great deal of fun and with whom I felt I could be completely myself) to the company of SMAV staff. My friendships with the mayor and public health officials further alienated Zone staff: these men were their superiors, and I believe some worried that I was a spy.

During the last months of my fieldwork, my relationship with many of the SMAV staff had degenerated greatly. I felt I was no longer welcome inside the medical service offices and was rarely engaged in conversation. It was uncomfortable but I was thankful that I had managed to interview staffers back when relations were still good. And indeed, whatever animosity SMAV staff had toward me, I had in turn begun to feel toward some of them, particularly the head doctor, who performed the workers' weekly medical exams. Over the course of months I had listened to sex workers complain of the doctor; she was brusque, they said. Disrespectful. They complained that she often inserted the speculum roughly and without lubricant. A SMAV secretary crossed boundaries to tell me that when they had run out of soap to wash the speculums, the doctor said loudly in front of a group of workers waiting for their exam that she did not care whether they were washed or not. Following this incident, I made a choice. As the closest link between the sex workers and the city, I arranged for a private meeting between sex workers and the Director of Public Health, who was to make a rare visit to the Zone. The meeting, I hoped, would give the women the opportunity to voice many of their concerns directly to a government official. The meeting did not go as I had hoped: the most articulate and politically informed worker was not present and the workers complained less of the collective problems of service, mistreatment, and administration that they had spoken of to me, and focused more upon an ongoing dispute that some women had been having with Marco, a former male prostitute employed as a janitor, who also ran errands for sex workers. The meeting did not create any great changes for the women and caused the further degeneration of my relationship with the SMAV. While my choice to arrange it was largely altruistic, it was an altruism tempered by rationalism and self-interest. I knew my time in the field was coming to an end and I had little to lose.

The Galactic Zone at the Crossroads of City, State, and Nation

As a fieldsite a brothel is predictably awkward, but the Zone, due to its temporal and spatial locations, was uniquely awkward. During the period of research, Tuxtla and its zone were administered by the local branch of the conservative National Action Party (PAN), one of Mexico's two main opposition parties. Throughout the country, these two parties were beginning to successfully challenge the entrenched and corrupt seven-decade rule of the Institutional Revolutionary Party (PRI), whose policies had aided the decline of rural subsistence agriculture, increased migration to urban areas, increased poverty and social dislocation, and engendered a guerrilla uprising.

Major roads throughout the state were often blocked by *campesinos* protesting government policies or, alternatively, by government supporters. Marches and protests also took place in Tuxtla's main square. As the PRI struggled to maintain control, phones were tapped and researchers' areas of investigation were circumscribed. Deportations of tourists and intellectuals alike were not uncommon.[4] The entire state of Chiapas was militarized, and there existed a general atmosphere of repression and (often justifiable) paranoia.

My close contact with the PAN created unexpected problems, specifically with the *priista* state offices of the National Migration Institute (INM) in the highland city of San Cristóbal de las Casas. When I arrived in the field, I first made my base of operations in San Cristóbal. I did this, ostensibly, for practical reasons: I had living quarters there and was affiliated with a local research institute that would assist me in securing a research visa from the city's office of the INM. I had no connections to Tuxtla, other than the entire purpose of my research. I was not eager to leave San Cristóbal, a charming and temperate city that I had first visited nearly a decade before.

But while San Cristóbal was in many ways a comfortable and supportive environment, the PRI-run INM, quite concerned with the presence of foreign rabble-rousers and potential Zapatista supporters, offered neither comfort nor support. During my stay in Chiapas, deportations of those suspected of engaging in political activity were common. I did my best to please the staff of the INM, particularly the imposing migration official, *Licenciada* Mazariegos, who inspired in me something close to sheer terror. I arrived for our appointments (and there were many) with my hair combed (unusual for me), conservatively dressed, tattoos covered, and carrying what I always hoped were the appropriate documents (they never were). I would be called in from time to time to answer questions such as "What is your relationship with the PAN?" In retrospect, this strikes me as rather funny, as I was perhaps the only suspected foreign PAN supporter in the state, in contrast to the legions of suspected foreign EZLN supporters. Over and over, I would truthfully explain that my relationship with the PAN was professional and in no way political. Indeed, despite my relationship with PAN officials, my political views were quite contrary.

As a researcher and foreigner working in an increasingly xenophobic state, I tried to remain invisible to authorities. Happening upon a caravan of Zapatistas in San Cristóbal for dialogues, I returned home immediately, knowing that accidental proximity alone could be enough to get me deported. My efforts, though, were not always successful. During the late spring, when the land conflict erupted in the Zone, television news crews came to cover the event. I was urged by colleagues to leave quickly and did, but not soon enough. That night Miguel and I appeared on the evening news, sipping Cokes and eating tacos in his food stand. I did finally receive my research visa, however, nearly six months after the initial paperwork was begun.

With time, I grew accustomed to the field, the fear of deportation, and the leers of unknown men. I became so comfortable in the brothel that I was able to knock on the doors of women engaged with clients if it was truly important enough to do so. I had conquered the INM and secured my visa. I was working well with the local *panista* officials. On my thirty-first birthday, there was a surprise party for me in the Zone: pirate taxi drivers brought a cake, as did the workers. Miguel supplied forks and plates and beverages. The municipal police who guard the Zone gates, along with janitorial staff, set off fireworks, and I was showered with gifts. I had been accepted. I was undertaking a project on the other side of Chiapas, removed from the land conflicts so central to the work of others in the region, just as I had intended. I felt I had arrived— until a convergence of local, national, and global politics caused an explosion in the Galactic Zone, threatening its very existence.

The Zone had been built upon communal *ejido* lands, constitutionally protected lands that at the time of the Zone's 1991 construction were not to be bought, sold, or rented. The site, belonging to the *ejido* Francisco I. Madero, had been chosen as part of *priista* Governor Patrocinio Gonzalez Garrido's pet project, "Project *Zona Rosa*," which sought to give the state increased control over commercial sex in Chiapas, even as it withdrew support from other sectors of the economy. A deal had been made between the ruling body of the *ejido* and the city and state governments (both then run by the PRI). Documents in the municipal archives described the deal as an exchange of land for public works projects within the community of Francisco I. Madero while documents from the *ejido* described the land transfer to the city and state as a donation. A representative of the Secretary of Agrarian Reform approved the deal, declaring there was "no legal impediment to the donation of land . . . as long as the *ejido* receives multiple collective social benefits" (Archivo de Tuxtla Gutiérrez, Expediente Zona Galáctica 1991). The representative instructed local officials to file the proper paperwork at the federal level in order to finalize the matter. They never did.

More than seven years later the *ejido* registered a claim against the municipal government, now run by the opposition PAN, demanding restitution of, or payment for, their lands. *Ejidatarios* threatened violence and gave municipal authorities until April 2, 1999, to pay up or hand over the Galactic Zone. The conflict received a great deal of press coverage; newspaper headlines exclaimed, "400 *Ejidatarios* Could Take Over the Galáctica" and "Eviction Feared in the Galactic Zone."

As much as I loathe admitting it in such a public forum, my first response to the conflict was concern that I was about to lose my fieldsite. My second response was guilt and shame about the self-centered nature of my first response. Third, I worried for my informants, sex workers above all, who would lose their sole source of income. Despite my many criticisms of regulated prostitution (particularly the aspects of social control and exploitation not unique to prostitution, but found in all highly gendered service-oriented work), I knew that most Zone workers would probably seek similar employment in other brothels throughout southern Mexico, brothels that offered no access to medical care, little security in terms of safety from violent clients, and perhaps, most important, did not distribute free condoms to workers, as the Galactic Zone's medical service did. During my many months in the field I had begun to lose sight of the benefits of the Galactic Zone. Its potential loss reminded me of its complex and sometimes positive nature as a place of work. Finally, I became intrigued by the conflict itself and despite my stubborn intention to research something, anything other than land disputes in Chiapas, I found myself drawn in.

My personal political inclinations were once again called into question as I tried to understand the conflict. Working with groups on all sides of the dispute, I struggled with the notions of "truth" and "neutrality." I met with the *ejidatarios* and their representative on numerous occasions. They were friendly, open, and very funny. Of the sex workers, they said, "They are beautiful." Their problem, they said, was with the city and the profit that the municipal government was making on their communal lands.[5] They spoke of the struggle for land by the poor and its centrality to Mexican history. Their representative was brash and humorous and charismatic. He spoke passionately of their cause, smoking cigarette after cigarette with equal passion. Whether it was the content of our talks or the dizzying effects of inhaling so much tobacco smoke, I left each meeting feeling their cause was just.

The problem was that after each meeting with city officials, I felt the same way. When I was denied access to the files on the history of the Zone in the Municipal Archives, I turned to the mayor for help. He put an arm around me and said, "We are friends, aren't we?" I felt duplicitous, but it was true—we were friends. I was immediately granted access to the files and prayed that I would find nothing incriminating that would threaten our friendship.

After months of meetings, interviews, and archival research I came to one conclusion: I had no idea what had actually transpired between *priista* government officials and the ruling body of the *ejido* back in 1991. It was clear that some sort of land deal was made, elements of which were perhaps unlikely to show up in archival documents. It was not inconceivable that the deal involved corruption on all sides and uneven profit among some of the parties involved. I believed that the city's present and previous *panista* administrations had simply inherited (and on occasion mishandled) this problem. I further felt that were the city still under *priista* control the current land dispute might never have occurred.[6] Despite these beliefs, I did not think that the *ejidatarios* were simply opportunists and continued to feel that, as communal and subsistence farmers throughout Mexico and the world were losing their lands, their activities deemed nonproductive in the new global economy, their argument was valid. My inquiry into the conflict taught me a great lesson: I learned to be comfortable with the many contradictions surrounding the dispute and the unknowability of certain social facts.

During my inquiry into the conflict, each group saw me as a potential ally. The *ejidatarios* urged me to publish something about the dispute quickly in order to garner publicity for their cause. The city, in their efforts to prove the public utility of the Zone as a means of finally and legally expropriating the land, publicized my teaching of English to sex workers as one of the Galáctica's many social benefits.[7] I was careful not to proclaim my alignment with either side and struggled to retain some semblance of neutrality, though I simply wished the matter to be settled and the Zone to remain open. April 2 passed without violence and the matter remained unresolved.

My struggle to appear neutral came to a head on May 26, when the city decided to hold a Mother's Day fiesta for sex workers some two weeks after the event. The fiesta, to which local media were invited, provided the city with the opportunity to further showcase the social benefits of the Zona, to attempt to instill middle-class values of domesticity and femininity in workers, and also perhaps to divert attention from the *ejidatarios* who arrived on that day with surveyors to measure the Zone in order to determine its market value. As I arrived at the brothel wearing my white labcoat and exited the pirate taxi, I immediately ran into the *ejidatarios* and their chain-smoking representative. They had never seen me in my labcoat, which was, at least to me, a symbol of the city government. I felt exposed. I was fearful that the *ejidatarios* would believe that I was actually a municipal worker and that I had misrepresented myself when interviewing them, but nobody questioned my allegiance.

Throughout the morning, as *ejidatarios* walked about with tape measures drawn and dropping plumb lines, city officials gave speeches reminding Zone workers of their "primordial function" to raise their children with love and guidance, and distributed aprons that read "For Mama. Compassion, Affection, Support. DIF Municipal. Tuxtla Gutiérrez, 1999–2001," along with a few condoms. I nervously removed and put on my labcoat in a ridiculous effort to manipulate my identity. It was nearly one hundred degrees out and I was working up a sweat. It was awkward and absurd and after some time I simply gave up and, exhausted, joined sex workers who sat under a tent listening to a Honduran reggae-rap band that featured lithe female dancers and a male dwarf. Maintaining neutrality in the midst of so many unknowns was tiring, and as I sat with the sex workers I knew it was their side I would ultimately take.

Conclusion

> Chaos should be regarded as extremely good news.
> —Chögyam Trungpa Rinpoche (in Chödrön 1997:xi)

My year in the field shaped me as no other experience has. For an anthropologist, after fieldwork, "things are never quite the same again" (Watson 1999:2). It highlighted my weaknesses and strengths, not only as an anthropologist, but also as a human being. I matured politically and intellectually, learning to embrace the contradictions of reality and awakening to the inadequacy of "theory." The many awkward moments I experienced in the field were often more illuminating than my moments of comfort: I learned, at least briefly, to glimpse the truth of Chögyam Trungpa Rinpoche's proclamation quoted above. The *ejido* conflict enabled me to truly recognize the importance of land in Mexico, and I came to understand more deeply why the many researchers who came before me had focused on this issue.

Participant observation, the mainstay of ethnographic research, offers the anthropologist "an intimate knowledge of face-to-face communities and groups" (Marcus 1995:99). But such intimate knowledge can at times be confusing, marred by questions of ethics and one's own selfish interests, threatened by politics and the unknowability of social facts, and compromised by efforts to remain both engaged and neutral. Fieldwork is like sex: It is often messy. It can be awkward, especially at first. It requires some flexibility. It is best when spontaneous and, no matter what one's proposal may say, simply cannot be planned. Like sex, even bad sex, fieldwork is always productive: it produces sensations, emotions, intimate knowledge of oneself and others.

Notes

   * This paper was written with the support of the American Association of University Women.

1. An *ejido* is a system of communally held lands.
2. After nearly seven decades of maintaining power at the federal level the PRI was voted out of office in 1999 and replaced in 2000 by Vicente Fox of the PAN.
3. This prosperity is due, in part, to the extraction of wealth from the countryside and the privileging of the urban sector in government spending.
4. I found that, while clients are not generally stigmatized as consumers of sex, there is sometimes a certain shame attached to their activities in the Zone, particularly when found out by "decent" women.
5. Following the Zapatista uprising, there was an influx of foreign supporters of the movement. This phenomenon came to be known as *Zapaturismo.*
6. The Galactic Zone was actually not a particularly good source of revenue for the city; its importance was more symbolic than economic.
7. While the motivations of the *comisariado ejidal* and the timing of their actions are open to speculation, there were many observers who believed their actions were linked to Tuxtla's place in the Mexican political system. While I was discussing the situation with the sex worker Magda, she gave me a pop quiz on Mexican politics in order to prove this point. "Who is the president of Mexico?" she asked. "Zedillo," I replied. "And what party does he belong to?" "The PRI." She continued, "And who is the governor of Chiapas?" I answered, "Albores." "And what party does he belong to?" "The PRI." "And who is the mayor of Tuxtla?" she asked. I was catching on. "Paco Rojas and he's a *panista*," I answered. "There you have it," said Magda, "That's why I said it's [the land conflict] purely political."
8. According to Article 93 of the Agrarian Law, lands may be expropriated for the greater public good.

Michael V. Angrosino

CHAPTER 2

Disclosure and Interaction in a Monastery

I am a cultural anthropologist/oral historian, and this essay is a reflection on a project I conducted for the centennial of Cassian Abbey (a pseudonym), a Benedictine monastery. During the period of research (one month of intensive interviewing, plus several short follow-up visits), I lived at the monastery and adhered to the monastic rule. I am a practicing Roman Catholic who has tended to look on monasticism as a revered but increasingly irrelevant anachronism. Living briefly at the monastery was a welcome spiritual and emotional respite from the racket of the "real world," and the research allowed me to interact with the monks as real people, and not as holdovers from a glorious but fading tradition. But I knew that the monastic life was not one to which I would be personally suited on a long-term basis, and thereby hangs a tale. . . .

Setting the Stage

At the time of the research, there were thirty-five monks in residence at Cassian, another dozen or so having been given special permission to work outside the monastery as teachers, pastors, and chaplains. The Cassian community supported itself through the management of extensive agricultural properties, supplemented by the hosting of religious retreats, workshops, and conferences. The monastic community founded, and for many decades ran, a small liberal arts college whose campus is adjacent to the monastery grounds; however, the college and the monastery are now separate administrative entities.

Like all Benedictine foundations, Cassian is autonomous in governance, although it has "fraternal links" to the other monasteries around the world that also follow the Rule of St. Benedict, which requires monks to devote equal time to prayer, study, and practical work. The monks of Cassian pray in common four times a day, and celebrate Mass together on a daily basis. Each monk at Cassian has his own small but comfortably furnished room in which he may keep a few personal items given as gifts. Unless he is ill, however, he is expected to spend most of his time with other members of the community, and not shut himself up in his room. Most items of material culture are owned in common. The monks have access to clothes, toiletries, small appliances, and cars that are the general property of the community, although they must receive permission to "borrow" such items. All meals are taken in common.

Cassian is governed by an abbot, who is elected by a vote of all vowed members of the community (the "chapter"). Nowadays, the Abbot of Cassian, like most Benedictine abbots, rules by consensus, and often consults with the senior members of the community, although the monastery would never be confused with a democracy. The abbot's second-in-command is the prior, who is responsible for the day-to-day workings of the community and for maintaining discipline among the monks. The other important office in the monastery is that of novice master, the monk who supervises the training of all newcomers to the community.

There is a further hierarchy within the ranks of the monks, with the novices occupying the lowest status. After a three-year novitiate, a candidate who shows promise will take temporary vows and enter into a probationary period lasting five to seven years. After that time, he will be allowed to make a permanent profession of his vows. Like all Catholic religious orders, the Benedictines require members to take vows of poverty, chastity, and obedience. Benedictines, however, add a fourth vow: stability, the pledge to remain affiliated with the monastery in which profession took place. Each vowed member, whether temporarily or permanently professed, is referred to as "Brother." Most monks at Cassian keep their given names, although a few adhere to the old tradition of adopting a new name upon entrance. Some members of the community are selected by the abbot to study for ordination to the priesthood; after ordination, they may properly be addressed as "Father," but only during the exercise of their sacramental duties. At all other times, they are "Brothers" like everyone else, since there is not supposed to be any distinction within the chapter between those who are ordained and those who are not. In practice, however, the priests have greater prestige and are said to be granted more privileges than the lay brothers.

Research at Cassian: The Ethnography of Self-preservation

My project was developed in consultation with the abbot, who had already commissioned a historian to write an official account of the monastery based on monastery documents and college archives. The abbot thought it would be a good idea to provide, in addition, a more personalized glimpse into the world of the monks. Knowing of my professional interests from conversations during earlier visits to the monastery, he encouraged me to develop an oral history of Cassian and strongly "suggested" that his brothers cooperate. In a meeting of the chapter, I explained the oral history method and outlined the advantages of keeping such a record for posterity. The method involved audio-taping one-to-one interviews developed from a general, open-ended prompt ("I'd like you to tell me about your personal experiences here at Cassian, and about some of the historical traditions passed on to you by earlier generations of monks of this community") supplemented by an informal question guide to make sure that major topics (e.g., discerning vocations; governance; living according to the Rule; memorable experiences in prayer, study, work, and leisure activities), as identified in the literature about monasticism, were dealt with. Each interview was transcribed, and the draft transcription returned to the subject for corrections, after which a final transcript was prepared. All tapes and transcripts, as well as detailed indices, were deposited in the monastery's library.

The monks all seemed very enthusiastic at first but proved to be considerably less than forthcoming in the interviews, in ways that seemed to me to go beyond appropriately monkish reticence. The whole project, in fact, turned out to be far more interesting in terms of what the participants failed to reveal—and the ways in which they managed that concealment—than of what they put on the record. My orientation toward symbolic interactionist theory provided me with a way to explain this apparent anomaly, and also to link the monks' response to my own anomalous role as a quasi-insider researcher.

People whose lives are being constructed in the act of storytelling have reason to want to control information; they disclose only what they must in order to create a desired impression on the "audience" (the interviewer most immediately, but also those who will later access the tapes and/or transcripts). They will therefore mobilize whatever storytelling or other performance techniques they have reason to assume will resonate with the intended audience. The manifest content of the interview may therefore be false, due to cognitive or emotional disorder or artful skimming of details, or because of outright lying. But the interview itself remains a true, microcosmic reflection of culturally sanctioned interpersonal processes. The content may constitute new territory, particularly for the interviewer, but the performance dynamics must be part of the cultural repertoire of both the interviewer and the storyteller if the deception is to succeed. Even when we are engaged in an act of flat-out lying—indeed, perhaps most of all when we are lying—we must mobilize strategies of interaction (e.g., gestures, body language, deployment of emotionally charged metaphors) that are meaningful within the culture and that are common to both the storyteller and the audience. To lie is to engage another in a game. There would be no point to the deception if the audience were not in on the game at some level. Therefore, both parties are demonstrating ways in which culture, which after all is the focus of ethnographic research, is negotiated—constantly re-created in the course of social interaction.

When a researcher sets aside the manifest (and potentially deceptive) *content* of an interview in favor of looking at the interactive *form* of that interview, the analysis necessarily involves a degree of self-study, since the persona presented by the interviewer is an integral part of the process of the co-creation of the narrative form. The storyteller must present him/herself in such a way as to project an image designed to connect (either positively or negatively) with the particular audience. The resulting story will probably be different from the story those same informants generate with a researcher who presents himself in a way that they have learned to think of as a different kind of audience. If one looks only at content, one would see contradictory accounts; if one looks at form, however, one learns a great deal about how people of a given culture go about categorizing strangers and incorporating them into their system of symbols.

Conceptual Framework

In *The Presentation of Self in Everyday Life* (1959), Erving Goffman elaborated on G.H. Mead's (1934) insight that "self" is a process rather than a fixed entity. Moreover, the process by which the self unfolds is inherently dramatic, in that it involves the actualization of one or more roles in relation to an audience, which may be either physically present or implicit. Goffman was also strongly influenced by Simmel (1950:307), who suggested that people who enter into the presence of others are faced with a problem of information control. A social situation is therefore like a theatrical performance in that it requires the actor to reveal certain things while keeping others hidden. The performer in any social situation is, in effect, claiming to be a certain kind of person, and is demanding to be treated as such. He or she cannot therefore "tell all," lest priority in constructing his or her identity be given over completely to the audience.

I believe that a number of the monks had a special need to practice image control in my presence. On the one hand they knew that they did not have to go into great detail in explaining the institution of monasticism, which might have been deemed necessary for a non-Catholic interlocutor, but they did feel that they had to defend their personal choices. As is patently obvious, the vast majority of Catholic men in the United States do not enter the priesthood or religious life. Since one can be a "good Catholic" as a layman, and since our culture leads us to suspect the psychosexual worst about people who elect lives bound by vows of poverty, chastity, and obedience, a monk feels compelled to put the best face on his choice. A Catholic would be expected to know that in the modern church "vocation" is taken to be a general call to follow God that is attendant upon baptism, and is not restricted to the priesthood or religious life. He would therefore want to know how a monk knows that *this* way of living out his vocation to follow God is the right way. A monk, in other words, needs to justify himself to a fellow Catholic who has made markedly different choices.

Every social situation is a temptation to commit fraud, and since the possibility always exists that the performers are *not* what they hold themselves out to be, even legitimate performers must put on a kind of show to convince others that they are genuine. The monk who *really* feels a specific call from God has the same problem, dramatically speaking, as the fraud who is trying to cover up his psychological inadequacies by claiming to have a vocation. His problem, however, is compounded when he is talking to someone who takes the very notion of a call from God as a real possibility, and who therefore presumably enters the interaction with some preconceptions about what the call should be like.

Performances in which the self is constructed for presentation to an audience do not arise out of thin air. In preparing to present ourselves to others, we spend time "backstage" with those who help us prepare our public presentations (e.g., teachers, counselors, friends, family). We cannot possibly go on stage without such preparation, lest we slip, thereby spoiling the show and leaving others with the wrong impression—wrong not necessarily in the sense of inaccurate, but in the sense of "the one I didn't want them to see." A deliberate falsehood made up on the spot would be an insult; but a consistent fraud that carries through the network of relationships from which the performer emerges is simply evidence of the workings of an ongoing cultural process.

Monks live in a situation that differs in some important ways from the ordinary backstage-and-frontstage setting. For one thing, their backstage is far more explicit and absolute than in the outside world, where a multiplicity of influences exist from which a person might choose. The preparation of a monk is based on very clear-cut rules of behavior—rules that, indeed, are hallowed by nearly two millennia of practice—and enforced by equally clear-cut norms of behavior modification. Someone on the outside may have several different backstages from which to draw (family, school, peer group); the monks have only one. Moreover, in the monastery, the backstage *is*, to all intents and purposes, the frontstage, as the monks rarely need to "perform" for anyone but their own community. When they do so, therefore, they must necessarily experience a contradictory sense of heady liberation mixed with a palpable fear of the unknown. Within the community, the norms are adhered to. With the occasional outside audience, the mask of the austere, serene, almost wraithlike holy man can serve, since it keeps the monk from falling into an unaccustomed situation in which he is unsure of the cues. (It also serves the needs of that outsider audience, which in general prefers to deal with anomalous figures like monks via stereotypical, culturally sanctioned images.) But what to do with a "quasi-inside" audience?

One of the greatest performances of all is that which we undertake to convince others of our normality. Except for the brave few who deliberately cultivate eccentricity, most of us spend much time and energy making ourselves seem normal, the penalties for deviance being so great in most social situations. It is not that most of us are *not* normal (whatever that means!) but that really normal people have to spend as much time cultivating the impression of normality as do those who are deviants and are striving to cover up.

In *Stigma* (1963), Goffman described the ways in which people with something to hide interact with others so as to seem normal. People are often stigmatized for some trait, attribute, attitude, or behavior that others find objectionable. They may therefore be so anxious to demonstrate their normality—to give the lie to the stigmatizing response they receive from others—that they tend to overplay their normalizing projections of self. In Robert Edgerton's (1968) felicitous phrase, referring to adults with mental retardation, they assume "the cloak of competence." This dynamic is kept in motion by the fact that in life, as in certain poorly performed plays or movies, the effort to seem normal is sometimes more obvious—and offensive—than the original stigmatized characteristic. A person who studiously avoids all social mistakes is apt to seem more disordered than the person who casually errs every so often. The lives of supposedly normal people are more apt to be entangled in webs of inconsistency than are those of deviants who have perfected seamless cover-ups.

Because the oral history interview is an intensely personal, focused kind of interaction, it throws the processes of self-presentation into high relief. An analysis of the symbolic function of the form of dissimulation adopted by stigmatized informants demonstrates that unfactual discourse, convincing or otherwise, is not simply noise in the system, but significant information that people socialized in a particular backstage community think constitutes normality. Philip Bock (1988:150) pushes Goffman's analysis to its logical conclusion, pointing out that since we are all stigmatized relative to *some* other social group, "guilt lies at the basis of all social organization." If we accept this point of view, we might say that adopting the "cloak of competence" is something we all do, and that there are culturally meaningful ways to go about it. The question therefore becomes: how do two parties (in this case a monk and his "quasi-insider" interlocutor), each of whom needs to justify himself to the other, assume a "cloak of competence" designed to project a "normalized" self-image that is mutually acceptable?

Stories and Interactions

I ultimately realized that the monks who were of approximately my own age seemed particularly intent on covering up. The older monks were by and large comfortable with the fact that they were humble sinners who stood in need of God's grace, just like everyone else; they were willing to admit to failings both trivial (one old brother told me with a rueful sigh that he occasionally filches an extra cup of pudding for dessert) and serious (one senior member of the community told a very detailed story to explain why he harbored an angry grudge against a former, now retired abbot—a narrative for which he asked me to turn off the tape recorder). The older brothers apparently felt that admitting to their failings did not compromise their status as men seriously seeking God. Although the senior did not want his tale of anger and bitterness on the permanent record, he clearly had no problem telling it to me—it was part of the way in which he wanted me to relate to him. In this light, it does not matter whether the story is factual or not. I do not have any reason to think that this particular brother invented the story of his grudge; but even if he did, I would still have to ask the same questions: why this story? why now? why tell it to me? I think that in this case he wanted, in his own way, to reassure me that honestly seeking holiness does not guarantee automatic perfection, probably because I had given him some cues of my own that I was impatient with my own maddeningly slow progress toward enlightenment.

The younger brothers, on the other hand, seemed to think that I would question their sincerity unless they appeared in the most saintly light possible, since I was of their generation yet had made decidedly different choices in life. If the older brother wanted to let me know that it was okay not to achieve instant sanctity, the younger ones seemed intent on making me feel like a slacker. Their vocation to religious life was not a sign of their failure as men, but the sign that they had achieved holiness. My vocation to a lay life was therefore not a voucher of my psychological health but an indication of my spiritual shortcomings. I was susceptible to this ploy because, in my spiritual insecurity, I had made it evident that I had a great deal invested in being thought a "good Catholic," particularly while in the hallowed halls of the abbey.

I might also point out that my own "normalizing" act continues by means of what I am doing in this paper—retreating behind the veil of social science theory. Doing so gives me legitimacy (I had sound academic reasons, and not just nebulous spiritual ones, for being at the monastery), provides me with convenient social distance (I can present myself to my professional peers as one whose spiritual interests do not stand in the way of hard-edged, objectifying analysis), and offers grounds for self-justification (the project was not altogether successful as a formal collection of historical materials, but its very failure could be used to interesting theoretical purposes).

Backstage at Cassian

Monks are not "stigmatized" in the ordinary sense of the term, but they have chosen to live in small societies that are separated from the world to one degree or another, and their life choices are treated with some skepticism by the larger society. Monks, like many devout Catholics—indeed, like many dedicated Christians of various denominations—like to characterize their choices as "countercultural," and to see the way they live their lives as "witness" against the overly individualistic, materialistic, competitive tendencies of the larger society. But there is no escaping the fact that society at large remains unimpressed by that witness, preferring to assume that professed holy people are self-deluding naïfs at best or outright charlatans at worst.

My monastic informants have been prepared for social encounters by a backstage that is a small community whose members interact far more frequently and intensely with one another than they do with outsiders. The intimacy that defines a small, enclosed community makes privacy an especially "delicate and sensitive commodity" (Wilson 1974:132). Community life, therefore, is marked by numerous stratagems and tactics that aim to establish and sustain the privacy that the requisite intimacy tends to inhibit. Such tactics are fairly obvious as they are happening, although they are usually not captured on audiotape, and must be separately catalogued in the researcher's notes. For example, there is a tendency to speak in hushed tones, or with the hand acting as a kind of defensive screen at the mouth, even when no one else is visibly present. In the same way, the monks all typically preferred to sit very close to me during the interviews, sometimes at distances that would be considered proxemically inappropriate, even uncomfortable, in noninterview social settings. At first, this tendency could be chalked up to their lack of practice in the ordinary social graces, but it also likely expresses a desire to carve out a separate, special place for *this* encounter in the midst of an environment in which everybody is "always in your business," as one of my informants put it.

In communities where one cannot usually escape intimacy, there seems to be a need to establish spheres of self-selected intimacy that cannot be easily invaded by the all-too-present others. Choosing physical proximity was more typical of the older monks; the younger ones may have been wary of having their posture interpreted as a sexual come-on, for reasons to be explained below. Although my own inclination was to move back, I was concerned that doing so might give offense. After several such sessions, I therefore developed a strategy of reaching out, ostensibly to adjust the tape recorder, but in the process pushing my chair back a few inches. Perhaps correctly interpreting my symbolic gesture, the seniors did not move in closer to reestablish their preferred distance.

Nevertheless, the concern with privacy remains a major factor in social interactions in the monastic community. "There can be no secrets here," one monk told me with mixed satisfaction and regret. This situation imposes a certain degree of stealth upon all its members and, because everyone is engaged in such concealment, the ability to do so is rarely challenged or compromised. But there seems to be a line—no less clear for being largely invisible—beyond which concealment must be interrogated. As soon as anyone seems to be *too* obvious in behaving secretly, curiosity is kindled, and everyone tries to find out what is going on. Since it would be considered inappropriate to come right out and ask someone what is going on, however, gossip and rumor become the coin of the realm. It is therefore not surprising that such tales—rarely, if ever, substantiated—form an inordinately large proportion of narratives generated by the project.

For the most part, stories told about figures from the past were mild and inoffensive. But one piece of inflammatory current gossip was making the rounds at the time of my research: one of the younger brothers was said to be HIV positive. This brother had been quite candid about his homosexuality when he first came to Cassian, but he had made it clear that he had abandoned that lifestyle long before he even contemplated joining the monastery. He certainly never said anything to me about his health status, and he seemed completely unaware that others were talking about him. It struck me that this young brother was almost painfully intent on erasing all signs of his homosexuality—his vocabulary and body language became almost a parody of machismo, leading me to suspect that he was gay even before he told me so. As noted above, the normalizing cover-up only ended up calling attention to itself. I therefore assumed that, given an inch, the others took a mile, and, knowing him to be gay, jumped to the conclusion that he was HIV positive. What I took to be their groundless conjecture, however, proved to be true, for shortly after the project ended the young brother did develop full-blown AIDS. After his death, his family briefly threatened to sue the community, which they accused of having failed to provide proper medical attention. There seemed to be no credible evidence that his care had been compromised, but it was also clear that the brothers had completely stopped talking about the situation. When it was merely a matter of speculation about someone who appeared to have something to hide, many people felt free to discuss it with me; when the awful truth was known, no one could talk about it, since it was precisely the sort of thing that played into outsiders' worst suspicions about what monks are like.

The desire to avoid perpetuating this stereotype might account for the younger monks' preference for relative physical distance from me during the interviews, as noted above, despite the attraction of creating a zone of privacy that the interview afforded. It was not entirely surprising that they would not discuss the matter with me on subsequent visits—after all, I was only a quasi-insider, and the community felt the need to close ranks against threats from outside even after the lawsuit had been withdrawn. But I was made to understand that they did not discuss it among themselves either, and their silence and embarrassed avoidance could well have been interpreted by the dying man as a lack of care and concern.

"Privacy" does not refer simply to people's desire to be left alone. Rather, it refers to a situation in which people suspend or disengage from one set of relationships (even if only temporarily) in order to activate a new or different set of relationships *with* the implicit consent of the partners in all those relationships. "Privacy, then, is the simultaneous activation of one relationship and the disengagement from another" (Wilson 1974:135). The degree to which we are successful at achieving new relationships and disengaging from existing ones is a measure of the authority we have over ourselves. The more intimate a new relationship, the greater degree of disengagement will be required from the others. Any inability to keep those others at bay indicates a proportionate loss of authority. Power, in contrast to this personal authority, is the ability of persons to prevent those to whom they are related from establishing new, intimate relationships with others.

In the monastery, the abbot is the ultimate power, although that power is ordinarily kept in bounds by the reciprocity of trust, discretion, respect, and honor. The vow of obedience, however, makes such reciprocity inherently asymmetrical; it is impossible for discretion to fully counteract the effects of authoritarian hierarchy. In effect, members of the community never feel that they are left alone. This is also the means by which they are typically prevented from satisfying themselves in respect to any relationships outside the hierarchy. While encouraged to develop "fraternal bonds" with all members of the community, monks are explicitly warned against forming "particular attachments." In the monastic community, one must be a brother to all, but a friend to none. Personal freedom has been usurped in favor of the good of the community. The monks profess to see this trade-off as a necessary and desirable element of living in community, and they speak with what comes off as circumspect pride about the process of having had their egos "tamed."

Nevertheless, their awkward eagerness to enter into the relationship with me, the visiting, quasi-insider researcher, demonstrates that the process has not been fully completed in most cases. For the monks, the interviews constituted a sanctioned alternative relationship. I was there on the sufferance of the abbot, of course, but I was not obligated to be obedient to him—I alone could keep secrets from him if I so chose. There was thus a whiff of danger in talking to me—the possibility, at once frightening and attractive, that because I would probably not carry tales to the abbot, they could assert their personal authority with me in ways that they would not dare in relationship to one another. But my discretion could not be taken for granted, given the possibility that in what they perceived as my anxiety to prove myself a "good Catholic" I might rat them out to the abbot. This fear, I believe, accounts for the many gaps on the tape resulting from the monks asking me to turn the machine off while they told me something off the record, or when they stopped altogether and made a conscious decision to go no further on or off the record with a train of thought. They could assert their personal authority with me—choosing what to tell and what to conceal—because I was outside the bounds of obedience. But being outside also meant that I could not be entirely trusted to reciprocate with trust and discretion. In a telling contrast to the proxemics of the interviews with the other monks, the abbot conducted his interview while sitting behind a table that separated him from me. In effect, he was attempting to draw me into the hierarchy of the monastic community, even as the monks used the same interview process to transgress the norms of that hierarchy.

Reflections on the Experience

During the course of the project, it occurred to me that, like most anthropologists, I was striving for acceptance by being as much of a "participant" as possible in the life of the community. But because the essence of membership in this community—the vows—was one I could not share, I could never be a true participant. The monks' vows could be construed as liberating in some ways—poverty, chastity, and obedience free a man from humdrum concerns and allow him to focus on the works of God— but they also have the result of foreclosing all other choices. I realized that although I had made many other commitments in life, I had never made any that so clearly had that same ring of finality (and the threat of divine sanction). And I suspected that I never could.

On the face of it, an ethnographer conducting an interview by recording the supposedly innermost thoughts of people for posterity would seem to be cast in the role of invader of privacy, and we often think of less than cooperative informants as asserting their own privacy against the researcher's nosiness. But in the Cassian project, the informants had long since learned to surrender their privacy, and to submit to constant, if benevolent, surveillance. Moreover, they believed that this situation represented a step on the way to spiritual perfection. As such, they could look on the interview not as an invasion of privacy, but as an opportunity to make a personal choice about privacy. The very fact that they had not been told how they were to act once they had signed up for the "suggested" interview made that interview's interactions substantially different from anything else in their lives. The interview was the only context in which they could licitly choose not to disclose everything on demand. Dissimulation was therefore not a passive/aggressive strategy, as we might assume, but a positive assertion of individuality that had long been vigorously—albeit voluntarily—suppressed.

The "person" may be defined as the more or less integrated compendium of the distinctive roles enacted by an individual in relevant social settings (Turner 1978:380). Small, enclosed backstage communities place considerable value on the achievement of high role integration, a process that has been referred to as a tendency to "anchor self-conception" (Turner 1978:380). The interview becomes a stage on which this anchoring can be practiced and achieved, without the threat of the negative consequences experienced in relationships within the backstage community. The monks practice a rigorously honest "examination of conscience" as part of their daily prayer, and also make a regular confession of their sins in the course of the sacrament of reconciliation. Their self-conception is thus anchored only to the extent that one or more significant others allow it to pass scrutiny. The opportunity to try out alternative ways to be oneself in a nonjudgmental setting is thus a welcome invitation. It is also, to be sure, an invitation to lie (or, perhaps less pejoratively, to playact), but it is precisely in our playacting that we learn to integrate our sometimes disparate fantasies about who we are and how we want others to react to us.

The monks' decision to withhold personal information from me reflects not just a spiritual value of self-abnegation, but a positive assertion of their otherwise suppressed individuality. In other words, they withheld information *because they could*. The kind of person who does so is exhibiting an "anchored self-conception" very much at variance with the one officially sanctioned within the monastic community, and the persona created in the course of the interview deviates from the norm of the backstage community. But it is still in fact a product of the interactions that shape the community in the first place. One can only choose to deviate from something that is a well-known and established norm. But one can only choose to deviate when in the presence of an "audience" that permits such deviance. I was complicit in the monks' dissimulation precisely because of my unwillingness to make a vowed commitment to adhere absolutely to the norms of their community. I was withholding an important part of myself, and thereby gave them tacit permission to withhold parts of themselves in return.

Conclusions

Could the research be considered a success under these circumstances? If one adheres to positivistic standards of scientific discourse, then the answer is no, since the content of the taped interviews is incomplete and in some ways misleading, for all the reasons discussed above. (Those tapes are now accessible only with the permission—never granted, as I understand it—of the current abbot, the successor to the one with whom I developed the project.) On the other hand, the taped narratives are true representations of the encounters between the monks and a particular audience—a spiritually insecure practicing Catholic hiding behind the cloak of competence suggested by his manipulation of social science theory. Analysis of the form and style of their response to the particular stimulus represented by my particular persona can tell us a great deal about the challenges and tensions of the monastic life and its place within contemporary Catholicism even when such matters are not spelled out in so many words.

This orientation toward formal/stylistic, rather than content, analysis of life history/oral history narrative data may in part represent a "postmodernist" view of reality as being necessarily situational and of identities as negotiated rather than fixed entities (e.g., Best & Kellner 1991). But "it is generally accepted [by oral historians] that the memory process depends on that of perception [which] enables us to reconstruct it on a future occasion, or to reconstruct *some approximation* [emphasis added] of what we comprehended" (Thompson 1978:110). In a similar fashion, anthropologists Langness and Frank (1981:87–116) have concluded that autobiography is an act of "self transformation" and that for all save psychotics, personal experience is "ordered" (i.e., remembered) according to categories that are constructed so as to be meaningful at the social level. My own formal analytical approach to narrative data and the corollary assumption that "lives" are not neutral, objective, fixed entities but rather shifting, constantly negotiated refractions of particular relationships has been heavily influenced by current thinking among literary scholars of autobiography (e.g., Eakin 1985; Elbaz 1987; Leibowitz 1989; Adams 1990; Zinsser 1995; Conway 1998; Evans 1999).

A researcher without so much baggage (or, at least, with different baggage) might have elicited a more straightforward, factual account from the monks. But he would not have been able to stand in the same interactive space, and hence would not have been able to evoke the same psychological interplay that characterizes the search for personal and communal identity in the monastic community and that can be evoked through a formal/stylistic analysis more efficiently than through a content-based analysis of narrative ethnographic data.

Ida Fadzillah

CHAPTER 3

Going Beyond "The West" and "The Rest"

Conducting Non-Western, Non-native Ethnography in Northern Thailand

Camera and notebook in hand, [the anthropologist] is looking for the savage, but the savage has disappeared.

—Trouillot (1991:35)

One reason for the disappearance of "the savage" is that he (or in this case "she") is now taking on the role of anthropologist and assuming multiple levels of familiarity that are transforming the relationship(s) of the observer to the observed. The ethnographer is no longer obviously distinguishable from her subjects, having emerged herself from the colonial, political, and historical morass that has come to define the non-West. In my experience as a Malaysian ethnographer of rural Thailand, fieldwork created certain moments of intellectual and social tension that served both to underscore the "savageness" of my own identity and to dissolve the significance of the native–Westerner distinction altogether. These tensions produced insights and observations that rested uneasily in the world of the village and in my own world, leading in turn to new spaces of significance for this anthropologist to ponder.[1] In this chapter I tease out moments of cultural overlap and dissonance, some expected, some unexpected. I also explore how research subjects themselves contribute to the construction of the anthropologist's relationship to the field.

Previous ethnographies on Thailand have emphasized conformity and stability,[2] thereby shaping my pre-fieldwork vision of Thai villages as spaces of logically patterned behaviors and attitudes. Imagine my surprise, and indeed outright confusion, when I encountered instead a research site that seemed to me out of focus, a space of constant and multiple movements, positionings, and posturings. Also, the "facts," the logic, and the reasoning given to me by villagers about their lives seemed to change on a daily basis, as if they themselves observed the world as made up of layers of constantly shifting ideas they struggled to understand. To put the picture of these people's lives into manageable perspective, I had to recognize that the reasons behind my blurred vision lay not with my own lack of insight, but within the shifting terrain of my research site, a place where belief systems and preconceptions continuously competed for ideological dominance.

I reflect here on how the identity I carried into the field helped to create very specific social relationships and stereotypes that affected the fieldwork process in both positive and negative ways. Through this exercise I hope to highlight how the "outsider" anthropologist exists within a space of multiple labels and affiliations. My own ethnicity, religion, and citizenship played a part in what information I was able to garner, and from whom. I believe that, no matter who the ethnographer is, analyzing these aspects of his or her identity is just as important as analyzing the research subjects' identity, since both affect the research outcomes.

The Life of the Ethnographer: Splitting Identity

I became an anthropologist the moment I had to decide where to conduct ethnographic research. In my mind, the choice came down to "anywhere but Malaysia." My parents strongly urged me to "come home" and do research, my mother even asking "why don't you want to stay in Alor Setar? [3] You can stay with Uncle Ibrahim's family, and he can help you get contacts and data!" My parents, however, did not know two important ethnographic "facts": first, that a top-rate ethnographic study had already been conducted in Kedah. James Scott's *Weapons of the Weak* (1985) had in fact inspired me to pursue an academic life based on fieldwork. To follow in his geographic footsteps seemed too daunting a task. And, second, from my perspective as a fledgling ethnographer, "real" anthropologists did not study their own culture; they were supposed to go "away," returning only when they had tenure.

And so I chose Northern Thailand. Though close enough to Malaysia to allow for family visits, Thailand was far enough in both the Malaysian and American popular imaginations to satisfy my requirement of going "away": it was a land perceived as mysterious, different, and, dare I say, "exotic." I specifically targeted the north of Thailand because my topic focused on female notions of beauty and sexuality, and, according to some academic texts, Northern Thailand was perceived by the general population as the birthplace of the country's most beautiful women (see, e.g., Phongpaichit 1988; Bond et al. 1997). Northern Thailand was also where a large percentage of the country's prostitutes originated, and I was interested in the complex notions of female identity, sexuality, and worth such a place fostered. My research thus became focused on teenage girls in a moderate-sized village in Chiang Rai Province that for the purposes of this chapter I have named Baan Khmer. I lived in Baan Khmer for eighteen months and talked to the girls and women of the village about their perceived futures, especially the choices they felt were available to them in terms of jobs, education, and relationships. Through attention to their future opportunities I came to better understand the girls' own concepts of success and failure, of duty, and of sacrifice.

While my methods and goals were clear, I found my position as an outsider in the village more confusing. I began research in 1996 with the assumption that, as a Malaysian who had lived in the United States for most of her life, I was indeed a foreigner. What I had not anticipated was that, as a Malay Muslim, I was not as foreign to the Thai villagers as I had thought.

The geographic border between Malay culture and Siamese culture has been fluid and overlapping for generations. One of the first official treaties negotiated by the British cemented the geographic border between Siam and Malaya in 1826. Under that treaty, the Siamese agreed to accept the southern boundary of Kedah as the farthest extent of direct Siamese control on the west coast of the Malay peninsula (Steinberg 1987:142). In 1909, the Siamese ceded four of their Malay dependencies in the south— Kedah, Perlis, Kelantan, and Trengganu—to the British, who promptly incorporated them into Malaya, which in 1963 became Malaysia (Steinberg 1987:193). The creation of a national border south of the narrow neck of the Isthmus of Kra[4] accomplished several things, including identifying the people to its north as Thai and the people to its south as Malaysian. It thus divided a once relatively unified society of Malay Muslims, leaving a sizeable group to become the Muslim minority in predominantly Buddhist Thailand, and another to remain part of the Muslim majority in Malaysia.

This historically shifting border between Malaysia and Thailand has left in its wake quietly fragmented populations, religions, and stereotypes. While geography textbooks might portray these older cultural/religious identities as of no particular consequence, the people themselves remember. As someone whose family has lived in Alor Setar for generations and who grew up hearing stories and observations about life across the border, I should have been more cognizant of the ramifications of these collective memories.

The Ethnography of Life

Though I decided to undertake research in Thailand because of its difference from my own country of origin, I was stunned by the similarities between certain things Thai and Malaysian. Most obviously, the people and village architecture look remarkably similar. And the weather was tropical in both places, though admittedly more temperate in Chiang Rai. The same fruits were available and sought after, in both areas the *batik* (or *batek* of Thailand) sarong for women was commonplace, and both shared certain customs. For example, the older people enjoyed chewing betel nut, and the younger people did not. I found that the most unnerving moments I experienced in the field were the times when I forgot my own Malay traditions and then realized that I had committed a Thai cultural *faux pas* as well.

Once, as I stood in the soccer field watching schoolchildren release home-made hot air balloons, I unthinkingly put my waterproof bag full of notebooks on the ground and prepared to use it as a cushion. The girls with me shrieked and physically stopped me in mid-act. "Books are sacred!" One girl, flustered, explained to me, "You should never sit on them!" As she said that, I remembered being reprimanded as a child for sitting on my schoolbooks. I was shocked and embarrassed that I had forgotten some of my own lessons in tradition. I was also reminded that more knowledge or memories of my Malaysian culture would have helped me better understand the experiences of these Thai girls. Additionally, I shocked my Thai companions, who before this incident had assumed my competency in Thai customs, primarily based, I believe, on our shared Southeast Asian heritage.

There are also several linguistic similarities between the two regions, of which I was aware in advance. It was another matter altogether to hear those similarities on a daily basis. Malay words spoken in a Thai context (or vice versa)—Thai being so phonetically, semantically, and grammatically different—were jarring, their familiarity within such a foreign setting shocking my senses. "*Moot*! (Ants!)," a woman exclaimed, pointing to the ants making their way to our lunch table. "*Semut*" (pronounced "samoot"), the Malay word for "ant," would have signaled the same annoyance. "*Plek*" (a word I used often as a child, and in the field), means "strange" or "weird" in both Thai and Malay. "*Ngong*" in Thai and "*bengong*" in Malay both signify the feeling of being utterly confused.

It could be that certain words sounded similar to me not just because I am Malaysian, but more specifically because I am from a Malaysian state that borders Thailand. I grew up speaking the Kedah dialect, which is a form of heavily accented Malay peppered by several terms distinct from those used in the more standard version. To this day I have difficulty understanding the standard Malay spoken in the capital city of Kuala Lumpur, feeling more comfortable instead with the coarser, more "provincial" Kedah variety. There are several similarities between Kedah Malay and Thai, most of which I am not qualified to explain. The most glaring to me, however, is the habit, seen as rude by polite Malay standards, of the Kedah Malay speaker to frequently interject "*ha*" when listening to someone else talk, the same way American English speakers will add "oh" or "right." Standard Malay speakers do not (or should not) do this, nor do they use "*ha*" as an informal form of "yes" or acknowledgment, like Kedah Malay speakers. The Kedah "*ha*," however, is comparable in its use and meaning to the standard Thai "*kha*," the female form of "yes" that is frequently used by Thai women in their own conversations.[5]

These similarities, once I was settled enough in the field to notice, provided a sense of comfort and familiarity, in the same way that my Southeast Asian appearance did. I looked Thai,[6] and sometimes I was relieved that I could blend in with the local population. While this did not occur for very long within my small fieldsite (where everyone came to know me very quickly), physical incorporation into the social landscape provided much solace during my trips to the Chiang Rai city center and to Bangkok. Sometimes it also seemed to help with my research since I felt that by simply looking Thai I was more readily accepted by those who knew me. For example, there had been another American in the village I lived in, a Peace Corps volunteer who had lived there two years earlier and taught English at the local school. Villagers would laugh when talking about Patsy, who they frequently told me was "always smiling, so friendly," who "liked to go running, but would never wear a bra," and who "would always say *sawadii* [hello] when she passed by." The villagers were amazed that she preferred spicy food, especially *phad Thai*, which was thought to be an unusual trait for Westerners. When people spoke of Patsy I felt, perhaps incorrectly, that they would never apply the same standards to me, because as a fellow Asian I was not as "exotic" or different.

Near the end of my research, I stopped in Chiang Rai city to pick up my plane ticket from the travel agent. She recognized me when I walked in and smiled. As she handed me my documents, she informed me that she had given me a discount on the ticket; she gave me the "Thai" price (rather than the higher price charged to foreigners) because they now considered me Thai. Regardless of whether I was given a cheaper fare, or whether the villagers did see me as less of a foreigner than Patsy, these examples illustrate moments in which I felt most Southeast Asian, moments that led me to feel more at home in the field, and hopefully to gain greater insights into my research topic. These moments were rare, to be sure, but need to be acknowledged and appreciated for the comfort and feeling of familiarity they afforded in otherwise unfamiliar social territory.

Life in the Field

The fieldsite I finally settled on was easily accessible by car, bus, and airplane, though not yet by train. Baan Khmer village is located almost halfway between Chiang Rai city and the Mekhong River, which forms a natural border between Thailand and Laos. The village is nestled between tall hills hiding Buddha statues and abundant rice fields. One mile northeast, in stark contrast to the village, is a new international golf course–resort, which consists of condominiums, a restaurant, and a hotel. The resort has begun hiring local women as caddies, following the Thai tradition of providing female-only caddies and porters.

Baan Khmer is a "typical" Northern village. It has a temperate climate and is always approximately ten degrees cooler than the central states surrounding Bangkok. I was surprised to find tall bamboo grasses interspersed with rose bushes in every garden. Many of the more affluent Thai residing and working in the capital city of Bangkok often build weekend getaways in the North, to which they travel once or twice a month.[7] The villagers of Baan Khmer do not get many weekend visitors in their area, though the residences of one or two are widely known. The main income of the village is from rice farming (either on one's own fields or via sharecropping), orchard farming,[8] and overseas labor, with Baan Khmer women and men migrating, legally and illegally, on two-year contracts to Saudi Arabia, Taiwan, South Korea, and Brunei, to name a few.

Buddhist temples (*wats*) appear every mile or so along the roads leading into the villages. Observant travelers can glimpse glass mosaics, in the shapes of dragons or serpents, or gargoyles, glinting in the sunlight as they decorate the tall spires and pointed roofs. Baan Khmer, the name given to a collection of three smaller villages lumped together by government officers, has three *wats*. One is so run down and old that nobody frequents it; another, of the *Mahanikaya* sect of Theravada Buddhism, attracts a devoted few, but is dusty and houses only a handful of monks. The third, located on a steep hill between the main village and the secondary school, is the most influential by far. It is of the *Thammayut* sect,[9] and its abbot is famous throughout Thailand. During the week of the celebration of the abbot's birthday, vans of people drove by our narrow side street, wending their way toward the monastery in vehicles with Bangkok license plates.

Baan Khmer itself owes much of its good fortune to the presence of such a respected abbot. For example, the people with whom I lived ran a restaurant and a large part of their income, perhaps fifty percent, came from out-of-towners who commissioned meals to be given to the monks on a daily basis. These out-of-towners paid money to the restaurant, and every morning the wife cooked the food, after which the husband drove to the *wat* and deposited the food for the monks in place of the absentee merit-makers. Along the road heading into the village were several small shops selling sundry goods, the most prominently displayed of which were offerings for the monks (toothpaste, towels, razors, incense, matches) bundled up in yellow cellophane and ready to be exchanged for merit. The village, though small, also sold begging bowls and saffron cloth (for making monk's robes), which could be donated to the monastery on auspicious occasions.[10]

The abbot's influence on the everyday landscape of the village could be seen at almost every turn. Everyone wore Buddhist amulets around their necks, even small children and adolescents, and on the walls of seventy-five percent of the houses and businesses I entered in Baan Khmer, next to pictures of the Thai king and queen, and posters of naked Thai women in various states of undress, there was invariably a picture of the abbot next to the Buddhist altar (which was always above head level, and which held a Buddha statue, lit incense, and usually some lottery tickets).

Despite the overwhelming presence of Thai Buddhist influence in the village, one of the most interesting conclusions of my research was how nonhomogenous Baan Khmer turned out to be. In the past, Northern Thai villages have been portrayed in academic literature as homogenous communities[11] of ethnic Thai Buddhists who practiced matrilineal descent and were members of spirit cults; this generalization has recently been criticized.[12] What I found in Baan Khmer were people who classified themselves, each other, and myself in various ways at various times: regionally (as "Isan," or Northeastern Thai; "Lanna," or Northern Thai; central Thai; Southerners; "dark," or Asian, foreigner [*khaek*]; and white, or Western, foreigner [*farang*]); ethnically (Lao, Thai, hill-tribe member, Thai-Chinese, Thai-Indian, or *luuk khrung*—the offspring of a *farang* and a Thai); and religiously (Buddhist, Christian, Moslem, or animist).

In the village where I worked there were hill-tribe families who identified themselves as both Akha and Mien;[13] a jewelry storeowner and his wife who were Thai-Chinese and frequented a Chinese Buddhist temple in Chiang Rai city; a *farang* married to a local Thai woman; and a Thai-Indian Muslim who managed the garment factory. There was also a Christian church down the road, as well as rival Buddhist temples.

These characteristics of ethnicity, religion, regional affiliation, economic status, and prestige were noted by the villagers, who used their observations to consciously and subconsciously "rank" themselves and others in the social hierarchy. In Southeast Asian society, a person cannot be acknowledged as a social being until she is ranked within this system, which dictates not just perceived status, but also the appropriate manners and language to be used in social interaction. To occupy a recognized space of significance one had to be labeled according to place of origin, language spoken at home, educational level attained, and amount of money accumulated, among other things.

My experience as a field researcher became unnerving when I realized that all the villagers, from the eight-year-old boy in my household to the grandmothers of the village, were studying me as critically as I was studying them. While this is within the normal experience of anthropologists in the field (the prefaces of ethnographies are full of stories of unwitting anthropologists whose outlook on life changed after such moments of realization), I was unprepared for my experience as an Asian American[14] studying in Thailand. The idea of being an Asian as well as an American did not fit comfortably into the villagers' frame of reference. I was either an American or another Asian. Because of these apparent contradictions I often had the opportunity to watch and listen to people actively negotiating my place in the social hierarchy. I was an anomaly. In some respects I fitted nicely into their model of an "American." I was a doctoral student attending an American university, a marker of some wealth and social prestige. I was also married to a *farang* and had lived in the United States for most of my life. To the villagers I lived and socialized with, these attributes made me a *farang*, and thus earned me, and themselves, a higher social status.

But in other ways I was very much Asian: I am ethnically Malay, a Muslim, and from Malaysia. My family members all reside in Malaysia. I am dark-skinned, short, and have large eyes and wavy hair. Additionally, I did not spend a lot of money, a characteristic that was interpreted by some to mean that I was either poor or, worse, stingy.[15] These characteristics automatically signified me as a *khaek* to many of the villagers. *Khaek* is a derogatory term in the Thai language used to denote people with dark skin and a Muslim background, such as Indians and Thai Muslims, most of whom are ethnically Malay and come from the south. *Khaek* refers to a foreigner who is placed lower on the social hierarchy than other Thais. For instance, the discourse surrounding *khaek* is that they are poor, dirty, immigrants, eat strange food, and are darker and thus less attractive. This term is not only demeaning but also misleading in that those often identified as *khaek*, such as Thai-Indians, are not usually foreign but have been Thai citizens for generations.

The White-Skinned Foreigner

The term *farang* is a complicated one, coded with subtle markers of power, status, and hierarchy. Most people who are white[16] and from the West are classified by Thais as *farang*. An examination of the term *farang* alongside its contrasting term *khaek* illustrates a striking jockeying for power between the labeler and the labeled. This type of examination is also timely. As Cook and Jackson (1999:19) put it:

> Thai studies have yet to deconstruct the indigenous and often homogenized category of the farang, a ubiquitous Thai cultural-ethnic term which conflates "Caucasian" (race) and "Western" (culture). But leaving aside the ambiguities of the term, critical reflexivity by foreign researchers in understanding how being positioned as a farang impacts upon their study is poorly developed and has yet to be integrated into critical reflection on the academic enterprise of Thai studies. A deconstruction of the cultural conceptions involved in the notion of farang would help us unpack the curious inverted stereotypical images that Thailand and the West present to each other.

The people I lived with, those I went to the Buddhist temple with, and those I interviewed (the majority of the village) labeled me a *farang*, something that rather shocked me. As an Asian, even as an Asian American, I had never seen myself as white. Now I was forced to view myself through the eyes of my informants as a *farang,* and to sort out what that identity meant. To be an Asian living in the United States meant being invested with the history, politics, and prosperity implied by the term "American." Yet, in my mind, ethnicity is very different from nationality. Living in America did not, therefore, qualify me as "white." In fact, my years in the United States have accentuated the differences between my ethnic identity and history and those of the "real" Americans I knew.

Back in Baan Khmer village my friends explained to me that they saw me as a doctoral student who had lived in America for many years, was married to a white American (an unquestionable *farang*),[17] and was obviously rich (for how else could I have afforded to live in Thailand for a year?). Since I had also traveled extensively,[18] and spoke English as my first language, I was clearly a *farang*.[19] Because I was perceived as a *farang*, others were very respectful toward me, deferring to me during religious and social situations even if they were male and older (markers of being at the pinnacle of the Thai social hierarchy), something which I found embarrassing and confusing. For someone who came from a Southeast Asian community with a similar sense of status, it did not look or feel right to be one of the most respected people in the room. Also, as a graduate student with no real job or regular source of income, I felt this formal respect to be completely unwarranted.

The deference paid to me was also annoying, for because I was considered a *farang* my companions sometimes became overprotective of my body and my research. One example of this occurred when I was helping wash dishes in preparation for an upcoming religious ceremony at the *wat*. Several out-of-town people had arrived the night before to attend. As I rinsed the cups and saucers being handed to me in assembly-line fashion, an old woman across the yard saw me and exclaimed, "Hey, aren't you my cousin's daughter from Khon Kaen?[20] I need to give your mother something!" and started walking toward me. Before I could tell her of her mistake, the girls washing dishes next to me quickly stood up and stopped the approaching woman in her tracks. "No, auntie," they said, "this is the *farang* studying women here." They gently steered her away and, as she left, someone else from our group shouted to her "Don't disturb her! She is doing research," and passed me another cup to rinse.

My status as *farang* was not absolute, however, even in the eyes of some of my Baan Khmer friends. One girl, Nok, was asked to interview a native English speaker, transcribe the interview, and then hand in a picture of the person with the assignment for her English class. She asked if she could interview me and I agreed. After we conducted the interview I helped her to transcribe it. The problem came when she received a picture of me to attach to her work. After staring at the picture for a while, Nok decided not to include it with her assignment. A little hurt, I asked her why. She responded, "Because you don't look *farang* enough."

While the general respect I received was flattering and at times useful, I also felt as if my identity as a Malay Muslim had been somehow shunted to the margins and replaced by "American." My perspective of the villagers, I knew, was framed though multiple lenses. However, I had not realized until this fieldwork experience how much of myself was firmly Malaysian, when I felt that identity being challenged.

The Dark-Skinned Foreigner

I noticed early on that the people who were most closely associated with me and my research (my neighbors, teachers, and students, for example) used my *farang* label to endow themselves with higher status. I would hear my acquaintances correct visitors to the village who would see me and ask, "Who's the *khaek*?" "No," my landlord liked to say, "she's actually an

American, a 'doctor,' a *farang*." My host family, whose close relatives lived within a mile of each other, had political alliances with the former headman of the village. The current headman had his own following of villagers who lived farther down the main road and attended a different Buddhist temple. When I walked by on my way to interview others, I heard the headman's supporters comment on the *khaek*. They neither made eye contact nor spoke with me. While this was in part because of my observed alliance with my host family, I never saw these people act toward others (also associated with my host family) in this way, or use the term *khaek* to refer to any of my host family's clique.

Khaek is akin to a slur. I found that it was mentioned only in relation to someone who was not present at the time, or who was thought to have no understanding of the Thai language. When I first arrived at Baan Khmer, it was assumed that I did not understand Thai well, and thus I would frequently hear the term *khaek* used in reference to me. Later, as I became a recognized fixture in the village, I noticed that some people still referred to me openly as *khaek*, even though they (and everyone else) knew that I understood the negative connotations of the term. Finally I came to the conclusion that perhaps as a *khaek* I was assumed to understand the literal meaning of the term, but perhaps not its symbolic capital. Or perhaps they just did not care. Either way, despite my position as an observer of the culture, I felt insulted and demeaned whenever I heard that term, and through a mutually unspoken understanding never conducted any interviews or observations in the headman's section of the village.

By the end of my fieldwork the label of *khaek* was used sparingly toward me in my presence, but the concept behind the label was frequently made apparent to me as people talked about the Indians and Muslims in the area. There was a substantial Muslim population in Chiang Rai city, but few Muslims in the village itself. The one exception (excluding myself) was the supervisor of the small weaving factory on the outskirts of the village. I saw him in the restaurant, and he always only ordered vegetarian fried rice. "It's because he's Muslim (*khaek*)," Jeew, the restaurant's proprietor, said, "and he doesn't trust us to use a clean pan to make his food," referring to the fact that many Muslims believe they cannot eat food that is cooked in pans in which pork has been cooked. She said, "We don't know him very well; he just comes in here once or twice a week. He smells kind of bad." Someone else in the village later told me, "His wife is very nice. She brought us a dish she cooked once, but it was something I had never seen before. It smelled funny, so I threw it away instead of giving it to my family." These statements shocked me, and made me feel uncomfortable. There were also statements directed at Southern Thais, the majority of whom are Muslim. Examples included: "They talk really fast, and it's not 'real' Thai." "They are really short and dark, not very pretty."

Conclusion

Villager perceptions of my identity constantly impacted on many aspects of my fieldwork experience. Was I *farang* or was I *khaek*? The symbolic and social connotations of those labels were very distinct, and dictated not only my own behavior in an interaction, but the behavior of the other participants in that interaction as well. Was this confusion about the fieldwork experience a "feminist dilemma" of the sort explored by Wolf (1996) and others? Partly. As a feminist ethnographer exploring issues of gender, identity, and power, I was prepared to confront my own subject position in the field. What was unnerving, however, was that the issues I had to actually confront were not centered clearly or cleanly at any one time on any specific aspect of my identity. Rather, the issues of power and control, and especially of acceptance and rejection, emerged constantly and simultaneously, the effect of which was a feeling of perpetual struggle on my part to maintain any kind of consistent identity at all. Thus there were moments when I engaged in reinterpreting my own identity as diligently as those of my research subjects. I became, in essence, another subject in my own fieldwork.

The fieldwork process is charged with the energy and emotions of its participants, and its participants include both the fieldworker and the subjects of her study. It is crucial, however, to acknowledge that the fieldworker is often under as much scrutiny from her research subjects as they are from her. Rather than seeing this as a problem of fieldwork, I believe close examination of such two-way scrutiny adds to academic understanding of the contributions of cross-cultural research. "Natives" have always assessed and positioned ethnographers, and native perceptions of the "other-ness" of the researcher (whether it be their country of origin, ethnicity, religion, or class) have always influenced the type of information made available to that person. Thus the confusion that arises from the rapid-fire creation of simultaneous positive and negative stereotyping, judgments, and generalizations signals a moment of possible revelation and, paradoxically, clarification for the ethnographer as to the cultural constructions of the research subjects. These uncomfortable moments reflect instances when the researcher herself is situated, for better or for worse, within the realm of her research subjects. She can then begin to view their world from the inside, thus taking full advantage of the value and complexity of the ethnographic experience.

Notes

1. Such tensions are seen by some as one of the strengths of extended field-work (e.g., MacClancy 2002; Bourgois 2002).
2. Exceptions to this, however, include Mills' (1999), Morris' (2000), and Tannenbaum's (1999) work on modern Thai society.
3. Alor Setar is the capital of the Northern Malaysian state of Kedah (known as "the rice bowl of Malaysia"). My entire family comes from this city and most still live there.
4. A thin and swampy area of land stretching north to south that connects Thailand to Peninsula Malaysia.
5. In the Northeast Thai dialect the women say "*ja*," and in Northern Thailand the women use "*jaw*."
6. Although Northern Thai are typically depicted as taller and more fair-skinned than other Thai, many of the inhabitants of the village where I worked had dark skin and curly hair very similar to my own.
7. People in Bangkok comment, with all seriousness, that it is often quicker to drive to the airport, sit on a plane for one hour, and then drive to their Northern houses than it is to try to drive home from work in Bangkok rush hour traffic.
8. Northern Thai fruits are famous all over the country. It is said by Bangkok natives that the best mangoes, lychees, and tamarinds come from Chiang Rai province. The North is also famous for its flowers—orchids and roses, for example—but it is Chiang Mai province that earns the most praise in this case.
9. Founded much more recently than the *Mahanikaya* sect, the *Thammayut* sect was a creation of Thai royalty, and advocates a much more rigorous lifestyle for its monks. *Thammayut* monks are allowed to eat only once a day, and are expected to follow more precepts (see Keyes 1984 and J. Potter 1976).
10. For instance, it was considered important to make extra merit for oneself and one's family on one's birthday or on the occasion of someone's death. In such circumstances it was not enough to offer food to the monks on their daily "begging" schedule. Instead, it was important to go and visit the *wat* and talk to the abbot and offer him something more "lasting" than food, such as toiletries, essentials, or uncooked rice, which could be stored until needed.
11. See, for example, the ethnographies of Konrad Kingshill (1991) and Jack Potter (1976).
12. See Tannenbaum (1999) and Van Esterik (1999) for specific critiques.

13. Two predominant hill tribes found in the uplands of Northern Thailand.
14. I use Asian American here not as a label of citizenship, but rather as an indication of the perceived cultural fidelities I was allegedly displaying. The villagers noticed more "Americanisms" in me than I was ever aware of, often labeling me "American" in ways I did not always appreciate.
15. For more on the stigma on stinginess in Malay culture see Scott (1985).
16. The complex ideology of "whiteness" in the West will not be dealt with here; rather, I am using the term as I observed the villagers using it, to refer to all Westerners who were obviously not of African descent.
17. An interesting perspective on race being traced not through one's own background, but through that of those one desires to be, is presented in Elise Lemire's book titled "*Miscegenation*": *Making Race in America* (2002).
18. A villager once commented to me, shaking his head, "You *farang* travel so far all the time and always seem to know where you are. We Thais, we're so scared of traveling far, because we can get lost even when visiting the village down the road!"
19. People would come to me asking for English lessons or help in getting jobs in the U.S.—not for goods or medical supplies, the more traditional commodities anthropologists dispensed as a matter of course in the field.
20. A major city in Northeast Thailand.

CHAPTER 4

Multiple Roles, Statuses, and Allegiances

Exploring the Ethnographic Process in Disability Culture*

Recent critiques of ethnographic practice have challenged the ability of traditional fieldwork narratives to adequately represent the fragmented nature of contemporary social settings. In response to such challenges anthropologists have begun to engage new approaches to conducting ethnography. The idea of "multi-sited" research (Marcus 1998; Clifford 1997b), for example, has become increasingly common, fieldwork "at home" is more widely pursued (Gupta & Ferguson 1997b), and innovative sites such as the Internet (e.g., Edwards 1994; Gold 2001) and business and research organizations (Forsythe 1993; Mouly & Sankaran 1995) are being identified. It is now not unusual for an anthropologist to be employed in the organization he or she is researching, and, as Forsythe (1999) and Hogle and Downey (1999) point out, occupying the dual roles of employee and ethnographer—where one's informants are also one's colleagues and supervisors—can produce a variety of unique personal and professional dilemmas. In fact, the more roles and statuses ethnographers occupy in relation to their informants, the more likelihood that conflicts of interest, ethical dilemmas, and/or points of contention will occur.

This chapter explores several personal and professional quandaries that I confronted while conducting ethnographic fieldwork on the pursuit of sexual intimacy for men with cerebral palsy. While engaged in this research and during the write-up period, I occupied multiple roles and statuses in relation to disabled informants, including nondisabled anthropologist/ethnographer, employee and long-time friend of my key informant, disability rights advocate and ally, and disability studies scholar.[1] I will argue that critical-reflexive exploration of these quandaries, borne of multiple roles and statuses and their consequent allegiances, both enriched my understanding of the sexual situation of disabled men and led me to question the conceptual assumptions of both disability studies and anthropology.

The Nondisabled Anthropologist as Disability Ethnographer

Sherry Ortner (1995:173) comments that ethnography "has always meant the attempt to understand another life world using the self, as much of it as possible, as the instrument of knowing." For the anthropologist, ethnographic process is mythically founded in the fieldwork experience, in the self's encounters with other people who are presumably culturally or subculturally different from the ethnographer, and in the attempt to apprehend their lived experience and their interpretations of the world. This process culminates in an interpretive rendering by the ethnographer: the ethnographic product, or the "written representation of culture" (Van Maanen 1995:5).

Over the last several decades, however, many anthropologists, myself included, have become increasingly self-critical of the motivations, the assumptions, and the asymmetrical power relations that may be inherent in our conception of ethnography vis-à-vis the "other" (e.g., Clifford 1986, 1988; Abu-Lughod 1991; James, Hockey & Dawson 1997). Criticism of ethnography has been most severe in terms of the ethnographer's alleged power to represent or interpret the "other" in the final written product, but the fieldwork encounter itself is also seen by many as inherently asymmetrical in terms of power (Clifford 1986, 1988). Anthropological complicity in the colonial endeavor has especially fueled this disciplinary self-critique, as has heightened suspicion of anthropological motives in the postcolonial era. Moreover, anthropologists are increasingly denied access, especially to Third-World countries.

Anthropological debate concerning the asymmetrical power relations in ethnographic encounters with, and representations of, the other has paralleled the implicit or explicit questioning by feminists and representatives of non-English speaking peoples and ethnic minorities as to the motives and legitimacy of social science research conducted by nongroup members (e.g., Oakley 1981; Bourne 1983). In disability studies, this wariness has taken the form of questioning the motives of nondisabled scholars and researchers writing about disability. The claiming of disability identity and disability culture by disabled people has rendered problematic traditional social scientific inquiry on disability issues. Self and group boundaries are monitored much more closely in research now than in the past, with the purpose of protecting disabled people against possible exploitation by researchers.[2] This discussion has been ongoing for several years and shows no sign of cooling off, as demonstrated by a 1999 essay in the *Chronicle of Higher Education* (Cassuto 1999) and the subsequent rejoinders from numerous influential disability studies scholars.[3]

Another paper presented by a noted disabled disability studies scholar at the 2000 meeting of the Society for Disability Studies continued this debate (Vernon 2000).

Although I am nondisabled, I have been immersed in disability culture in the East San Francisco Bay Area for many years. Since 1984 I have worked as a personal assistant for disabled men, socialized with disabled friends, and even lived, for a couple of years, with a disabled friend for whom I also worked. In these roles, my nondisabled status is not an issue, and in the case of being a personal assistant it is necessary. However, given the recent political context of disability research, my decision, as a nondisabled person, to conduct ethnographic research with some members of this community in the mid-1990s caused me a certain amount of concern. Sensitive to the above issues of nongroup membership and purported exploitation by researchers, I wondered how disabled men would greet me as an ethnographer rather than as an employee or friend. That the research I wanted to conduct was on disability and sexuality made me even more anxious. I wanted to explore the social and cultural barriers that men with cerebral palsy confront in their attempts to negotiate sexual intimacy with others. But what right did I have to delve into disabled people's intimate and private sexual lives? What were the underlying power relations that I was reproducing here? Would ethnography be seen in this case as simply voyeuristic?

The disabled researcher, Tom Shakespeare (1997:177), describes the trepidation he felt when a book he co-wrote on disabled people's sexual lives in the United Kingdom (Shakespeare, Gillespie-Sells & Davies 1996) was about to be published: "What would other people think? How would the disability movement react? What difference would our book make? Had we done the right thing?" Shakespeare and his coauthors, however, are all disabled, so they were not concerned about being considered exploitative outsiders by either their informants or their readers. I, on the other hand, was acutely aware that there were disability studies scholars and members of the disability community who might question my right, as a nondisabled person, to research and write about disabled others, especially given my focus on their sexual lives. I realized that I could not responsibly conduct research on disability issues without scrutinizing the underlying power relations involved in my ethnographic fieldwork and without taking the subject position of disabled people more fully into account vis-à-vis myself and nondisabled people in general (Shuttleworth 2000b).

For instance, I realized that I had experienced more sexually intimate relationships than many of the men I was interviewing. I wondered if this experiential asymmetry would be a reflection of inherent asymmetrical power relations in our ethnographic encounter. Although I certainly do not consider myself an expert in the area of dating, there are fewer interpersonal barriers for me as a nondisabled person, a clear reflection of the cultural attitudes and social practices that make it difficult for many disabled people to negotiate sexual intimacy with others. Yet, does this asymmetrical power relation necessarily invalidate my perspective in writing about disabled men's experience and interpretation of their sexual situation?

For many years the disabled men I worked for had been conveying to me their belief in the need for research on the barriers to their sexual expression. The men with whom I was conducting pilot interviews implored me: "If you don't do it, who else will?" Whatever criticism I might receive from other disabled people, I proceeded with the blessing of these men. During the research, I recorded as accurately as possible what they perceived were the significant sexual issues in their lives. While my research is aimed at emancipatory goals and is as participatory as possible, like Shakespeare (1996, 1997), I view the researcher's interpretation as a significant contribution to qualitative research. Furthermore, informants are not passive in the ethnographic process and often subvert anthropologists' agendas according to their own interests (see, e.g., Ong 1995; Frank 2000; Shuttleworth 2000b).

Disabled people in the United States and in other English-speaking societies have long had to contend with, and continue to experience, considerable stigma, prejudice, and lack of societal access.[4] As a result, Mitchell (1999) suggests that nondisabled scholars will likely have to endure a certain amount of necessary suspicion. The fact is, even for nondisabled social scientists like myself who claim an informed sensitivity to the multifarious oppression of disabled people, the trust and respect of this community will emerge only as a result of the cogency and relevance of our work to their lived situations (Shuttleworth 2000b). Despite a desire by some disability studies scholars to move beyond this debate and to address the representational and dialogic aspects of other inclusion issues in ethnographic research process and practice (Corker & Davis forthcoming), for those of us researchers who are not disabled, our nondisabled status can never be taken for granted if we choose to engage with and publish within the disability studies community.

The Disability Ethnographer as Ally

As my research progressed, I found myself immersed in disability studies' perspectives and became a more outspoken disability advocate, especially with regard to sexual rights (Shuttleworth forthcoming). This immersion in disabled people's struggle for equal access in U.S. society meshed, intellectually and emotionally, with my long-term engagement in disability culture and began to obscure the easy insider/outsider–disabled/nondisabled division that I had been making.[5] Did my long-term relations with disabled people in several different roles make me an insider while conducting research in the disability community? I certainly have an intimate knowledge of disabled people's practices and behaviors. In fact, as a personal assistant, I have what might be termed an intimate, embodied relation to these practices and behaviors and I have also witnessed many instances of disabled people's stigmatization and exclusion, often becoming more upset than my disabled employers and friends themselves (see Shuttleworth 2000b). What is missing of course is the actual lived experience of this oppression.

I continued to be immersed in disabled people's daily lives as a personal assistant, friend, and advocate the entire time I was writing up my ethnography. From this highly engaged position, I could not distance myself from my fieldsite in the ways that many ethnographers have traditionally done (Clifford 1997b). In fact, my multirelational engagement with the disability community kept relevant issues continually in my awareness throughout this last phase of the ethnographic project. Unlike my previous experiences of doing ethnography,[6] I did not have the luxury of removing myself from the field to focus on the analysis and interpretation of the material I had gathered. In this sense, although my work is certainly theoretically rigorous, I feel it remains substantially grounded in the exigencies of everyday life in the disability community. Additionally, I believe my multiple engagements acted to bind me even closer to disabled people's struggle for equal access in U.S. society. Some disabled colleagues and friends began calling me an ally, an achieved status in the disability community that includes not only being an advocate for disabled people in terms of particular issues but also having more comprehensive involvement in disabled people's lives.

However, the depth of my involvement in the disability community creates, if not an ethical dilemma, at least some points of contention with my anthropological background. It puts me at odds, for example, with those anthropologists who argue for the separation of scientific and moral models in anthropology (D'Andrade 1995). Despite continued calls for a more socially responsible and politically committed anthropology (Berreman 1973; Scheper-Hughes 1996), many anthropologists endure a certain amount of stigma within the academy for engaging in identity politics (Knauft 1996). Anthropologists may also be "uneasy about the usefulness of performative moralization in anthropology" (Cohen 1998:xxiii).[7] Additionally, too strong an identification with one's research subjects may lead to accusations of "going native." Granting anthropologists unfettered license to either identify strongly or align themselves with oppressed groups might also be seen by some as an unacceptable assault on the still lingering claims to objectivity for the ethnographic process. From my perspective, however, attempting to create or maintain an inviolable space between the academy and the community constitutes a distancing tactic that suggests a false separation between the life of the mind and the insecurity and messiness of everyday involvement (Shuttleworth forthcoming).

It is common knowledge in the disability community, although not within anthropology, that many anthropologists studying disability have only weakly allied themselves with the Disability Rights Movement and with academic disability studies. Very few of the small but growing number of nondisabled anthropologists who study disability regularly attend or present at the annual Society for Disability Studies Meeting, for example. While some have presented papers there in the past, they often do not return. Perhaps they are reacting to the identity politics at these meetings, or perhaps they fear that their own lack of engagement with disability studies perspectives might be attacked by disability activists and scholars, many of whom, as already noted, are suspicious of "outsider" research. I argue, however, that to engage with both disability activists and scholars about the issues affecting disabled people's lives and to ally oneself with their struggle for full societal participation do not necessarily require anthropologists to compromise the ethnographic product.

The Disability Ethnographer as Employee and Friend

My work as a personal assistant for disabled men and my tendency to socialize with disabled friends predate my role of ethnographer in the disability community by over a decade. I have written at length elsewhere about the embodied understanding of significantly disabled men's everyday bodily practices and the hermeneutic perspective I developed during my role as a personal assistant (Shuttleworth 2000b). I want to focus here on the quandary that my roles as personal assistant and friend for one disabled man created for me in the face of my anthropological background and my desire to maintain an ethical ethnographic practice.

It was during intimate discussions on sexuality with a disabled friend and employer, Josh (pseudonym), that I first conceived of writing an ethnography of disability and sexuality. Josh has cerebral palsy and uses a wheelchair to get around, and an alphabet board and head pointer for communication. In the mid to late 1990s, I lived with him and several other people in a large house that he owned in the East San Francisco Bay Area. Josh and I would talk into the early hours of the morning, and he often mentioned the barriers that he felt he faced in his search for sexual intimacy.

My work relationship with Josh consisted of assisting him with personal care and also with practical actions such as taking notes in university lectures and facilitating his communication in these lectures and at city government meetings that he attended. One feature of our friendship was that I often extended my assistance to him beyond what he required of his other personal assistants. For example, I would get him set up so that he could masturbate after I went upstairs to my own room. I also accompanied him to strip clubs, facilitated his communication with strippers, and, prior to the formal conception of the research, facilitated his encounters with several sex workers. Josh's primary goal was to find someone with whom he felt comfortable enough to initiate a long-term sexual arrangement. If I had simply been Josh's employee, my involvement most likely would have stopped at assisting him in communicating at strip clubs. The hook for deeper involvement was my long friendship with him.

Josh was thirty-one years old at the time. Still a virgin, he desperately desired some sexual experiences. Yet he lacked the interactional skills necessary to establish an emotionally meaningful, or even casual, sexual relationship because of early social exclusions. He also felt that he suffered significant sexual discrimination because of his impairment. He was thus thoroughly incapable of expressing romantic or sexual interest to any of the many women that moved in and out of his life as personal assistants, friends, or acquaintances. Multiple sociocultural impediments had rendered his sexual self-agency immobilized. As he would often tell me, "I feel blocked" (Shuttleworth 2000a, 2000b, 2001).

I presented Josh with the avenue of sexual therapy and surrogacy,[8] but he balked vehemently at taking the therapeutic route. According to him, there was nothing he needed help with, he just wanted some sexual experiences. Although applying the therapeutic model to the sexual difficulties experienced by disabled people can be read as a further sign of their sexual exclusion (Shuttleworth 2000b), I thought therapy, and perhaps some work with a sexual surrogate, might help Josh become less blocked intersubjectively. At this point I had not started the formal phase of fieldwork and was simply conducting some impromptu interviews with him.

Josh instead chose to purchase the services of sex workers. To him, exchanging money for sex seemed more honest than working with a sex surrogate. Despite feeling ethically uneasy and a little anxious, given Josh's need for assistance, I opted to help him. This consisted in calling women whose numbers were obtained from a local sex newspaper, explaining Josh's impairment, and asking if they were open to having a session with him. If they said yes, I would facilitate the sexual encounters (see Shuttleworth 2000b).

When the formal fieldwork started, Josh wanted me to continue helping him. My anxiety and awareness of the ethical and legal dimensions of this were much heightened once my research was given the official stamps of approval by my dissertation and ethics committees. Yet Josh was still looking for someone with whom he felt comfortable, and he continued to need my assistance. I could not remember any anthropological accounts of ethnographers engaging in, or helping informants engage in, illegal activities.[9] I began comparing what I was doing to an urban ethnographer assisting a drug addict to get a fix. The threat of getting caught was also very real; the elaborate process of setting up first encounters revealed the serious concerns that these women sex workers had about the police.[10] Although I continued to assist Josh, I breathed a sigh of relief when, about six months into the formal research, he announced that his interest in finding a comfortable sexual arrangement with a sex worker was waning.

The Ethnographic Salience of Ethical Dilemmas

Disability ethnographers are increasingly incorporating critically reflexive perspectives into their writings (e.g., Davis 2000; Frank 2000; Shuttleworth 2000b; Corker & Davis forthcoming). Strongly influenced by anthropological works on reflexivity, especially Clifford & Marcus (1986), these researchers consider it of paramount importance to reflect on the sources and uses of their knowledge and methods along with their particular roles and statuses vis-à-vis their informants. Indeed, my own experience of engaging reflexively with the issues and dilemmas outlined above positively enhanced my understanding of the life-worlds of my informants. Reflecting on the ethical quandary I faced with Josh, while simultaneously trying to position myself professionally between anthropology and disability studies, also led me to look more critically at some of the theoretical and methodological assumptions of both disciplines.

My ethical concerns about facilitating Josh's encounters with prostitutes and his communication in strip clubs were intensified by my sensitivity to anthropology's long-standing taboo on sexual interactions between researchers and research participants (e.g., Kulick 1995; Ashkenazi and

Markowitz 1999; Herdt 1999).[11] In addition to concerns about the legality and morality of my actions, I was constantly anxious about whether the assistance I provided to Josh was inappropriate in the context of ethnographic fieldwork.

By reflecting on the reasons for the anxiety I experienced during the initial stages of my fieldwork I began to see how certain social institutions (in my case anthropology) deem some contexts appropriate for sex and others not. Transposing this general insight to the fieldwork I was doing led me to wonder why sex work and sex surrogacy, both negatively sanctioned in U.S. society, are sometimes seen by disabled men as their only avenues for sexual expression. As a result of this critical questioning, I was able to comprehend the degree to which sexuality is considered a personal project of the self in U.S. society. I also began to realize why contexts such as surrogacy and sex work, which deviate from the ideal of self-sufficiency in making sexual connections, are so stigmatized. In the United States, sexuality as a reflexive project of the self (Giddens 1992) relies on the rhetoric of autonomy and self-sufficiency. Those who fail to find a sexual partner in the sanctioned self-sufficient ways are thus subject to negative judgment. These insights deepened my understanding of the cultural terrain that Josh and other significantly impaired people encounter in their search for sexual intimacy.

I also feel that the intimate data gained by assisting Josh with his sexual quest, in corroboration with other men's stories, has led me to an enhanced understanding of the struggles many disabled people face in their desire for sexual expression. As the facilitator of Josh's quest, and as an almost around-the-clock discussant, I was privy to a wide array of his thoughts and feelings on this phase of his sociosexual life, leading up to his establishment of an emotionally meaningful long-term sexual relationship (Shuttleworth 2000b). I do not believe that I would have been pushed to the same productive levels of ethical reflexivity had I simply entered the disability community for the purposes of conducting research over one or two years. While I recognize that some might challenge my decision to assist Josh in the ways that I did, I argue that my choice to do so, and the associated ethical dilemmas I experienced, led to important insights about the realities of ethnographic research, and of the challenges faced by the participants in my study. In addition, the mutual trust that Josh and I developed over the course of our relationship, my loyalty and compassion toward him and his trust in me, raises important questions concerning the rapport building that is so essential to the ethnographic enterprise. For example, is the "natural" rapport that is built up in the course of a pre-ethnography friendship a more ethical beginning than the rapport building meant solely for the instrumental purpose of conducting an ethnography? Which of these would generate the more emotionally accurate ethnographic description of informants' circumstances?

A Reflexive Interrogation of Allegiances

I also found (and still find) it very productive to reflexively interrogate my allegiance as an advocate for and ally of disabled people, and as a disability studies scholar, in relation to my allegiance as an anthropologist/ethnographer. I came to question both the assumptions underlying traditional anthropological notions such as "culture," as well as the conceptual biases of disability rights/studies perspectives. In terms of the latter, my anthropological exposure to diverse theoretical approaches, and to the notion that there are multiple and competing stakeholder voices among informants, continually enables me to uncover obscured aspects and underlying assumptions of the Disability Rights Movement and its academic offshoot that true "insider" researchers may miss (e.g., Shuttleworth 2000a, 2000b, forthcoming).

A critical reflexivity also enables me to confront more fully the assumptions underlying some traditional anthropological notions and taboos. Anthropologists have been authoritatively dismissive of certain developments in disability studies. For example, claims about the existence of a disability "culture" have been too easily dismissed by anthropologists as a dilution of their traditional use of this concept (see Kasnitz & Shuttleworth 1999, 2001; Shuttleworth 2000b; Scheer 1994).[12] While initially skeptical of claims about the "culture" of disability culture by some disabled people in English-language contexts, I have since come to question anthropology's rights to primary ownership of this term.

Without my immersion in the disability community as a personal assistant and friend, my participation in disabled people's collectivist movement, and my involvement in disability studies, I would never have begun to reflexively question my anthropological assumptions from the perspective of the "other." Indeed, in a recent article (1999), Kasnitz, a disabled scholar, and I come to the conclusion that "culture" as a signifier must remain open to transformation in the context of people's struggles in the world. I would warn anthropologists that participating in negotiations with others over the meanings of some of our much-beloved concepts is mandatory unless we wish to forfeit a say in what these terms will come to mean in the larger society.

Conclusion

For the anthropologist, the lack of a formal social role among one's informants (other than researcher) could be construed as an asset in an age of objectivity. However, a perspective from within the social field also informs the cultural description that is the heart of ethnography. Experiential accounts of the ethnographer's role, position(s), statuses, and allegiances in the social field, and a critical-reflexive exploration of some of the issues and dilemmas that emerge, can only enhance ethnographic understanding. The conceptual assumptions of both public and academic representatives of those under study, as well as anthropology itself, can be challenged using such an approach.

Critical reflection on my role as an ethnographer/anthropologist in relation to the multiple roles and statuses I hold within the disability community and the dilemmas I faced because of my multiple allegiances thus functioned to subvert my assumptions as both anthropologist and disability studies scholar. Yet the most significant insight from reflecting on these dilemmas remains the expansion of ethnographic understanding of disabled people's sexual situation. Without accompanying Josh on his sexual journey and having my ethnographic ethics tested, my research would have lacked an important aspect—an experiential sense of what is at stake for disabled people as they strive for sexual expression.

Acknowledgments

My research among men with cerebral palsy in the San Francisco Bay Area was assisted by a grant from the Sexuality Research Fellowship Program of the Social Science Research Council, with funds provided by the Ford Foundation. The writing of this chapter was assisted by the Ed Roberts Postdoctoral Fellowship in Disability Studies, University of California, Berkeley, funded by NIDRR and the Department of Education #11133P020009. I am grateful to Devva Kasnitz for her comments on an earlier draft and to the editors for critical feedback that sharpened the final version of this chapter.

Notes

* Earlier versions of this paper were presented at the Society for Applied Anthropology's 2000 Meeting, and published in *Disability Studies Quarterly* 21.3 (2001):103–113.

1. Disability studies is the academic offshoot of the Disability Rights Movement. The central idea of the Disability Rights Movement, which was subsequently taken up by academic disability studies, is that impairment is not the cause of disability, as in the medical model, but that disability is due to sociocultural environments that restrict access in multiple ways to persons whose bodies, bodily movements, or behaviors fall outside of a narrow aesthetic and/or functional range. Some anthropologists who study disability engage with the theoretical debates within disability studies, but most do not.

2. Some disability studies scholars, and many of those now claiming a disability identity, maintain that previous social science research, mostly conducted from a medical perspective, has been irrelevant to the goal of improving disabled people's position in society and their quality of life (see Oliver 1992, 1996; Stone & Priestly 1996). Disabled researchers such as Oliver (1992, 1996) have even argued that traditional social science research has in fact played a role in the oppression of disabled people and that an emancipatory approach, which reverses the social relations of research production by putting disabled people fully in control of the research process, is now necessary.

3. This debate centered on Cassuto's argument (1999) against the desire of some disability studies scholars to label other scholars as "disabled" or "nondisabled." Cassuto maintained that this distinction implicitly perceives nondisabled people as less qualified to study disability than disabled scholars. The ensuing debate registered a wide range of responses. There were those scholars who agreed with Cassuto that this distinction pointed to an implicit bias toward and preference for disabled people doing disability research. At the other pole were those scholars who thought that curiosity about a scholar's disabled/nondisabled status could simply be a desire to know one aspect of the researcher's social position.

4. Since disability rights/studies perspectives emerged in English language contexts such as the United States, the United Kingdom, and Australia, disabled people's exclusion has been well documented in these societies. The extent of disabled people's exclusion in other societies is a hot topic and its evaluation often depends on whether the ethnographer brings a critical perspective to bear (Shuttleworth in press).

5. Clifford (1997b), in fact, points to a growing number of ethnographers who find it difficult to draw the distinction between insider and outsider. These ethnographers "define the spatial practices of their fieldwork in terms of a politics of location, of tactically shifting insides and outsides, affiliations and distances" (1997b:210).

6. During the mid-1980s I conducted, at several different locations in the East San Francisco Bay Area, a life history of a woman who was dying of cancer, as she moved from one daughter's home to another daughter's home. She died before I wrote up the study for my anthropology master's thesis. In the early 1990s, I also conducted ethnographic fieldwork at a geropsychiatric hospital in the East San Francisco Bay Area. When I finished the research, I wrote up the study and went back six months later to present my findings to staff.

7. Although respectful of the "critically applied anthropology" of Nancy Scheper-Hughes, her colleague, and the decision of those anthropologists who would follow her politically engaged path in their ethnographic process, Cohen nevertheless maintains that "the language of time is strewn with the best of intentions, reflexive articulations from the moral to the militant" (1998:xxxiii). In other words, critical and politically engaged ethnographers can never be certain that their position is unassailable. Cohen's wryly cast barb is meant to remind these kinds of ethnographers that morals are manifested in their social iteration. Thus, the danger for ethnographers taking a political stand is that their position becomes reified and they become morally righteous.

8. Sexual surrogacy is a therapeutic process that has been proven effective in treating psychogenic sexual problems such as fear of intimacy, premature ejaculation, performance anxiety, the inability to achieve orgasm, and developing or regaining sexual confidence. Since many disabled people do not have the opportunity during adolescence and young adulthood to develop their sexual self-esteem, sexual surrogacy is sometimes presented as an option for them.

9. Rabinow (1977) describes his experiences with a prostitute in Morocco, but his portrayal suggests that prostitution is not viewed as negatively there as it is in the United States.

10. Prostitution is illegal in the United States. For many, the most humiliating part of being involved in prostitution is being arrested. In 1987, average arrest, court, and incarceration costs for prostitution amounted to nearly $2,000 per arrest (Pearl 1987).

11. These works, which began to appear in the mid-1990s, take anthropology to task for the discipline's traditional silence around sexual interactions and relations in the field, a silence that effectively functioned as a taboo. Perhaps the most significant reasons given for this silence include anthropology's early- and mid-twentieth-century aspirations to the scientific objectivity of other sciences along with a similar aspiration toward professionalism in the discipline.

12. At the same time, some anthropologists are questioning the assumptions underlying the culture concept itself (e.g., Abu-Lughod 1990). Others continue to use it uncritically.

CHAPTER 5

"He's Not a Spy; He's One of Us"

Ethnographic Positioning in a Middle-Class Setting

> One friendly critic of our discipline . . . has defined an anthropologist as
> a person who respects every culture-pattern but his own.
>
> —Herskovits (1977:37)

Ravina High, the Western Australian government secondary school where
I conducted ethnographic research during the 1998 and 1999 school
years, erupted into serious conflict toward the middle of my fieldwork
there. Throughout the course of my research after this situation arose, I
was committed to documenting as many different perspectives on this
breakdown of relations between staff and management as possible. This
approach created a number of difficulties and significant challenges, particularly when it came to comprehending the views put forward by the
school leader, the Principal of Ravina High.

An incident following a feisty union meeting is etched firmly in my
mind. The meeting was marked by angry responses on the part of the
school staff to attempted reforms to the workplace emanating from the
principal's office. Afterward, I joined some of the teachers for lunch in the
staff room. As I moved toward a vacant chair, one of them asked me what
it felt like to be a spy at a union meeting. It was a perplexing question.
Naturally enough I was uncomfortable about being positioned as a spy,
and unsure of how to respond. A friend of the questioner, who by this
point was also a friend of mine, seemed to sense my discomfort. She came
to my assistance, exclaiming, "He's not a spy; he's one of us."

I very much enjoyed my fieldwork experience at Ravina High. I reveled
in my interaction with students during the various classroom activities I
sat in on. I delighted in the many conversations I had with teachers and
school administrators in the staff room and corridors of the school, over

a glass of beer in the pub on a Friday afternoon, at parties and other social gatherings, and during the numerous semiformal interviews I conducted with them. I was also pleased with the access I was granted to formal meetings that were held throughout the period of my research—of the School Executive, the School Council, the Parents and Citizens Association, and the Staff Association, all of which are key components in the day-to-day running of the complex organization that is Ravina High. Fieldwork was an exhilarating experience for me.

The teacher's observation, reported above, that I was "one of them," suggests I was successful in gaining strong rapport with at least some of the staff at the school. However, while her comment brought me some pleasure, I also found it disturbing. The reasons for this will become clearer as this chapter develops. It is sufficient for now to point out that this statement, which clearly positioned me alongside those teachers who were increasingly opposed to the school administrators, inadvertently reminded me that, despite my intentions to represent all sides of the conflict, I had lost contact with Grace, the Principal of Ravina High, and the initiator of many of the controversial changes.[1] While I did endeavor to rectify this loss of contact by spending as much time as I could with Grace over the final weeks of my fieldwork, this effort was, in many ways, too little, too late. I argue that this "failure of ethnography" (Devine 1996) was driven by the critical imperatives that accompany many ethnographers when they choose to explore "the bourgeois, middle-class life of mass liberal societies, which industrial capitalism has produced" (Marcus & Fischer 1986:111). Given that a major aim of this essay lies in exploring the epistemological implications of ethnographic positioning (Straight 2002:5), the following descriptions of key events that unfolded during my time at Ravina offer some insights into the ways in which I was simultaneously positioning myself and being positioned by others in the field. My initial encounters with Grace are an important starting point.

The Woman in the Principal's Office[2]

Grace is a dynamic woman. When I first met her in November 1997, I estimated that she was in her mid forties. With her round spectacles, wispy short hair, small stature, and slight build, her appearance belied her strength and determination. Our encounters, which, as I have already hinted at, were more frequent in the initial stages of my project than in the middle and later phases, usually took place in her expansive office. We also chatted over cups of tea in the staff room and occasionally when we

happened to meet in one of the corridors. Usually profound and intellectually energetic, the conversations with Grace were satisfying and enjoyable. Particularly fascinating was her penchant for presenting a new idea
seemingly every time I spoke with her. While I usually found these ideas
stimulating, the rate at which she wanted to get things happening in the
school sometimes left me feeling dizzy, even a little exhausted, although
the proposed changes would have very little impact on me.

Grace's position as head of the school meant that she was my primary
research sponsor, a situation accentuated in these devolutionary times,
where centralized educational bureaucracies are being dismantled in favor
of creating autonomous educational institutions through school-based
management and administration (Whitty, Power & Helpin 1998:3). The
devolution of central authority made negotiating my way into Ravina
High far easier than expected because it meant I could avoid the tortuous
process of seeking permission for my research through the central office.
Grace's enthusiastic support for the research project, and her facilitation
of a process of negotiation with the school staff that was close to ideal,
helped make my passage into Ravina High surprisingly straightforward.

Recognizing the value of having someone from outside the school look
with fresh eyes on the various taken-for-granted operational processes of
the institution, Grace was very keen for my project to go ahead. While she
was comfortable with my initial aim of investigating how cultural difference was understood and taught, she also encouraged the open-ended
intent behind my desire to investigate the culture of the school, particularly as seen through the eyes of its teachers. Indeed, she appeared even
more comfortable with, and encouraging of, this larger project than the
more focused work on cultural difference. "This will be good for the
school," she assured me, "and you should not be afraid of presenting us
with a warts and all account."

Social Conflict and Ethnographic Positioning

Because managerial innovation was such a key theme for the adults at
Ravina High when I was there, my initial research interest in the teaching
and understanding of cultural difference quickly gave way to a focus on
organizational change. Devolution and Local Area Education Planning
(LAEP), two of the more popular concepts circulating at the time, became
my major research foci.

In terms of local management, the school already had control over its
$900,000 annual budget. A local decision-making body, the School

Council, had also been formed. Comprised of members of the school administration, parents, teachers, students, and interested members of the community, such as the local mayor, this group was charged with the duty of evaluating and approving decisions made in and about the school. At the same time as this local decision-making capacity was apparently increasing, the size, if not the reach, of the central office of the Education Department of Western Australia was diminishing. For example, district officers were taking on increasing amounts of responsibility for overseeing the running of schools in their local area, duties that were previously assigned to people working in the central bureaucracy. Grace was disdainful of the bureaucratic "interferers" in the district office, a standpoint that eventually contributed significantly to the demise of her principalship.

Local Area Education Planning provided further impetus for change. This process involved representatives from schools that shared common student-catchment boundaries meeting to discuss ways in which they could collaborate to make better use of available educational resources. Or at least that was the theory. In reality the LAEP process was rarely discussed at Ravina High in terms of cooperation or collusion. Rather, the mergers of some schools, enforced under the LAEP banner due to their lack of numbers, led many Ravina staff to conclude that their survival as an entity depended upon their ability to attract more students. In terms of relationships with other schools, a competitive rather than a collaborative atmosphere prevailed.

Enthusiastically embracing the devolutionary moment, Grace appeared to enjoy the competitive edge encouraged by both LAEP and school-based management. At the beginning of 1998, Grace introduced a specialist sporting program into the school that attracted students from various metropolitan and rural areas. She also restructured the school timetable in order to offer upper school students a greater range of courses. In the wake of these changes, Grace set about finding further ways to make Ravina High a better, more dynamic educational institution.[3] Despite applauding the competitive spirit of LAEP, Grace showed her dislike for bureaucratic process, and her lack of confidence in its ability to achieve desired reform, by ceasing to attend LAEP meetings in second term. Dismissing them as a sham and a waste of time, she got on with "running the school," a phrase she often invoked as a means of justifying her absence from meetings the district directors required her to attend.

Dynamism was a key issue. While Grace was very careful to avoid casting too many aspersions on the staff of Ravina High when talking with me, she often implied that the organization rested on its laurels, relying on its reputation as "a good school." Grace's attempts to shake the staff out of what she perceived as a kind of inertia were summed up picturesquely by one of the deputy principals in a meeting at the beginning of the 1999 school year, when he talked about how Grace had disturbed the "beautiful, tranquil millpond" that was Ravina High in the early to mid 1990s. Having recognized fairly early in my research that I was another of the principal's innovations, I slowly came to believe that Grace's initial call for me to present a "warts and all" picture of the school was not necessarily the straightforward granting of license I had imagined. I sensed that she was also extolling me to identify what needed changing, and to join her in the reform program, a positioning that I resisted as best I could. Given that Grace was my major sponsor, however, this was difficult to achieve in any direct way.

Grace also endeavored to position me as an assistant in her battle with the bureaucrats, whom she often spoke of in disparaging terms. Toward the end of my first semester in the school, she urged me to make a presentation of my findings to the staff as part of a professional development program she was planning. "The staff have expressed an appetite to hear what you have to say," she assured me, "and it would be good if you could see your way clear to present your research findings to them next semester." Aside from the fact that I did not feel ready to talk with the staff about my project, I was not sure on what evidence Grace's perception of their "appetite" to hear from me was based. Any conversation I had with teachers on this topic failed to support the principal's statement. What Grace appeared to be aiming at was a boycott of the district office professional development activities planned for the first day of second semester. She was keen to develop an alternative school-based program, thereby sending a clear message to the district officers that their efforts were neither needed nor appreciated.

Deliberately mobilizing a strategy apparently employed by a number of staff in response to Grace's reform program, I passively resisted her request by ignoring it. Aside from the fact that such a presentation would have been premature, I was uncomfortable with the sense I had of being manipulated into supporting her efforts to undermine the education bureaucracy, a collective she once described as a "juggernaut sucking us dry of all our resources."

As I was being pushed and prodded in different directions by a variety of parties in the school, I was also trying to position myself in methodologically useful ways. Having decided to focus on teachers and organizational change, I arranged to do some intensive "teacher following" in the second half of 1998. I altered my research strategy so that, instead of attending classes involved in communicating ideas about culture and multiculturalism (e.g., English and Social Studies), I followed eight teachers and the principal through the course of their working day. Shadowing nine people for a fortnight each meant that I had a research program that would keep me occupied for the vast bulk of the nineteen-week second semester. I tracked five teachers through the ten-week third term, and the remaining three through the first six weeks of fourth term. My intention then was to follow Grace in weeks seven and eight.

This new research strategy was intense, allowing very little room for involvement in other school activities. As a result, apart from my attendance at the weekly meetings of the School Executive and the occasional School Council and Parent and Citizen's meetings, I had very little contact with Grace during this period. Unfortunately, the conflict between Grace and the teachers escalated at the same time, making it impossible for me to spend any intensive time with her at all. Whereas she had previously been quite accessible, by the fourth term her time was increasingly taken up in crisis meetings with her superiors, union representatives, parents, and key collaborators. In hindsight, it would have benefited my research enormously to have spent a fortnight shadowing Grace in third term. As it turned out, two part-days in the middle of fourth term were all we were able to manage. In reflecting on this failure I identified several useful methodological and epistemological points regarding ethnographic research in middle-class settings.

The Cultural Critique of Middle-Class Lives

Marcus and Fischer's influential exploration of "anthropology as cultural critique" (1986) offers some important insights into what they claim is a hidden commitment underpinning much of the anthropological enterprise, namely, the critique of Western middle-class lives. Given the important role schools play in the reproduction of capitalist societies (Bowles & Gintis 1976; Bourdieu & Passeron 1977), it is not surprising that these institutions come in for special critical attention.[4]

In their important review of critical approaches to ethnographic studies of schooling, Levinson and Holland (1996:19) point to the lack of attention given to teachers. They conclude that critical ethnographers must scrutinize the actions of school officials, even if they are not prepared to discuss the research relationships formed with such people. I suspect that an ideological commitment to the critique of bourgeois, middle-class life in mass liberal societies underpins much of this critical research on schools, thereby making it difficult for researchers to know how to write about the relationships they formed with adults in their fieldsites. Some report on the assistance and positive reception they received from the teachers, yet their accounts of schooling all too often fail to develop the characterization of teachers beyond ghostly thin representations (see, for example, McLaren 1986; Reed-Danahay 1996; Fordham 1996). I argue that a loss of focus on portrayal as the central purpose of ethnography, caused by the emancipatory ideology of the critical researcher, along with an ensuing "race to critique" (Goodman 1998:55–56), prematurely closes off key pathways to the development of productive, useful relationships with significant people. This ethnographic failure results in unnecessarily "thin ethnography" (Ortner 1995) and diminished accounts of schools and schooling (Forsey 2000).

By the beginning of 1998 I was determined to maintain a strong focus on teachers and teaching at Ravina High. However, I had not really thought about how I might position myself for this task. I paid even less attention to the anthropological privileging of the subaltern that Marcus (1995) has brought to our attention. In retrospect I needed to think more about the ethical, methodological, and epistemological significance of the downward inclination of anthropology's critical gaze. In doing so I may have been able to overcome what turned out to be a significant lack in my overall research project—the failure to engage in a meaningful way with Grace at the time when her reform projects were reaching their zenith. Had I approached my research with a commitment to positioning myself in the interstitial spaces (Mulcock 2001), my final account of the turmoil produced at Ravina High over the course of 1998 and 1999 might have been considerably enriched.

Mobile Positioning in Interstitial Spaces

In August 1998 I attended a lecture sponsored by the Western Australian Institute for Educational Research. The speaker, who had conducted several impressive ethnographic projects in British schools, responded to a question about power and the researcher with the following candid observation: "When I am with students, I hate teachers. When I am with teachers, I hate administrators. When I'm with principals . . . well, who can you hate?" This comment offers some important insights into the sort of mindset criticalist researchers often adopt in the field. Although I would never go so far as to suggest that I came out of my fieldwork hating anyone, the above observation, made with some degree of levity, helps me to understand why I largely ignored Grace, and her perspective on the changes she was implementing, through the second half of the 1998 school year. My own bias toward left-leaning unionist positions, combined with anthropological and sociological prejudices against those deemed to hold power over less powerful others,[5] kept me further away than I should have been from the productive spaces under discussion in this volume.

The ways in which ethnographers position themselves affect the stories they tell just as much as they affect the types of relationships formed in the field. Sympathetic downward gazes, punctuated by highly critical upward glances, may be emotionally and ideologically satisfying, but they do not necessarily make for good research. As the call for deeper, richer, "thicker," more nuanced understandings of power and its social effects is being issued (Abu-Lughod 1990; Ortner 1995), those of us committed to a politically engaged, critical anthropology need to ensure that we position ourselves in ever more productive ways and places.

My training as a biology teacher undoubtedly helped draw me toward Mulcock's discussion (2001) of the significance of social interstices in ethnographic research. She suggests that anthropologists need to be prepared to find themselves locked into these frequently uncomfortable, in-between spaces, where support or otherwise for the various parties one encounters is continually challenged and complicated by the ambiguities and struggles of social life. In biology, "interstices" refers, most commonly, to the spaces between the cells of living organisms. These cells are bathed in fluid; far from being inert regions, the interstitial spaces are filled with nutrients and waste material that move backward and forward through the cell walls according to physiological status. Mulcock's model suggests that it is not always possible, or even desirable, for anthropologists to fully penetrate particular cell membranes to become, as with the essential nutrients, part of the cell contents. Indeed, she goes further, suggesting that being caught in anthropologically and socially awkward interstitial spaces is potentially useful and productive (2001:42), particularly if the researcher is seeking to document and understand a configuration of conflicting perspectives.

Mulcock reports having little choice about her interstitial positioning, her attempts at penetrating the cellular groups she moved among repeatedly repelled by subtle social forces resulting from the "chemistry" (or lack of it) between herself, her research participants and her research topic. My position was quite different, as the story opening this essay implies. Rather than being prevented from entering particular cells, I found myself lured too far into them. The danger I faced was the possibility of losing my ability to absorb, however partially, the ideas and values of other important contributors to the social world in which I was immersed.[6]

The discomfort I felt when one of Ravina High's teachers suggested that I was "one of them" was an important moment in my research, one in which I was inadvertently called to return to the interstices. Given that I spent considerable amounts of time in the second half of the year moving among the teachers and recording their perspectives on what was happening to the school, it is easy to see why some assumed that I was aligned with those pitted against the principal. And, as a left-leaning former teacher, I did find myself drawn to taking sides in ways that tapped into "deeply entrenched moral imperatives" (Turner 1974:35).[7] Although I had not yet articulated at that point my thoughts on the need for passionate detachment and mobile positioning in ethnographic research, I did heed the call to return to the interstices. By then I had abandoned my plans to follow the remaining teachers, opting instead to spend the bulk of my time in the staff room, which had become the primary locus for up-to-date commentary on rapidly declining relations between the principal and her employees. As already indicated, I had limited access to Grace by this stage, but I "followed the conflict" (Marcus 1995) as best I could.

In bringing this essay to a close, I want to couple the need for cultural relativism with the aforementioned commitment to mobile positioning and interstitial spaces, a project that seems especially vital for a "repatriated anthropology" (Marcus & Fischer 1986:111). Admittedly, these two positions might initially appear contradictory—but if anthropological training is part of an enculturation process that produces a certain disdain for "the bourgeois, middle-class life of mass liberal societies produced by industrial capitalism" (Marcus & Fischer 1986:111), then we surely need to contemplate some deprogramming if we wish to adopt ever more productive positions in our research endeavors. Such an approach might have allowed me to give greater priority to following Grace.

The Critical Ethnographer's Mindset in Middle-Class Settings

The anthropological commitment to detailed description and analysis of "other cultures" needs to be applied with greater rigor than it currently is in home settings. Cultural relativism plays a key role in such description and analysis, yet, as George Marcus (1983) so cogently demonstrated, this important and much-vaunted dimension of the ethnographer's conceptual tool kit is too often overlooked by ethnographers involved with elite subjects in their own society. This phenomenon can be explained in part by the tendency to conflate cultural relativism with moral relativism (Fernandez 1990), which all too often leads researchers in home settings to distance themselves from their elite research subjects lest they appear complicit in the injustices inflicted on the victims of capitalist domination (Marcus 1983:23).[8]

Herskovits, whose vicarious observation about the failure of anthropologists to respect their own cultural patterns opened this essay, offers some very useful insights regarding the need to adopt a culturally relativist mindset regardless of the setting. His own social positioning is interesting in this regard. As a Jewish man coming to grips with the horrors of the Second World War, he naturally enough condemned the evils of Nazism, yet he maintained that if we are to really come to grips with what happened in wartime Germany, we have to commit ourselves to grasping what made life meaningful to the people of that time and place (Herskovits 1977; cf. Fernandez 1990).[9] Herskovits believed that cultural relativism, or "the tough-minded suspension of disbelief" (Fernandez 1990:159), was vital to developing such understanding. In order for this to happen, researchers need to develop their "capacity to resist those habitual responses that arise out of the cultural conditioning . . . and group processes of identity formation to which we have been exposed" (Fernandez 1990:149).

Reflecting further on my own research experiences, I have become acutely aware of how my early cultural conditioning toward social critique has been strongly reinforced by anthropological training. I would go so far as to suggest that critique of the "bourgeois, middle-class life of mass liberal societies" and its concomitant privileging of the subaltern are cultural imperatives for many anthropologists. The effort required to resist these tendencies—as part of our cultural conditioning, group processes, and identity—is taxing, but necessary to the continued development of productive research practices in home settings. I share the discomfort felt by many school researchers with the ways that power is wielded over those who are further down the pecking order in school environments. Nonetheless, in thinking about power, we would do well to remember Foucault's observations (1980) about the productive capacity of power and the need to move beyond an exclusive focus on its destructive potential and realities. If we are to deepen our understanding of how power is both used and abused, then we need to be prepared to adopt Herskovits' "tough-minded suspension of disbelief," a stance that should push us away from cellular biases and toward the more awkwardly productive spaces of the interstices.

Had I been better primed to recognize the complex array of power that exists in any social setting I might have been better prepared to position myself more usefully at Ravina High. I might have avoided the methodological and epistemological trap of characterizing Grace as the teachers' oppressor. I might also have recognized, more readily, how the teachers were wielding their power over Grace in ways that were productive for them, but destructive for her and some of the good ideas that many people acknowledged she had.

I argue that ethnographers involved in studying power in any setting need to adopt a mindset whereby they commit themselves to engaging as meaningfully as possible with a wide range of interlocutors. Ethical, methodological, and epistemological concerns make it imperative that this be done with the purpose of understanding elite lives and perspectives, not as a means of "getting the goods . . . so that [our subjects] can be opposed" (Marcus 1998:27). Such research should aim for a better appreciation of the production of power and the role of various players in this production (see Ortner 1995). Goodman (1998:57) is correct in asserting that "clear, authentic ethnographic portrayal will likely be more educative than the ideological insights of the researcher who made the observations in the first place." It is important to remember that, as with villagers on remote islands, we are observing ways in which people come to grips with their lives in the particular historical and social moments in which they find themselves.

My ethnographic apprenticeship at Ravina High led eventually to my doctoral dissertation. During this apprenticeship I learned something of the value of committing myself to a nuanced critical *appreciation*, rather than critique per se. It is only in retrospect that I have come to consciously recognize the importance of resisting the tendency to privilege the subaltern at the expense of understanding as many perspectives as possible. I have already indicated that my contact with Grace in the crucial second half of my project was far too superficial. I did spend some time following her, and she did allow me to conduct an extensive interview with her, but my research was "thinner" (Ortner 1995) than it could have been. Had I gone into my fieldwork thinking more about the need for mobile positioning, with a greater awareness of how the anthropological privileging of empathy can allow the researcher to be manipulated by the interests of research participants, had I been primed to seek out the interstices rather than particular cells, and had I committed myself to a tough-minded suspension of my own critical proclivities, I might have spent more time with Grace and deepened my understanding of her perspective, her reasoning, and her practice. Almost certainly my research would have been the richer for it.

Notes

1. Both "Grace" and "Ravina" are pseudonyms.
2. This subhead is inspired by Wolcott's work (1973) titled *The Man in the Principal's Office*, in which he reports on the time he spent following a primary school principal through many of his working days.
3. Clearly notions of building better, more dynamic schools are subjective and very much open to debate. In this instance I am reporting the ways in which Grace constructed and discussed what she was doing.
4. For some comprehensive accounts and critiques of these critical approaches, see Anderson 1989; Davies 1995; Levinson & Holland 1996.
5. See Nader (1974:289), whose questioning of the anthropological bias toward the powerless has resonated down the years.
6. Haraway's influential ideas on "situated knowledges" (1991) offer strong support for this perspective. Problematizing the premium so often placed on seeing "from the peripheries and the depths" (191), she argues for "passionate detachment" and "mobile positioning." She also draws on biological metaphors to make her case: "One cannot 'be' either a cell or molecule—or a woman, colonized person, laborer, and so on—if one intends to see and see from these positions critically. 'Being' is much more problematic and contingent" (192).
7. By the time of the union meeting in question, I also felt I had some valid reasons for doing so. I was particularly disturbed by severe chastisements given to two staff members who were largely supportive of Grace. The dressing down she gave them appeared unjust to many of those involved with the school at the time, including me.
8. For example, Reed-Danahay (1996:17) defends her deliberate distancing from the teachers involved in her study on the grounds that she needed to gain the trust of the people living in the French village where she conducted her research. While she does not defend her disapproval of the teachers, ultimately this is what emerges from her text. The teachers are presented as "selecting on behalf of a class power not their own" (Connell 1995:91) in ways that the author is uncomfortable with, but are not afforded the opportunity to defend their actions (see Forsey 2000).
9. As a former student of Herskovits, Fernandez wrote this paper as a means of deepening our appreciation of his mentor's ideas regarding cultural relativism. He argues that Herskovits' stance on this important anthropological theme has often, and all too readily, been misunderstood.

Jonathan Telfer

CHAPTER 6

Dissent and Consent

Negotiating the Adoption Triangle

This chapter considers various dimensions of undertaking ethnographic research within the conflictual, politicized, and feminized field of adoption in South Australia during 1994 and 1995. While my study clearly characterizes the domain of adoption as a site of contestation, this fact, minimally reported in the relevant literature, only became apparent to me as I attempted to move among the various interest groups within my field. I quickly came to recognize how voluntary and state-sponsored organizations constituted around adoption occupy not only different but also antipathetic positions (Bourdieu & Wacquant 1992) on the rights of adoptees, adoptive parents, and relinquishing parents. The feminized nature of the field presented further dilemmas for a male researcher, as did my status as an adoptive parent. While the latter aspect of my identity proved to be pivotal in winning the trust of key agents in some adoption organizations and informal networks, it also meant that access to other arenas was denied. The intricate combination of several factors—the field itself, my gender, my position as an adoptive parent, and my personal style—yielded a rich variety of ethnographic opportunities, constraints, obligations, and predicaments.

Fieldwork on Adoption

My initial interest in undertaking anthropological research on adoption was fueled by personal as well as scholarly concerns. As the adoptive father of two Korean-born children, I found that a myriad of questions arose for me before, during, and after the adoptions. These questions concerned identity, senses of affiliation and kinship, and varieties of relatedness and relationship experienced by those whose lives have been deeply affected by adoption in one way or another. As I embarked on my research, it became clear that the questions I sought to deal with concerning intercountry adoption were embedded in broader patterns of relatedness around adoption practices and policies. In order to explore adoption as a field, I could not restrict my focus to intercountry adoption and exclude the practices around local adoption, such as the regulation of knowledge, information exchange, vetoes on contact or release of identifying information, adoption reunions, and the like. Rather, my fieldwork had to encompass as many parts of the social domain of adoption as possible.

The adoption-related organizations relevant to this study can be divided into two primary categories. At the time of my research the first of these comprised two sections of the South Australian Department of Family and Community Services. One section was devoted to issuing identifying information about adoptees and relinquishing parents, and regulating the vetoes that agents could place on contact with biological relatives or access to information. The other section of the department provided local adoption services, assessed prospective adoptive parents, and liaised with women (and, to a degree, men) who were relinquishing their children for adoption. This section was also responsible for monitoring the intercountry adoption services provided by a single licensed adoption agency, which assessed and educated couples adopting from overseas. It then monitored the family's progress in the twelve months between placement of the child and the legal adoption order being issued in court. This group of agencies regulated information about and access to other persons or adoption processes. For many agents, the staff of such organizations wielded enormous power over their struggles for certain relationships or identities (see Telfer 2000).

The second category of primary organizations largely involved support services for adult adoptees who were seeking biological relatives, birth mothers who had lost a child to local or intercountry adoption, and those whose lives had been otherwise affected by adoption. Some of these groups were primarily constituted around lobbying for, or resisting, legislative and policy changes concerning adoption. A number sought to reduce or extend access to identifying information, or contact with biological relatives, in relation to local adoptions that had taken place decades earlier. The support offered by these groups was taken to be extremely valuable by the agents involved, since many group members were undergoing taxing, often emotionally perilous pursuits of identity or other life-changing enterprises. The atmosphere in the groups tended to be highly charged, and information, relationships, and expectations often precariously balanced.

All agents involved in the field held varying views pivoting on the taken-for-granted acceptance of what is known as the adoption triangle: adoptees, adoptive parents, and relinquishing parents (see Sachdev 1989). Contestation over the legitimacy of the rights of various agents in this triangle of relationships illustrates how the field of adoption is a "field of struggles aimed at preserving or transforming the configuration of . . . forces" (Bourdieu & Wacquant 1992:101). The triangle was taken as emblematic of the moral and personal stances of all concerned with adoption and had a telling influence on my fieldwork. The frequently competing interests of the groups I approached, for example, meant that they were naturally suspicious of one another and rarely had any direct contact. Given the critical nature of relationships between anthropologists and informants in the field, the delicacy of simultaneously working with individuals and organizations representing all points on the triangle demanded conscientious attention (Amit 2000b).

Challenges in the Field

When initially approaching various adoption organizations of which I had hitherto been unaware, or barely aware, I had no way of appreciating the scale of mutual suspicion and limited potential for interaction between certain groups. For example, with regard to local adoptions, groups organized around relinquishment might have little or nothing to do with those organized around adoptive parenthood. At the same time each might assume that the other was opposed to the aims and pursuits of their own group. Such assumptions about conflicting agendas between selves and others tended to reflect, and help constitute, the pervasiveness of the adoption triangle as a working concept. I wished to probe the cultural dynamics of this triangle through participant observation, including the worldviews and social practices of agents that depicted the "other" as not only quintessentially different, but also as a potential threat. My own biography was a vital contributor to this process. As Finnstrom notes, "the sharing of experiences . . . works as a tool of intersubjectivity in the endeavour to represent and demystify the other" (2001:256).

The people I worked with were mildly puzzled by my desire to learn about adoption from a variety of perspectives. As an ethnographer seeking access to groups with antipathetic views of each other, I was bound to face a number of personal and ethical challenges, especially with regard to confidentiality, obligations to those who assisted me in my work, and my own reflexivity. As it happened, I found that some agents would, in the early months of fieldwork, ask me occasional questions (albeit tangentially) about other organizations with which they knew I was involved. I interpreted this as being as much a litmus test of my own practices regarding confidentiality as an authentic effort to obtain precious information concerning competitors.

My own experience as an (intercountry) adoptive parent created concerns for some. For example, Paula (pseudonym), a birth mother, told me during our first meeting that I was the first adoptive parent that she had ever talked to. She had assumed that adoptive parents were terrible people, "just wanting kids at any cost." My willingness to respond to her questions about my own reasons for adopting, and my attitudes to my daughters' possible searches for, and reunion with, birth relatives were not what she expected. Paula had been reunited with her then twenty-four-year-old son and was happy to narrate her experiences, finding "therapeutic value" in the process of talking to me. I am reminded, as I write this, of Rapport's words: "Narrative awareness, by the anthropologist as well as by the individual, does provide the potential means of, and the route to, existential freedom" (2000:90). Paula and I met several times over the ensuing months, but our meetings were discontinued when her relationship with her son broke down, so that further discussions concerning her relinquishment, search, and reunion were no longer helpful to her.

While apprehension from organizations constituted around relinquishment or adopted persons required careful consideration on my part, potential pressures from organizations supporting adoptive parents merited equal deliberation. At times I was confronted with assumptions about my partiality to the interests of adoptive parents or intercountry adoption. I also faced another challenge as my project unfolded: Initially, all groups encouraged my research on adoption in general terms, especially given the paucity of such work in Australia. However, as implicit understandings (erroneously believed to be held by everyone) were made more explicit, this encouragement became less enthusiastic. A further factor, which, like so many developments in fieldwork, could not have been anticipated, served to overcome some of these potential obstacles, at the same time as it intensified others and introduced new demands onto the research process.

Fortuitously from my point of view, early in 1994, only two to three months into my fieldwork, the government of South Australia announced a review of adoption in that state. A review panel of four experts was appointed to take submissions from the public over several months. Advertisements were placed in the state's daily and regional newspapers, and an issues paper was produced to facilitate the preparation of submissions. The review and the consultative processes that came before it served to generate and intensify discussions within these adoption-oriented organizations, as well as introducing opportunities for reflexivity among members. While the review was welcomed and recognized as a valuable opportunity for change, it was also received with trepidation, anxiety, and, to varying degrees, suspicion. In many instances I was able to be part of the discussions and formulation of submissions. The precise point at which I became accepted, for the purposes of my own data collection, was somewhat lost in the preoccupation over the Review of Adoption.[1]

Negotiating Access

Seeking informed consent to carry out research on deeply personal matters in a field characterized by dissent was far from a homogeneous process. My attempts to negotiate access to relevant organizations and networks met with varying degrees of success. Apart from seeking to build networks of participants, I was interested in attending routine support group meetings and other activities. Some support group coordinators expected that, as a social scientist, I would only want to interview people. I found that it was necessary to explain that my methodology, participant observation, involved observing what was done as well as what was said. Initially, this methodological approach added to the fears that some held about my presence, given that I also planned to become involved in a range of other adoption-oriented organizations.

Perhaps not surprisingly, my requests to attend activities such as support group meetings for couples seeking to adopt from overseas, compulsory education groups for prospective adoptive parents, meetings and outings for parents of toddlers or teenagers, and other practices centering on intercountry adoption were generally eagerly acceded to. In fact, on occasion I had to tactfully decline invitations to assume the role of expert (as both a researcher and an experienced adoptive parent). My participation in some of these activities was, nonetheless, complicated by virtue of my gender.

Indeed, from the outset of fieldwork, my status as an intercountry adoptive parent proved to be something of a paradox. I soon became used to being introduced in some groups as "Jon Telfer, he's doing research on adoption and he wants to come to all our support group meetings and stuff—it's ok, though, he has adopted daughters, so he knows about adoption." In such situations, my status as having personal experience with adoption was represented as a distinct advantage. In other groups, however, this same status was a distinct disadvantage. Winning the trust of a particular group organized around adult adoptees was far from straightforward, for example. Some eight to ten weeks into fieldwork, I learned of this group through a social worker in the government department administering the release or withholding of information about adoptees and birth relatives. She passed my name on to the coordinator of the group for adoptees. The president of the group rang me at home one evening to ask me about the aims of my research and my general views on adoption. He also asked whether I minded answering some questions about my attitudes toward adoption information being available to my own adopted children, for example. We arranged to meet at the university the following week.

Our first encounter involved me taking the role of respondent rather than questioner. While the meeting was amiable enough, I was presented with a range of questions, not only about adoption, but also about my relationships with other social scientists who had worked in the same field. This, I learned, was due to my somewhat distant training as a social worker and my occasional part-time teaching across different disciplines in the social sciences. I also discovered later that the researchers my acquaintance had in mind were thought to be opposed to the interests of the group he represented. Allowing me access, if I were indeed a friend of the person concerned, was held to be unwise, maybe even dangerous, for the group members and their aspirations. The president of the group advised me he would take my request to the group at their next meeting and get back to me. Some weeks later he rang again. The group would allow me to sit in on their meetings, but would like to "get to know me a little first."

I was not altogether prepared for the two and a half hours of intense questioning that ensued at the first meeting of this group I attended. The atmosphere was, from my point of view, tense, inquisitorial, and, at times, antagonistic. The questions that flowed from the eighteen or so people present were personal and prying.[2] They included my reasons for adopting children, my culpability for taking them from their culture of origin, how I would feel about them eventually having contact with biological relatives, whether I was aware of the damage wreaked by adoption generally, and whether I was prepared to participate in the group at the risk of hearing some unpleasant, critical, and possibly very confronting accusations toward adoptive parents and adoption as a practice. I was reminded of Favret-Saada (1980:11) being asked "Are you strong enough?" in relation to her pursuit of knowledge about (secret) witchcraft in the Bocage of France. It was unmistakably plain that my actions, words, and values were likely to determine my future with this important group for the duration of my fieldwork. As it happened, I was commended on my candor, honesty, and commitment at the close of the session. I had passed what had been intended as, and was, a "trial by fire." I was advised that my willingness to listen was something they wished other researchers and others involved in adoption would emulate. I later learned that inquiries had been made about me in the period between my initial meeting with the president and my attendance at the group meeting, although I was never clear on who, if any, of my colleagues or acquaintances had been approached.

While this experience was personally testing, it was not the first occasion on which my access to particular groups or situations was problematic. Some weeks earlier, I had written to, and met with, the coordinator of a group constituted around the welfare and interests of relinquishing mothers. The coordinator and part-time social worker advised me that my request to take part in a range of activities, including sitting in on support group meetings, could not be accommodated. In addition to the obvious sensitivities of such groups, I was told, some women who attended support group meetings discussed their relinquishment (often many years ago) for the first time. My gender was a significant obstacle, although the coordinator did suggest that involvement would not be automatic for a female researcher either. As our discussion continued, it became plain that, while my experience as an adoptive parent was perceived as something of an advantage over other researchers, it was also held to be "pretty tricky," given that "many women's experiences of adoption, including adoptive parents, is very negative." Personal ethics, and those of the discipline, meant that I respected the views and wishes of the coordinator and her organization and did not press further for access (see Pels 2000). However, the coordinator did emphasize that, since the organization wished to support my research, they would publish a letter from me in their newsletter inviting participation. Paula, referred to earlier, was one of the two dozen or so relinquishing mothers who responded to my invitation.

The rejection of my request to attend the meetings of this organization meant that I had to grapple with the implications of not being able to secure full and unconstrained access to a group of people who appeared absolutely critical to my research project. I believed that the knowledge to be gained from participating in the activities of this support group would be extremely enriching, and would problematize the kinds of narrations provided in interviews. As events transpired I was indeed able to observe and participate in a support group and other activities that included birth mothers, through my involvement in another organization that attempted to meet the needs of all points on the triangle; adopted persons, adoptive parents, and relinquishing parents.

There was one other organization to which I could not secure immediate access. In the first few months of fieldwork I had been told about one or two organizations that focused their attention on political lobbying for privacy—groups opposed to the overturning of sealed adoption records. As far as I could determine, these groups consisted mainly of adoptive parents and, to a lesser extent, adopted persons. My efforts to secure access were not dismissed, yet a series of mishaps, such as the protracted illness of the president of one of the groups, consistently placed their activities beyond my reach.

As I have shown, my efforts to negotiate access to various adoption organizations met with mixed degrees of success. After only a few months of fieldwork, however, I had become well acquainted with, and apparently accepted by, a range of groups, networks, and organizations. At the same time, I continued my attempts to gain access to others and to build networks through word-of-mouth referrals and introductions from those I had already come to know. These processes inevitably placed me in predicaments that underlined my polysemous position as both "insider" and "outsider" in different parts of the field.

Inside and Outside the Field of Dissent

The significance of gender in my fieldwork would have been difficult to anticipate. The literature on adoption, largely based in social science disciplines other than anthropology, does not highlight adoption as a feminized field. Yet, as fieldwork progressed, the feminized quality of the field became increasingly obvious to me in a variety of ways. The first of these was simply that women predominated across the entire range of social practices associated with adoption. From couples seeking to adopt, to adoptees seeking reunions (first and foremost with the genetrix rather than the genitor), to social workers, counselors, and support group coordinators, women's interests and domains of expertise were, by and large, held to be primary in this field. The involvement of men was clearly seen as supplementary by most (Backett 1982). While men did take part in support groups, parent education courses, and the like, the *habitus* (Bourdieu & Wacquant 1992) of agents in this field meant that it was taken for granted that women were the prime movers in matters associated with relationships, relatedness, identity, and kinship (see Stivens 1985; Ernst 1990). My gender therefore marked me as something of a novelty. It also distanced me from my field of inquiry, just as my status as an adoptive parent located me within it.

Among all the influences and forces affecting my fieldwork, my position as an adoptive father weaved in and out of focus. The term "adoptive father" might suggest unidimensionality, yet being a researcher who is also an adoptive father was neither uniformly important nor consistently taken to have the same implications for my presence in particular contexts. The only consistent aspect of my adoptive fatherhood status was its veracity. Its declaration (and my determination not to conceal it, even in contexts where adoptive parents were thought to be despicable) yielded a variety of interpretations and reactions. For example, in many contexts associated with intercountry adoption, it was assumed that my own experience would ensure my understanding. Nonetheless, it was important for me to be on guard against my own assumption that I did already understand—a dangerous but occasionally enticing possibility for any "insider" ethnographer.

My meetings with some birth mothers, some adopted persons, and some relatives of adopted persons resulted in receptions ranging from cool to mildly hostile. For these individuals, my position in the adoption triangle meant that, however well-intentioned a researcher I was, my own biases were bound to "get in the way," as one young woman put it. For such people, the nature of my parenthood was beyond my own agency or locus of control (Flinn 1998). Nothing I could do or say would countermand such judgments. The immersion I sought in various groups was mediated by the ambiguous cast of a portion of my own biography.

When seeking to secure access to intimate, precious social knowledge across competing organizations, winning the trust of people in a field characterized, at least in part, by dissent, was a vexed issue as much as it was fragile and in need of a gentle and sensitive approach. My preparedness to disclose aspects of my own life (and that of my family) was often taken as an index of my trustworthiness. As one support group member observed, "You wouldn't really expect us to tell you everything about ourselves if you're not prepared to be as open as we are, would you?" Here the notion of informants' trust of me as an ethnographer was intimately linked to practices and expectations concerning confidentiality. I was told that, for some, concerns about confidentiality were exacerbated by previous researchers failing to adhere to their undertakings in this regard. I felt only slightly relieved by the fact that none of them were anthropologists.

In the first few months of fieldwork people frequently asked me about confidentiality. How did I propose to use the information about them?

Was information gleaned during an interview managed differently from my observations during an emotional support group meeting in which intensely personal matters were shared among group members? Most important, would information obtained in one group setting be revealed to members of other groups, even if inadvertently? In a sense, such questions can only ever be partially answered. Over and above my immediate responses, the passing of time and my preparedness to be observed while observing were necessary ingredients for building fieldwork relationships.

The development of trust, between myself as researcher and those whose experiences I sought to observe, listen to, and discuss, was critical, especially given the nature of the field in which I worked. Of course, the growth of trust is fueled by a myriad of practices, responses, silences, and commitments. Research participants, at least in fields such as adoption, need to be able to depend on the researcher's consistency and reliability. Some suggested that my quiet, easygoing demeanor assisted my entrée and acceptance into the field, along with my commitment to honesty and openness. This meant being clear about what I would and would not, or could not, discuss. However, in among all the exhortation above about the importance of patience, trust, and good faith in ethnographic research, the value of astute observation as a crucial element in the anthropologist's conceptual and methodological arsenal should not be overlooked. Indeed, observation and the anthropological insistence on analytically challenging the taken-for-granted (especially in relation to oneself) were enormously beneficial in my own efforts to grapple with the forces, cultural assumptions, and struggles within the field of adoption.

I have outlined here a variety of social factors that help fuel ambiguity in the lives of those who are deeply connected with adoption in one way or another. While these ambiguities are of ethnographic interest, it is their significance for my own fieldwork methodology, their ability to both facilitate and impede my research, that make them the subject of this chapter.

Final Reflections

Retrospective reflections on the experiences of fieldwork can be as valuable as they can be unsettling or uncomfortable. While my biographical position in relation to the field of cultural and social inquiry that I chose to pursue was problematic in a variety of ways, I could have achieved the kinds of access that ensued only through particular combinations of familiarity and strangeness, proximity and distance. In other words, I could not have achieved the access that I did if it were not for my own biography. I think it fair to say that certain aspects of professional practice in the field, certain casts of the professional persona, and some personal traits and predilections were not only useful, but also critical. Such traits will be familiar to students and colleagues, not only within anthropology perhaps, but in other social science disciplines that entail learning through sensitive, but professionally rigorous contact with persons and groups in a variety of social and political settings.

Notes

1. See Pieke (1995) for a more dramatic, but nonetheless highly pertinent, discussion of unanticipated events in fieldwork.
2. In so representing, I am aware that my predicament was neither unique nor unusual; the nature of anthropologists' disclosures about themselves seems to vary enormously.

Val Colic-Peisker

CHAPTER 7

Doing Ethnography in "One's Own Ethnic Community"

The Experience of an Awkward Insider

I finally succumbed to my "Croatianness" upon arrival in Australia. This was an unexpected development, as I left my country to escape—among other calamities of postcommunism—the high tide of nationalism. In the face of war, the politics of identity had become unbearably simple: we were divided into "good Croatians" and "enemies." I did not feel I belonged to either of these categories. In Australia, however, my Croatianness was imposed on me in a novel way. I became a person who speaks "with an accent" and was repeatedly asked where I had come from. I soon realized that my "ethnicity," evident in my accent, had become one of the most noticeable markers of my identity, at least in superficial social encounters.

Many migrants to Australia from non-English-speaking countries resent being asked, "Where do you come from?" They feel that the question defines them as outsiders. I always regarded such inquiries as "small talk," perhaps even signs of friendliness, but I sometimes resented my interlocutor's utter ignorance about my country of origin, once revealed. Several months after I arrived in Perth, Western Australia, a small incident made me feel like a second-class citizen for the first time: I encountered a large map of Europe in a university library that did not include Croatia. Instead, there was a blank dark blue area stretching from Slovenia in the west to Bulgaria in the east. The cartographers did not bother to draw in the countries in between, which were at war at the time the map was printed (1993). I hurried away, embarrassed. I was a person from a nameless land, from a country that was not even on the map. This event made me think about how migration had changed the way I felt about being Croatian. I was more willing to be a Croatian in Australia than when I was in Croatia. These thoughts were the embryo of my research project on the migration experience of Croatians in Australia.

My first Australian job, as an interpreter for the Department of Immigration, also clearly defined me as Croatian. Additionally, it provided a great opportunity to learn more about my "ethnic community." I was later awarded a scholarship to do a Ph.D. in sociology and decided to focus my research on the values and identities of two postwar "waves" of Croatian immigrants in Australia. I discovered that very little had been written about this large migrant group, and, remembering the dismal map and how little most Australians knew about Croatia, I developed a sense of vocation. I was going to make the most out of the dislocation of my identity and the discontinuity of my own life, broken in two halves by migration. I wanted to add ethnography on Croatian-Australians to the pandemonium of Australian multiculturalism. This personal motivation remained a great driving force throughout my project.

I set out to investigate the two distinct "waves" of Croatian migrants. The first wave had arrived on Australian shores from the late 1950s to the early 1970s as part of a massive southern European labor migration that fed the Australian postwar economic boom. Most of these people had working-class backgrounds and came from rural parts of Dalmatia.[1] They took jobs in Australian abattoirs, fed kilns in brickyards, cleaned hospitals, and toiled on fishing boats, on farms, and in market gardens. Many swapped their youth, strength, and health for a handful of dollars. They stuck together in the same suburbs and met regularly in "ethnic clubs." The later wave of Croatian immigrants started arriving in the late 1980s, having fled the economic recession and political crisis that led to the "war for Yugoslav succession" (1991–1995). In contrast to earlier migrants, this was a group of tertiary-educated, urban professionals who spoke English and in most cases found professional jobs in Australia. They took up residence across the metropolitan area and blended into middle-class neighborhoods.

My choice of research topic made sense: I was an "insider" and had pre-existing networks and contacts. I met many people from the older group through my interpreting work, while the younger group included my own friends and acquaintances and their social connections. I could hardly separate my private life from my ethnographic work, given that I was part of the recent wave of Croatian migration to Australia. Introspection thus became an important part of my work, reflecting the apparent tension between the roles of the detached observer and engaged participant.

The experience of doing research, as a sociologist-ethnographer, within my own minority community brought satisfaction as well as awkwardness, advantages as well as pitfalls. My argument below focuses on several aspects of this endeavor. The first relates to the heterogeneity of the migrant community beyond the shared "ethnicity" apparent to outsiders. The internal class division was the first thing I noticed about the "community," and it was also a source of awkwardness during my fieldwork, as elaborated below. The second purpose of this chapter is to advocate "insider's ethnography" (autobiographical content included), which, with ethical and methodological checks and balances in place, can be a fulfilling and productive experience. Third, I tackle the tacit cultural hierarchies that influence the life of Australian "ethnic communities," and the way they have been researched.

Ethics

Before I started my fieldwork, I knew the business of ethnography was awkward by definition. Ethnographers research people, "explore" them, ask questions, observe, photograph, make recordings, take notes, and pry into the details of their daily lives. Akin to journalists, ethnographers are nosey by profession. In my case, personal acquaintances and clients were to be my respondents. I decided to leave people I knew intimately out of my sample as I believed it would be too hard to separate the "backstage" data I gained as a friend — when "the effort of public image maintenance relaxes and the rockier terrain of everyday life . . . dominates the scene" (Friedman Hansen 1976:126) — from the data collected "frontstage" with the respondent's permission and awareness that "everything they say may be taken down and used in evidence." As several ethnographers have observed (e.g., Harrell-Bond 1976; Gow 2002), it is not always possible to maintain an ethical level of detachment from personal ties in the research context.

Before we begin our ethnographic fieldwork, ethics clearance procedures remind us that our endeavors may be intrusive and unpleasant to our subjects. And even if we succeed in conducting our fieldwork in a minimally disruptive manner, our respondents may not like the final product, the academic text that describes and analyzes them in a language many may not appreciate. The older migrants I interviewed were unlikely to read my English prose, and, while it was more accessible to the younger group, its content and analysis always had the potential to diverge from my respondents' personal tastes and opinions. I was therefore pleased indeed when several research participants read my descriptions of them and expressed their appreciation. I felt my work had been vindicated, even though it was not yet legitimized by the appropriate academic authorities.

In the light of these anxieties, I found comfort in recent methodological and theoretical shifts in sociology and anthropology that challenge the objectivity and authority once routinely claimed by researchers (e.g., Abu-Lughod 1991; Clifford 1988). According to Okely and Callaway (1992:1), these disciplines have, over the last few decades, been "liberated . . . from any vestige of a value-free scientism." Indeed, deconstructing the myth of the noninvolved objective observer is like shaking off a heavy burden: instead, our research now requires us to be conscious of the ways we are involved and engaged with our research participants, and to find strategies for ethically managing that engagement.

Ethnographers work with words, ideas, stories, and theories. We turn life into text. As Clifford (1986) has argued, the ethnography is a constructed artifact that creates and invents cultures rather than representing them. The final product of our research is more often determined by the nature of our discipline, political considerations, and the audiences we expect to have than by the nature of the reality we claim to represent. We know that the social reality we attempt to unravel through our "-graphies" and "-ologies" is far more complex than any research, however sophisticated, can capture. If we abandon our claims to reside within what Bauman (1992) called the "legislative reason," which services the structures of domination, in favor of "interpretive reason," which engages the process of reciprocal communication with its subjects, we might find ourselves at least partly liberated from some of the ethical concerns associated with the possible real-life consequences of the discursive (un)reality of the text.

The Issue of Representation

When I started my research, publications about Croatians, unlike many other migrant communities, were scant. Some of the materials I did find on Croatians were impressionistic, superficial, or incorrect and some, to make things worse, claimed authority as "government publications." The available sources were mainly self-published migrant memoirs and political pamphlets. More was written about Yugoslavs, most of whom were actually Croatians, a fact which was rarely stated. One of the reasons for this extraordinary neglect was that Croatia became an independent country only in 1991. Prior to that Croatians were subsumed, in migration literature and in official statistics, under the category of "Yugoslavs." Another reason was that, although large, the Croatian community was, until recently, typically working class. It lacked the resources and critical mass of professional and socially mobile members to have significant representation in the mainstream. As a result this group did not achieve much visibility beyond folk dancing and musical performances at multicultural occasions. While I was wary of assuming the authority to represent Croatians, I at least had some insider's knowledge about where they came from, and who they were. I felt that if I was to give them a voice, it might be a more authentic one than what a non-Croatian ethnographer could produce. This idea mitigated my concern about "travel[ing] uneasily between speaking 'for' and speaking 'from' " (Abu-Lughod 1991:143) the community I was part of.

The ontological opposition between the researcher and the researched takes different shapes and intensities in the reality of fieldwork. I shared the social position and migration circumstances with the recent migrant group and therefore felt more at ease with representing them, while for the older group I was a social researcher, a professional writer, a rather exotic creature, not-really-one-of-them. However, these people did not have an Australian voice because of the language barrier and they were eager to find a way of speaking through me.[2]

The difficulties of bridging the gap between the everyday language my respondents used in their narratives and the theoretical language of scholarship was another reason for the feeling of awkwardness I experienced with regard to the issue of "representation," especially where the older group was concerned, regardless of how much I empathized with them. I was attempting to mediate between academic discourse and the discourses these working-class people inhabited. This tension, which most ethnographers face as they move between everyday expression and academic prose, was less pronounced with the professional group, who tended to "conceptualize" and generalize their narratives during the interview. Less translation was required on my part to turn their reflections into a scholarly format: they largely represented themselves, allowing me to become more of a medium for, than a creator of, their message.

The Insider's Job: "Fieldwork Versus Homework"[3]

Although my academic colleagues perceived me as an "insider" doing research on my own "ethnic community," the insider status that was relevant for my fieldwork had to be granted by the community I wanted to research. The class gap and diversity of experience between the two waves of Croatian migrants, however, precluded the existence of any singular community.

The older migrant group was rather homogenous in terms of socioeconomic and regional background; they spoke similar dialects, played the same card games, and ran *bocce* (a bowling game) tournaments at their "ethnic" clubs. In many ways, these people formed a single community, as everyone seemed to know almost everyone else. Within these dense networks knowledge and gossip about others represented an important element of the feeling of belonging, thereby maintaining the "social transparency" of the Croatian village (Erlich 1966:455). This group was divided, however, along lines of conflicting political identification. Most identified as Croatians once Croatia became an independent country, but others stuck to their old "Dalmatian" identification, which many Croatians tended to perceive as "Yugoslav" (understood, briefly after the war, as anti-Croatian). Some also remained loyal to their "Yugoslav" identity after the country itself fell apart. Nonetheless, this politically divided community hinged on a consciousness of shared belonging (Cohen 1985:13). This consciousness was embedded in a multitude of common symbols and meanings: the language (a host of similar coastal dialects), cultural narratives and practices, homeland nostalgia, and shared social position in Australia. This large group of the 1960s arrivals resembled an estranged family: however bad the conflict, a family remains a family. The "common blood" cannot be denied.

In such a context I earned my insider's status primarily on the basis of language and cultural practices that I was familiar with by accident of my birth and early life in the coastal part of Croatia. My being able to communicate with my respondents in the language they recognized, not only as Croatian but moreover as their own dialect, was a crucial factor in the community's willingness to accept me in the unfamiliar role of "researcher." Some of my interviewees reported that they could speak only "survival" English. Being able to understand their dialect was also of great practical value to me in the attempt to unravel their narratives, especially in the case of highly culturally specific idioms and phrases, popular proverbs, and jokes. Had I come from another local cultural context, albeit Croatian, my task would have been considerably more difficult. Most of the time shared language helped to turn "fieldwork," with its wintry connotations of exposure and venturing out, into cozy and sheltered "homework."

My respondents belonged to all three political factions (Croatians, Yugoslavs, and Dalmatians) and did not expect me to take sides (except in one case). Paradoxically, this was largely due to the fact that I was not-really-an-insider: I was a generation younger, came to Australia at a different time, and was an "intellectual worker" doing something that this group of people perceived as "nonwork." My higher education detracted from my "insider's status." Although a potential source of power imbalance, it was almost completely redressed, however, by my younger age, short Australian experience, and gender. My respondents had more "life experience" and were long-term migrants and therefore more knowledgeable about "things Australian." My gender worked in the same direction: a woman's power is never as serious, as threatening, and as distancing as a man's. Being female helped me to establish rapport with men from this group, some of whom openly displayed their patriarchal prerogatives.

Unlike Skrbiš (1999), a male sociologist working "inside" his own Australian-Slovenian community, I did not encounter a sense of emotional distance because of my social position. Those who allowed me to interview them seemed happy to share their stories and experiences and regularly invited me to their homes. Once I arrived there, I had to accept their rules of conduct and hospitality, which balanced out whatever power I might have had in my role as an interviewer armed with a tape recorder. After some initial scrutiny, they treated me as a social visitor, rather than a researcher, thereby transforming the interview situation into something more familiar to them. The rules of social visiting required that I reciprocate for asking questions by disclosing information about myself: in most cases, bits and pieces of my own story were necessary to "break the ice." The information I provided then further defined my insider/outsider status. But, in sum, I was strange and different enough to be spared the close scrutiny that would have required me to belong to a political faction.

The need to collect signed consent forms often undermined my insider status. The older working-class migrants were generally uneasy about providing their signatures and expected detailed explanation. While filling in and signing forms is a common experience for most Australians, it is not so in Croatia, where things are more often done on the basis of trust, and with common friends as informal guarantors. By asking my respondents to sign a consent form I positioned myself as a cultural outsider, someone coming from the "Australian side." I had to justify this practice by citing university procedures, which required that I conform to "Australian rules."

To do my "homework" with the older group I typically needed to shed my researcher's persona and reach out to them in a more holistic way. My favorite migrant story was recorded across a table full of homemade sweets and through the expressive body language and tears of a woman who only felt comfortable when all the physical traces of "research" (tape recorder, papers, consent form) were removed from sight. Luckily, the amazing details of her story were unforgettable and I succeeded in recalling them on the basis of sparse jottings after I left her neat, spacious, and somewhat lonely-feeling suburban home. What I invested in that "session" were true emotions, not just researcher's curiosity: she struck a chord in me, and we together experienced a sort of catharsis. This human attachment, rather than just engagement in "role playing," made the inevitable retreat from the research field akin to betrayal, and the research itself akin to manipulation (cf. Rynkiewich & Spradley 1976; Stacey 1988, quoted in Burbank 1994:12).

My insider status in the recently arrived professional group of Croatian migrants was less volatile. These respondents easily accepted the interview as a formal occasion and behaved accordingly. Their interviews were therefore more structured and predictable, with less traditional "eating and drinking" hospitality involved, and less digressions from the questions I posed. As respondents from this group were mostly people from the fringes of my own social circle, my insider status was assumed. Similar background and migration history, as well as the fact that all but two interviews were conducted in Croatian, were enough to overcome the potential awkwardness of the interview situation. So, while in the older working-class group I acquired my insider status through the fieldwork—by giving "right" answers to their questions about myself and speaking the "right" dialect—with the younger group I partly lost it. By inserting the professional role of the researcher into the essentially private nature of our preexisting relationships I opened an unavoidable gap between us.

Translating Cultures

Many Anglophone Australian ethnographers have done their research in what were once called NESB (non-English-speaking background), and are now referred to as CALD (culturally and linguistically diverse), communities. Some have used interpreters, which I regard as a necessary evil but far too heavy-handed a method for the intricate job of ethnography. Some have heroically set out to learn the language of their respondents, often linguistically and culturally remote from English, in order to do their research. The late-nineteenth- and twentieth-century idea of doing anthropology started as an exploration of "exotic" cultures by Westerners: a great deal of colonial arrogance, and at first explicit and later tacit cultural hierarchies, underpinned this quest for knowledge. The modernist agenda and ethnocentrism of the West[4] melted down toward the end of the twentieth century, at least in the social sciences, as postmodernism issued in a "new self-awareness of the intellectuals" (Bauman

1992:94), ethnographers included. However, the assumption that Western—increasingly "English-speaking"—cultures are the most developed and in a way contain and comprehend all the other less developed "weaker" (or more "primitive") cultures and languages seems to be alive and well (see Talal 1986).

In recent decades, however, the increased presence in the academy of previously marginalized "others" such as women and "ethnics," for example, has somewhat eroded the interpretive arrogance of the white Western, predominantly male, subject. This is not to say that the quest for understanding or even interpretive effort should be banned beyond "one's own culture"; culture is a much contested concept itself and what it means to be an "insider" in a culture is an ongoing debate (Clifford 1986). However, much sensitivity and care is required in this area, and the increased presence of those researchers whom Abu-Lughod (1991:137) called cultural "halfies" should be valued and encouraged in the ethnographic genre.

The ability to effortlessly converse with my respondents in our native language (those proficient in English also confessed that speaking English would preclude them from expressing "fine shades of meaning") drew my attention to the problem faced by ethnographers who do not speak the language of the group they study. I found it hard to imagine a non-Croatian conducting in-depth interviews with older migrants through an interpreter and still being able to establish a relationship of trust. On a purely technical level, constantly interrupting the narratives for the purpose of interpreting would ruin their natural flow and consistency and would probably be fatal for their interpretive potential. Alternatively, how many years would it take for a non-Croatian to acquire the necessary language and cultural competence to conduct the interviews themselves? I thus propose that being a "linguistic insider"—a researcher who can effectively communicate with his/her respondents without an interpreter—is a minimum requirement for serious ethnographic fieldwork.

My data had to be translated into the English language and into the "Anglo" cultural context (cf. Talal 1986), as well as into the academic idiom. I was trying hard to preserve all those "fine shades of meaning" while doing this. When the time came for me to focus on writing up my data, I had to construct an orderly text for consumption by my supervisors, examiners, and eventually a wider, but primarily academic, audience whose understanding was situated within an Anglo-dominated discourse. I also had to be faithful to my sources. I could not think of a better kind of faithfulness than to carefully use my insider's knowledge of the cultural context my respondents were coming from, and in this way "harmonize" the translation with the "*intentio*" of the sources (Talal 1986:158). To simultaneously attempt to determine "implicit meanings—not the meanings the native speaker actually acknowledges in their speech" (162), is both a "big ask" and a serious task. While the production of academic knowledge, based on generalizations and the identification of patterns, inevitably means reducing, mutilating, and distorting the reality "out there," cross-cultural interpretation has a potential to skew it even further. In the course of my research, I embraced the role of the "halfie" ethnographer, thus cautiously claiming certain authority in bilingual and bicultural interpretation of meanings.

In order not to betray the voices of my respondents and to mitigate the effect of the translation between different discourses and registers I include the migrant stories in my writing. These stories illuminate migrant experience by "allowing glimpses into the lived interior of migration processes" (Benmayor & Skotnes 1994:14), something that theoretical language rarely, if ever, achieves. While the necessity of translating the stories into English and shortening them affects their authenticity, they are still the part of my ethnographic text that I like the most; this is where my respondents have a chance to "speak for themselves," where their "private language of intimate understanding [does not have to be] translated into a public language" (Pocock 1961, cited in Talal 1986:161).

Autobiographical Voice

My insider status meant that I was also constantly observing aspects of my own experience. I could identify with the younger professional group of my respondents in many ways, so my autobiographical voice was inevitably mixed with their voices. I hoped this awareness would save me from the slippery ground of extrapolating too liberally from my own experience and accepting biases I share with my respondents as "objective" truth. As Abu-Lughod (1991:141) observed, the problem with being a "native anthropologist" can be one of gaining sufficient distance. The "native anthropologist" must be able to resolve, in her own way, "the messy tangle of contradictions and uncertainties surrounding the interrelations of personal experience, personal narrative, scientism, and professionalism in ethnographic writing" (Pratt 1988:29). As Behar (1994:2) reflects, however, the introspective gaze also runs the peril of turning into "navel gazing," of leading the ethnographer into a "bubble of self-absorption." Given that my ethnography was inevitably autobiographical in parts, I felt pushed to acknowledge and explore my "positionality" throughout the research process. In this way my own experience became a valuable heuristic tool, a source of theoretical sensitivity rather than a source of bias.[5] I was constantly reminding myself that I was telling one of many possible stories about Croatians in Australia.

In hindsight, it seems to me that approaching the task of ethnographer heavily armed with theories, concepts, and methods and pushing aside the human and autobiographical dimension in the name of objectivity would have been counterproductive. Unless we approach fieldwork with an open mind *and* heart, ethnographic prose can result in an academic account that has little to do with reality. Using our holistic selves in ethnography is not only a rewarding social experience but, fortunately, is increasingly acknowledged among social researchers as a legitimate scholarly approach.

Conflicting Expectations

My Croatian subjects' expectations of my research were clearly subjective: the older group of migrants felt that my study could in some way rectify what they perceived as the "bad public image" of Australian Croatians. Some of my respondents, especially activists and leaders in the community, felt burdened with the images of "Croatian terrorists" that had developed in the Australian press during the 1960s and 1970s, and of bellicose Croatian separatists reinforced during the war in the 1990s. They saw my research as an opportunity to tell *them* the truth about *us*. Now that Croatia was an independent country, it was perhaps the right moment, as one interviewee put it, to "tell them that we have never been terrorists, we only wanted to be Croatians and not Yugoslavs."

Many of my interviewees felt rather alienated from mainstream Australian society, even after decades of living in Australia. They often expected me to be "on their side," to tell their "truth" to the world. In a couple of cases I had to walk a tightrope between sensitively refusing the awkward "us and them" political discourse, and being rejected as an outsider. The recent group of migrants, on the other hand, did not have the intense community-consciousness of the older group and did not see me as their representative in any way.

I felt as though I "betrayed" the older group of respondents in two ways. First, I could not accept the role of "political representative," and I did not believe that my academic work would have much power in changing the political image of Croatians in Australia. Second, I was unable to meet the expectations that arose around the culturally appropriate maintenance of relationships established during the research process. This was especially relevant with respect to the older women with whom I developed friendships akin to that of mother and daughter. In the rural communities they came from, people were bound by multiple ties. I was unable to limit my role to that of "researcher": as their stories unfolded, I sometimes shed a tear, and felt that I was unwittingly placed in the role of a confidante or even counselor. While allowing access to some excellent data, such relationships were not sustainable once the fieldwork was completed.

These issues were less complicated with the younger group. If they had any expectation from me, it was that I should not place them in the same box as the older group. They were keen to shed the position of an exotic ethnic "other" in relation to the "normal Australian self."

Conclusion

My status as a "halfie"—part of the researched group and simultaneously distanced from it—was a specific source of awkwardness for me. Throughout my research I felt that I had to be extra aware of my positionality and cautious about my methods, vis-à-vis the two subgroups, especially as my own autobiography was more similar to one group than the other. Additionally, the fact that the older group was not able to appreciate my work and read my exegesis of their narratives left me with what I felt to be the unwelcome and awkward power of representing them as a mute "other."

While it is important to reflect on our role as social researchers, we also need to be wary of the dangers of extreme self-consciousness, and with it the risk of "irony, of elitism, of solipsism, of putting the whole world into quotation marks" (Clifford 1986:25). Thus I am instead proposing a kind of self-awareness that recognizes the subtle but important difference between constantly reflecting on one's limitations and responsibility, and being paralyzed by them.

Representing "one's own people," or indeed any people, through ethnography means constructing an artificial, partial account of individuals' lives. During this process I kept in mind that there is a residue in every human social experience that academic language cannot penetrate—one that defies classification and scholarly analysis. Perhaps only nonverbal artforms can reach this level of experience, as words are always exclusive, limited, and final. However, if partial and limited truths are accepted and "built into ethnographic art . . . a rigorous sense of partiality can be a source of representational fact" (Clifford 1986:7). Following Clifford, I argue for a self-aware, "serious partiality." In spite of the limited power of the academic text I believe that by dismantling some of the especially resilient stereotypes that surround the "Croatian community" my research did repay something to this minority group, even as I "objectified it through," or "subjected it to," my form of social analysis. I also believe that, as a cultural "halfie," I was better suited to do the job than a complete stranger to the community would have been.

Notes

1. The coastal (Adriatic) province of Croatia.
2. Many early Croatian migrants were counted as "illiterate" in Australian statistics, although this actually only meant "illiterate in English" (Australian Bureau of Statistics 1997).
3. I owe this expression to Lavie and Swedenburg (1996).
4. The "West" historically has two meanings: a wider meaning of Christendom (versus the "East" of non-European and non-Christian civilizations), and its more contemporary meaning, which I use here to refer to the "developed" world, comprising many different countries and cultures, including those of Western Europe, North America, and Australia, which have claimed economic, political, and cultural domination through colonialist and neocolonialist strategies.
5. The dilemmas surrounding the use of autobiographical voice are not confined to native researchers. In Evans-Pritchard's (1976:241) words, "what one brings out of the field-study largely depends on what one brings into it."

Jim Birckhead

CHAPTER 8

"And I Can't Feel at Home in This World Anymore"

Fieldwork in Two Settings

Ordinary everyday life is full of awkward moments: misunderstandings, conflict, pain, sorrow, feelings of unease and dread, boredom and ennui, depression, and even despair. This is the human condition, given the basic dialectic between self and other(s), the tension between precept and practice, the "state of the world," the uncertainty and brevity of life, and the ultimate existential problem of what it all means. If existence in one's home lifeworld is not challenge enough to endure, doing ethnographic fieldwork serves to heighten the vagaries, contradictions, and pleasures of "normal" life as we attempt to absorb others' experiential worlds and deepest meanings in the name of anthropology.

I reflect here on my long-term fieldwork with fundamentalist Christian serpent-handlers in the southern United States (commenced in 1970), and on my more recent consultancy work with native title claimants in Australia,[1] to elucidate the awkward and fraught spaces as well as the creative and productive aspects of my ethnographic experience. Many of my more awkward moments in the field have derived from the fact that my basic focus as an anthropologist has been largely "existential" rather than "formalistic" (Henry 1964:xviii); that is, I have concentrated on the deep meanings people create and those realms of experience that suggest a " 'real' life beyond academic analysis" (Stewart 1996:73).

The serpent-handling work, at the beginning of my career, reflects a more traditional academic focus on pure research and theory, such as is required for a Ph.D. dissertation in anthropology. Although I successfully completed this research, I often felt awkward and self-conscious as I plied my trade among the "saints"[2] and anxiously struggled to find an "authentic" self or role among "them." Native title research, on the other hand, which I began some twenty years after receiving my Ph.D., is anything but pure; it is circumscribed and forensic, and very much implicated in racial politics and government policy. It is contract research, mandated by legislation and the Federal Court, and directed by lawyers, who issue "instructions" for the researcher to follow according to tight deadlines. In this process, the anthropologist as "expert witness"/researcher has a "paramount duty . . . to the Court and not to the person retaining the expert" (Federal Court of Australia 1998) to research and report on the authenticity of the people and their claim for native title over their "traditional country." As such, the anthropologist "is not an advocate for a party," a position in some conflict with long-held professional codes of anthropological ethics, which state that "an anthropologist's paramount responsibility is to those he studies" (Spradley and McCurdy 1975:609).[3] I often felt uneasy in this role and for even being involved in these "constructions of Aboriginal tradition for public purpose" (Ritchie 1999:255). As elders sometimes cynically mused, "the Court needs a White man to tell them who we are, when we could do it better ourselves."

I reflect first on my engagement with religious serpent-handlers in the southern United States.

With Signs Following . . .

> And these signs shall follow them that believe: In my name they shall cast out devils; they shall speak with new tongues; they shall take up serpents; and if they drink any deadly thing, it shall not hurt them; they shall lay hands on the sick, and they shall recover.
>
> —St. Mark 16:17–18

These are the five "signs" of holiness that true believers in serpent-handling religion must follow in order to be "saved." It is the serpent-handlers' belief that only a church "with signs following" and people who "follow the signs" can claim to be true disciples of Jesus Christ. While members emphasize the importance of working in all of the signs, media coverage has, not surprisingly, focused on "snake-handling" and poison drinking, especially deaths from these causes, to the exclusion of the more mainline Christian practices of speaking in tongues, Divine healing, and "casting out devils."

Scattered through the Appalachian and Deep South, the thirty-five to forty-five small, independent congregations of serpent–handlers, each consisting of some twenty-five to one hundred members each, conform nicely to what Gerlach and Hine (1970) refer to as a "segmented polycephalous interaction network" (SPIN). These groups are also classified as "crisis cults" (La Barre 1962), "thaumaturgical sects" (Wilson 1970), "revitalization movements' (Miller 1977), and "churches of the stationary poor" (Gerrard 1971).

When I made my tentative entry into the churches and lives of serpent-handlers in 1971, I was a recent but ardent convert to anthropology. I longed to "have a people" (Birckhead 1997, 1999), to survive the trial by fire of fieldwork, and to gain membership to the fraternity of returned ethnographers. It was also a part of my own personal search for meaning as a young man in the tumultuous 1970s. During my first sultry summer of fieldwork discontent, however, I agonized over my choice of fieldsite and over my real reasons for wanting to poke into peoples' lives at all (see Birckhead 1997).

My life "in the field" alternated between attending religious services of one to four hours each three or more times a week, spending time with saints informally outside of church, and having "time out" to let down, reflect, and write field notes in my rented room across from the University of Tennessee in Knoxville. The services ranged from poorly attended mid-week prayer meetings to the crowded, surreal, "Holy Ghost–filled" happenings on weekends during which the transformed hunting cabin/church house was awash in the total experience of hot pounding gospel rock, hand-clapping, and foot-stomping, punctuated by chilling screams of ecstasy and the innate fear that arose when serpents were "taken up," or people danced with fire or drank strychnine or brought out scorpions.

Night merged into day as I traveled in convoys of cars with my religious "brothers" and "sisters" to other Southern states to pray for "serpent-bit" saints, to visit Nashville gospel singers, or to "swap serpents" with handlers in far-flung parts of the network. During these periods of deep immersion, I lived and absorbed the visceral touch and feel of serpent-handling. I often had disturbing, vivid dreams of being attacked by snakes—dreams that I related to "saints" for their prophetic interpretations.[4] I loved the adrenalin high and intense drama of the serpent-handling life and was grimly captivated by the immediacy of the possibility of death. I also enjoyed spending time with the saints and being "Brother Jimmy," although at times I found their high-intensity, risky lifestyles confronting and emotionally exhausting. While in their midst, I assiduously observed their interactions as they followed their precept of living "spiritual" lives in a "carnal world," especially when it came to the "backstage" (Goffman 1959) repair work that took place when "signs" apparently failed; when a handler was bitten by a serpent or burned by fire, a strychnine drinker died in the faith, or a prophecy or exorcism did not result in the anticipated outcomes.

However, my successes notwithstanding, I continued to feel self-conscious and agonized over my role as observer. At times I felt like a voyeur, not much better than the reporters, television crews, and curiosity seekers whom I came to despise. Although I had explained to the saints in a general way that I was "studying," I never felt that they fully comprehended what I was actually doing in their midst. But they did create a space for me, making sense of my presence according to their own pragmatic and cosmic purposes.

A year into my fieldwork, a brother was serpent-bit during the Saturday night service of September 18, 1972 (Birckhead 1997:66–67). My feelings of awkwardness, of being out of place, and of not wanting to violate the privacy of this religious community emerge in the following excerpts from my field diary.

Serpent-Bite and Estrangement

Billy Jay staggered out, slipping into unconsciousness with his arms draped around the necks of two church brothers. He was being taken to Brother Jimmy's house in Carson Springs, followed by the documentary crew who had been filming the service up to the time of the serpent bite. The service continued with a pall over it and the fear of death, both for Billy Jay and for Jimmy, who had drunk carbon tetrachloride as well, and all on film.[5]

Outside, after the service, I fidgeted in the parking lot wondering what to do; to go to Brother Jimmy's house, where Bill was being prayed over, or not. I asked Brother Ralph and Sister Bea if they were going up, and they said "no, [we] could pray for him just as well at home." In the end, as I watched them drive away, I was left standing alone in the dark church car park, next to the gurgling stream at the head of "Snake Hollow."

After unsuccessfully trying to find Jimmy's house, I gave up and drove to Morristown, where I was staying for the weekend with a Methodist preacher and his family. I was tired and weary by this time, and felt like an ambulance chaser even wanting to see Bill, no doubt, vomit, swell up, suffer, and maybe even die. I did not know Brother Bill very well and would only be going to obtain information and watch a spectacle, like the film crew that was already up there with their cameras rolling. I would be just one more intruder thrust into the saints' lives during a time of crisis, and was anxious to disassociate myself from the film-makers and others of their sensationalistic ilk.

I had failed as a fieldworker, had allowed human and ethical qualms to paralyze me by not taking advantage of the opportunity to observe an important "backstage" scene. Seeking relief in sleep, I mulled over the events of the day and my reactions, or perhaps, overreactions. During my nightmarish sleep I handled a large, dead, slimy rattlesnake. Not even in sleep can I escape the terrors of the world of my field reality.

The next morning, cold autumn rain heavily falling, I still felt estranged from my role as ethnographer and longed to return to my "real" life in Edmonton, St. Louis, or Knoxville. I dreaded the afternoon baptism that I had been invited to attend. Dogged determination drove me on, down the winding road to Del Rio, Tennessee, where the pastor, Brother Liston Pack, lived across from the French Broad River, where baptisms were held.

A few saints were already there. I uneasily walked past the church brothers and sisters sitting in the kitchen and living room to the bedroom where Liston and Jimmy were talking. To my delight, Jimmy was alive and well (having survived the carbon tetrachloride[6] that he had consumed) and I was told that Brother Billy Jay was recovering. They asked me why I hadn't come up to the house last night. Jimmy reassured me that as a brother and valued friend of the church I am always welcome at his home and should have come up to pray for Brother Bill.

My spirits lifted, and I enjoyed the baptism in spite of the dreary weather. That night, after the Sunday evening service up at Snake Hollow, I found myself at Jimmy's house, with all of us sitting around Bill's bed, looking at his bruised and swollen arm, while one saint after another spoke about the time they had been serpent-bit. This was a taken-for-granted fact of life. When "the hedge is broken, a serpent will strike."[7] There was an air of joviality and camaraderie in the room. We sat around and talked like this late into the night. I reveled in these serpent-handling stories and now felt very much at home with "my people."

Thinking back, this was a common pattern during my work with serpent-handlers: feeling awkward, but gritting my teeth and persisting, to be rewarded by deeper access to the saints and their world. Perhaps it was my youth, basic shyness, and lack of self-confidence as a fieldworker, or the metamorphosis of consciousness required to be deeply open and sympathetic to people who routinely flirted with death and who seemed so aberrant to majoritarian views. More likely, it was the guilt and "bad faith" (Sartre 1953:47) of being "Brother Jimmy," who sought to absorb their spiritual meanings and convert these into social science schemas.

Hinson (2000:331) sees this as a process of "ontological colonialism" or "analytical assimilation" (332), whereby the "conceptual landscape now belongs to the ethnographer" (334) rather than to those being studied. I "paid the price" and endured. With repeated return visits over the years (Birckhead 2002) I have learned to feel at home with a more mellow serpent-handling self, relating now to more mellow, self-reflective "saints," survivors, and "backsliders" among those who "follow(ed) the signs."

Although research with serpent-handlers made me anxious in a number of ways, native title research, because of its legal and bureaucratic embeddedness, presented additional challenges and frustrations, as I will now explain.

Native Title Days, 1996–2003: Tracking *"Djurbils"* and Chasing Contracts

> Clearly, the recognition of indigenous peoples' customary title by the common law is problematic. It involves a collision between two systems of law which are founded upon fundamentally different conceptions of the world. In the process of recognising native title, the common law is therefore bound to distort the rights and obligations created by customary law.
>
> —Morris (1995:1)

The above quotation well summarizes the basic contradictions of native title, but leaves to the imagination the deep issues of conflict that may face an anthropologist attempting to work within the maelstrom of this "collision" of systems, laws, and worlds. Indeed, I found aspects of my native title work to be the most personally and professionally challenging of my anthropological career.

Unlike my serpent-handling research, I did not initially set out to do native title work. Instead I was invited by the working party for a claimant group, in late 1996, to be "their anthropologist." They were seeking a mature, experienced professional to work in partnership with them, someone who "had a good heart," whom they could trust and feel at ease with. As they had invited me to fill a role that was necessitated by legislation, such anxiety-provoking details as selecting a fieldsite, gaining entry, negotiating a role, finding people to speak with and a place to stay[8] were all arranged by the working party. It was even specified that a member of the community, Mudargun ("law man who moves quick"), would serve as my field assistant and accompany me on all research visits.

Things moved quickly once I had agreed to take on the consultancy. I was first flown up " 'ome," about a thousand miles from where I live, so that I could be introduced to the community, house by house, and could attend a weekend meeting at a nearby cattle station. Before I could be officially hired I had to be "approved" by the elders, a process I found awkward and uncomfortable.

A week later I flew to Brisbane to meet with the working party, the representative body,[9] and claimant lawyers. To my amazement and unease, one of the main agenda items was "Is Jim hired?" As it turned out, some members felt that because they had not been consulted about the invitation extended to me, I had not in fact "been hired." The lawyer for the representative body agreed, noting that they, and not the working party,[10] employed consultants. To my added discomfort, some questioned the propriety of my presence at the elders' meeting the previous week as not all the working party or elders had been party to that decision either.

The meeting also debated what type of document would be required for this claim: a "full anthropological report," which would stand up in court, or an "indicative interim report," which would outline the "evidence" to ascertain whether a full report was warranted. This issue was almost the undoing of the claim, with the working party wanting a full report and the lawyer for the representative body agreeing to contract only for a partial report. The discussion continued about my "being hired," during which we *dagay* (whites), the two lawyers and myself, were asked several times to leave the room. After a long interval, we were called back and I was told "you're hired, now tell us about yourself."

As the academic year drew to a close, and in spite of my initial positive feelings about working collaboratively with native title claimants, I found myself wondering what I had fallen into. Looking back, I wonder what drove me on: curiosity, the fact that I was flattered to have been asked to be "their anthropologist," my strong belief that anthropology should be applied to improve society, an existential quest for new experience (to step out of my home world and to be back in the field again), or my family's wish that I earn extra money to buy horses?

My anxiety proved to be warranted, not so much because of the normal interpersonal challenges inherent in doing fieldwork, but owing to an unending string of difficulties with the contract and the legal and bureaucratic management of the claim.[11] To start with, it took a year to draw up and negotiate the contract between the working party, claimant lawyer, representative body, and my university, with me being caught somewhere in the middle. This severely limited my access to the field during much of

1997. There was also the community's ongoing belief that their rich culture required nothing less than a "full anthropological report," and the fact that I had been contracted to produce only the "indicative interim report." Members of the community urged me to proceed as if I were doing a full report, on the understanding that their lawyer would negotiate with the representative body to amend the contract to provide me with necessary additional field time. This did not actually happen until late in 2001, when a new contract was drawn up for seventy days of fieldwork and writing to wrap up the reports, a new legal team and representative body, and the additional input of a historian, a linguist, an archaeologist, and a second anthropologist. In retrospect, the process for me had the nightmarish quality of being lost in a complicated labyrinth with no exit. One obstacle after another seemed to conspire to frustrate my research and keep me in a state of anxiety over the future of the claim and my involvement in it.

My frustration and unease were heightened by the cultural richness of the community I was working with and by the overwhelming level of access to cultural knowledge that I sometimes had. I had acquired the nicknames of "Jim Bob" or Banahm (little brother)[12] and I felt increasingly "at home" with my hosts, Nanna and Poppy, and with Mudargun, my field assistant. I often found myself sitting up late with Nanna, a respected elder, talking about her long life and her deep understanding of spiritual power and entities. I learned about "clever" people (Hume 2002), who possess special powers for good or evil; the names, locations, and meanings of *djurbils*, totemic increase sites that link people to their country (see Radcliffe-Brown 1929); not to cast my shadow across a grave in the old burial ground lest I get "caught" and die; and words and phrases from the language. Poppy usually shared aspects of his cultural knowledge with me while we did chores together, or while I drove him to nearby towns to buy chicken feed or go to the post office. He also pointed out to me specific *djurbil* sites, telling me the stories behind them and whom they belonged to. Discussion about such spiritual matters often continued as community people and relations dropped by Poppy and Nanna's house, or when Mudargun and I visited others in the community.

While this work was ethnographically rich and exhilarating, it was also very sad and poignant, and urgent. I was painfully aware that these old people would not be around for long. The following sketch reflects some of these feelings, and raises questions about our role as fieldworkers, as both "stranger and friend" (Powdermaker 1966) to the people who agree to participate in our research.

"How Death Enters Your Life—A Telephone Ringing"[13]

News of Nanna's death in November 2001 came inadvertently to me at the conclusion of a phone conversation with one of our lawyers, who mentioned almost as an after thought, " Oh, I think she passed away last night." I was devastated, as I had planned to see her the following week now that the new contract had finally been negotiated. I had so looked forward to her saying, "Boy, come sit on the bed with me and we'll talk."

My thoughts drifted back to the many stays with her and Poppy, and how they had always said their place was my home. I recalled the late-night chats with Nanna, and other nights when we were all in bed by eight o'clock. One such night, I was awakened at about 10:30 P.M. by the sound of a squeezebox being played by Poppy or Nanna, muffled singing and laughing between them. I lay in my bed in the sleep-out, smiling and feeling an inner glow, a temporary sense of being at home in the universe with these down-to-earth, deeply religious people—religious both in a tribal and a Pentecostal way.[14]

I remembered with bittersweet fondness how Poppy, who rose at 5 A.M., would bring tea and toast to my bed. He would pull the quilt over me, and say, "Don't you get up, my beloved. You just rest for awhile." He did this for Mudargun and Nanna as well.

So, it was with deep sadness that I met Mudargun at Sydney Airport for the 6 A.M. flight to Brisbane for Nanna's funeral, back in the community. We sat on the plane together, talking like brothers about our times with Nanna and Poppy. This was the end of an era. He had so much more to learn from them and felt a deep personal loss. It had also been a rare privilege for me to have known them so well, not just in terms of the native title research, but in terms of the warm human relationship I had with them, the worldly wisdom they shared so willingly with me, and their interest in my family, whom they had never met.

Hundreds of people came to Nanna's funeral, as she was a respected elder. The ceremony was dignified and profound: a mixture of Pentecostal and traditional tribal ways. I caught up with people I had not seen since my last visit a year and half ago, some of whom assumed that I was no longer working on the claim. Nanna's sister thanked me for coming up, saying dryly, "She talked about you all of the time and said that you would come back soon. But you never came back, did you?" Her words hit me hard with a dull thud, leaving me speechless. What could I say? This was hardly the time to launch into a defensive explanation of the litany of disasters beyond my control that had kept me away for so long.

Nor was it the time to explain that I lived in other worlds as well, with too many personal and professional commitments. Nevertheless, her words continue to haunt me, and I deeply regret that I was unable to go back to see Nanna before she died.

In summary, I believe that my native title research reflected a good match between the claimants and "their anthropologist," and that it was quite productive and successful to a point. Yet the bureaucratic delays and frustrations that I experienced limited my autonomy as an anthropologist, leaving me to feel awkward and foolish much of the time. Words can hardly express how compromised and disillusioned I felt as a professional when I was not able to keep up the momentum of field relationships because my university and the representative body, for example, took some five months to negotiate a contract that would allow me back into the field.

Once I was back in the field, but after the deaths of Poppy, Nanna, and many other old people, my work progressed well, but with an overwhelming amount of information to collect from people about their family history and knowledge of sites in a very short period of time. Fortunately, because I had "paid the price" and stuck by this claim through thick and thin, people trusted me and readily agreed to be interviewed, usually as a family group. These tape-recorded interviews with groups and individuals lasted between two and three hours, and were a sheer joy to do. After all the delays and frustrations the research seemed to be finally coming together to form a coherent picture of people and country. Under the second contract I stayed in motels rather than elders' homes, worked without a community field assistant, and had a "paramount duty . . . to the Court." I was no longer "their anthropologist" as such. Ultimately, however, I remained frustrated. I had to return "home" to write the reports in time for the Court deadline, thereby disrupting my further pursuit of this ethnography with people who were so willing to share their cultural knowledge with me.

"And I Can't Feel at Home in This World Anymore"

> The world is not my home, I'm just passing through
> My treasures are layed up somewhere beyond the blue
> The angels beckon me from heaven's open door
> And I can't feel at home in this world anymore . . .
>
> (Traditional religious song)

This religious lament, sung during my first service at the Holiness Church of God In Jesus Name in 1971 by saints who believed the "world" would soon end, points to the dual existential themes of "homelessness" and being "at home in the world" (Jackson 1995), and, by extension, to how the ethnographer attempts to find a home between worlds, or at least in some world. Weston La Barre (1971:27) evoked the occupational hazard of "the loneliness of the long-distance anthropologist," presumably caught somewhere between "the urge to be at home everywhere" (Novalis, in Jackson 1995:4) and the grim prospect of becoming "a stranger who can never go home, i.e., never find a point of rest in any society" (Nash 1963:164). Susan Sontag (1961) finds such a life "heroic," with its displacements (Behar 1996:21) and "involved detachment with all peoples" (King 1987:47), while John L. Wengle (1984) sees in the liminality of fieldwork a "quest for immortality" through the continual death and rebirth of ethnographic selves.

With "Brother Jimmy," "Jim Bob," and "Banahm" now put to one side, I once again inhabit the less awkward space of my "real," non-fieldwork life until my next project comes along. However, these field selves and the knowledge and experience on which they are constituted are never really laid to rest, but nibble at the edge of consciousness trying to break through. At times I experience a type of "otherness" to my self (Dabrowski 1967:37), like an alien among "earthlings," unstuck in time and place like Billy Pilgrim (Vonnegut 1972), and a sensation of being possessed by ghosts of the field. It is as if the field of my almost photographic memory, notes, photos, audio tapes, and video tapes still exists out there in a parallel universe, just as I left it, awaiting my return. Like a chapter in a good novel, I can revisit it at will and relive the experience.

These remnants, vestiges of field selves and field experiences, sit uneasily with my life in the "real world" in a modern managerial Australian university with its endless, tedious, and often meaningless meetings, Orwellian monitoring and "quality audits," and petty status distinctions. It all seems so banal compared to the intense drama of life and death in the field among individuals who live with strong spiritual meaning. While people generally find me "very interesting" because of my "exotic" pursuits, I have learned not to reveal too much to "lay persons," lest they "suspect (my) loyalty to the normal world" (Wagner 1997:94–96). The "field" does change one and, like religion, provides "another world to live in" (Santayana, in Geertz 1966:1), if only for a time.

In conclusion, my reflections on the awkward, sometimes alienating, and uncomfortable spaces of "living the ethnographic life" (Rose 1990) in two settings notwithstanding, I have to agree with Ruth Behar (1996:5) that despite everything: "Anthropology (ethnography) . . . is the most fascinating, bizarre, disturbing, and necessary form of witnessing left to us." With the benefits of hindsight I could, no doubt, have improved my methods for studying serpent-handlers and researching a native title claim, and perhaps been less anxious in the process. But, in the end, both settings required the personal engagement of being there, of being open to the possibilities of the respective situations, and therefore of being vulnerable as an anthropologist and as a human being. From my anthropological training in fieldwork methods, ethics, and politics, I accepted that "going to the field" would be challenging and confronting. With respect to serpent-handlers I underestimated how guilty and out of place I would sometimes feel, while with native title research I was caught out by the almost insurmountable roadblocks thrown up by the various bureaucracies that impinge on such claims. My strategy in both settings of persisting, of "paying the price" in spite of the obstacles, was, I believe, the correct one.

Notes

1. The Native Title Act of 1993 and its amendments in 1998 were the legislative responses to the 1992 Australian High Court Mabo Decision, which recognized that original or native title may still exist and be vested in any number of indigenous "tribal" groups across the country. The Native Title acts provide the mechanisms by which this title can be asserted and validated legally (through anthropological research as well) to establish the legitimacy of a claim group through principles of descent, long-term connection with the country claimed, and ongoing cultural practices reflecting a group's deeply held "traditional laws and customs."
2. Serpent-handlers often refer to themselves as "saints" and "apostles" and address one another as "brother" and "sister."
3. Another consequence of the anthropologist's having a "paramount duty . . . to the Court" is that the Court can obtain all research "evidence," including fieldnotes and tapes, diary entries, emails, photographs, and correspondence, thus compromising the usual promises of confidentiality that we offer people with whom we work in the field.
4. The poem "Holy Ghost People (Scrabble Creek, West Virginia)," by Adrie A. Kusserow (1998:209–210), conveys some of the experiential feel of serpent-handling religion.
5. Sadly, Brother Jimmy and Brother Buford died from strychnine that they later consumed during a "spirit-filled" Saturday night service on April 7, 1973. This brought about an invasion of media people and sightseers, and legal problems for the church. Indeed, I appeared as a defense witness in the Cocke County Court regarding the strychnine deaths. These events awk-

wardly transformed my fieldsite into a much more public realm, causing me to expand my frame of reference to focus on minority group identity and the media (Birckhead 1993).

6. Carbon tetrachloride is a sweet-smelling cleaning fluid or solvent. While not as dangerous as strychnine, when ingested it can cause damage to the liver, kidneys, and nervous system, and in some instances can cause death (Agency for Toxic Substances and Disease Registry 2003).

7. Serpent-handlers say that they are protected by the "anointing power of the Holy Ghost," which surrounds them like a protective shield or "hedge." This can be breached by a variety of factors, causing a serpent to bite (Birckhead 1976).

8. The working party decided that I should stay in the home of elders "Nanna" and "Poppy." They were Mudargun's tribal grandparents, and their knowledge was considered invaluable. I seemed to connect with them from the beginning and over time developed a close personal relationship with them.

9. Native title representative bodies manage claims. This includes contracting for legal and anthropological research to be undertaken, and liaising with claimant groups.

10. The working party, consisting of some fifteen people, comprised representatives of the main claimant family groups in the community and acted as a bridge between the community and the representative body.

11. This is not to suggest that there were no awkward moments in the field, but I was prepared for these from my experiences with serpent-handlers, and from previous work with indigenous communities on Cape York in far northern Queensland, Australia.

12. The name Banahm was given to me by Nanna and Poppy, as they felt that it was disrespectful for Mudargun to refer to me as "dagay" while I was living in their home. The name "Jim Bob" was given to me by Mudargun, who told whites in the area that I was "Jim Bob, a champion bull rider from Arkansas."

13. This quote is inspired by Oates 2001:15.

14. As in many Aboriginal communities, Christianity plays an important part in people's lives, often being interwoven with traditional "tribal" beliefs and practices.

PART II   **ETHICAL ENGAGEMENTS**

Sylvie C. Tourigny

CHAPTER 9

"Yo, Bitch* . . . " and Other Challenges

Bringing High-Risk Ethnography into the Discourse

The tapping noise of the shotgun muzzle against my window, or maybe the sudden set of Chuckie Dog's jaw, or the changing light pattern over my left shoulder, got my attention. As I rolled down the car window, a sawn-off gun barrel rose and pointed unhesitatingly at Chuckie Dog, who was sipping coffee in my passenger seat. Dark eyes appeared through a black ski mask and a voice mumbled[1] inches from my ear:

"You think you can fuck with me and not die, punk?"

Chuckie Dog's eyes looked icy. His right hand stayed in his pocket, suggesting it also held a gun. He smirked:

"Punk, you said 3G's and that be what we paid. Shit weren't that good, anyways. I thought you bring more 'coz you know the shit's no good. So it's you fuckin' with me!"

The Mask growled before a vaguely familiar voice spat out:

"How's tellin' you the truf 'bout the shit be fuckin' wiff you? You don't be wantin' it, you cain just be goin' on home, man. You don't make no deal and then fuck with it. Not with another set, man. Any set be buyin' anyways. You'se wantin' to start set trippin', man, and I don't stand for none'a that."

So, both youths belonged to sets on different turfs affiliated, however loosely, with the same gang. Getting rid of a set's leader can heighten leadership prospects, but "set tripping"—starting conflict between branches of the same gang—curries disfavor. Interfering with drug deals is even less forgivable. There was no time for me to try to figure out who was "right" about the value of some unknown quantity of drug, or about some prior agreement. As I pondered how to intervene, Dog answered:

(continud)

"I tole you if you'se gonna meet me here you'se better not diss me in front of her . . . "

I felt as though I had been slapped. The Mask answered:

"I tole you I ain't never gonna hurt doc, man, so shut up wiff that. You just gimme me my money, punk, or I'se gonna blow your fuckin' brains all over her dashboard. I ain't aksing no mo'."

They had agreed to meet this way. The quiver of the shotgun was less reassuring than the promise to not "hurt doc." Dog's and my whereabouts were predictable whenever I visited his family. Understanding why he had arranged this meeting, however, had to wait. While the enormity of the events distracted me, both voices grew louder and angrier. When I reawakened to the moment, both guns were drawn. I was hurt, disappointed, afraid, and very angry. I fell back on a fundamental street principle: "don't ever let yourself be disrespected."

"Stop that, now, both of you. And shut the fuck up.[2]"

Both men groaned but I barked loudly enough to get their attention.

"First off, 'doc' don't like being the stooge. . . . So go ahead, shoot each other . . . Better yet, shoot the dumb-assed honky bitch. Then your families and your sets will be real happy when cops land here. Young bloods[3] are gonna die and the man's gonna terrorize all your asses unless you cool it."

The standoff petered out; guns retreated, and the deal stood, but the next transaction would advantage Chuckie Dog's set.

This encounter happened while I was undertaking research on the survival strategies of socioeconomically marginalized minority families living with AIDS in inner-city Detroit; gang involvement was one of these strategies. It was a significant event in my ethnographic career.

Focus, Background, and Rationale

This chapter highlights a very narrow sliver of ethnographic reality: the rare, usually brief, high-risk moments that seriously threaten researcher or project. Using incidents from my own research, I aim to evaluate the broader, unarticulated significance of risk that is sometimes part of fieldwork and to initiate a dialogue about its meaning.

My first high-risk ethnographic encounter took place in a hospital emergency room in a suburb of Hartford, Connecticut, in the mid-1980s.

I was conducting research on stress, appraisal, and coping among women with ovarian cancer, when an upper-middle-class respondent's husband walked in on my conversation with his dying wife about her funeral preferences (Tourigny 1988). Because for months he had denied his wife's impending death, the conversation was encroaching on his beliefs about her future. Picking me up by the lapels, he held me a foot off the ground, spat at me, and threatened to bash my face in. I reassured him that the conversation presumed no time frame, whereupon he started crying; we spent hours discussing his terror at the prospect of losing her. But the rapidity and incongruity of the threat alerted me to the stark reality that our ethnographic choices—particularly those zeroing in on genuinely problematic elements of respondent reality—sometimes come unexpectedly and threateningly close to painful truths, and thus that risk is potentially ubiquitous and unpredictable.

An important reason for considering the role of risk and risk perception in ethnographic research is the extent to which these factors can consciously or unconsciously structure field experience. Increasingly, academic colleagues working outside the ethnographic tradition, particularly in the United States, seem to view work in socioeconomically deprived communities as inherently life-threatening. Such preconceptions have the potential to alter project design, funding availability,[4] and thus knowledge of those populations who may benefit most from our work.

Furthermore, our actual experiences of risk, and their consequences, constitute a major methodological issue. The researcher's feeling betrayed or threatened inevitably alters the way research itself proceeds, and impacts on our interpretations and analyses of the data collected before and after traumatic events. We need to start conceptualizing physical and emotional risk as inevitable aspects of fieldwork in order to demystify some of these processes: even if truly threatening situations are rare, risk itself is always present, though in varying degrees depending on the nature, location, and relationships of the fieldwork. The alternative is to muddle through unsystematically, leaving individual researchers to face the emotions triggered by difficult fieldwork experiences in professional and theoretical isolation, precisely when disciplinary perspectives are most needed.

The complex lives of AIDS caregivers who are young, poor, and engaged in drug markets and related gang work form the empirical backdrop for my analysis of the risks that I faced as an ethnographer working in inner-city Detroit. As the emergency room and the street-corner incidents illustrate, however, potential risks exist everywhere.[5] Conversations about other risks—such as the inevitable modifications complex issues of attachment and loss, proximity and distance, confidentiality and professionalism associated with ethnographic practice impose upon our lives—can proceed candidly only after we have addressed the issue of basic physical risk.

High-risk moments unfold with recognizable beginnings and ends and trigger immediate reactions. Yet their impact lingers, potentially tainting the project by altering field interactions and researcher perspectives. Additional challenges emerge involving the interplay between the experience of risk and the selection of theory to analyze resulting data. While we tend to seek narrow explanations centered on the moment, the encounter, or the personalities, multiple, interlinked paradigms are more often needed to explicate high-risk moments. Physical risk of the kind I describe emerges from within a complicated context (Tourigny 2001). While avoiding exposure to such risk without irretrievably compromising the project itself may be difficult, our interpretation of events depends as much on the precepts we bring to our research as on decisions made in the field. We therefore must allocate time and training to anchoring ethnography within a reliable set of applied skills hinging on sound ethical and moral principles.

The Research Project

The twenty-six inner-city residents with HIV/AIDS who enrolled in my five-year ethnography of socioeconomically vulnerable, AIDS-afflicted, inner-city Detroit households identified 88 caregivers who became auxiliary respondents.[6] The altercation in the car park involved two of 31 such auxiliary respondents between 12 and 22 years of age (Tourigny 2001). Twenty-eight participants died during the project, nineteen of AIDS, two in a single car accident. One was murdered by an ex-partner, and a client (or "john") allegedly killed another, a sex worker. Three died of gunshot wounds; one overdosed; and one suspicious death occurred in a crack house.

Basing my study on in-depth fieldwork, and using Bourgois' (1996) notion of "vulnerable ethnography," I sought to understand how socioeconomically marginalized households managed life with HIV/AIDS. Much of my involvement with youth resulted from contemporaneous de-funding of General Assistance[7] in Michigan, which eliminated cash assistance to purportedly able-bodied adults not heading households (Henly & Danziger 1996; Tourigny 2001; Tourigny & Jones-Brown 2001a, 2001b;). Unable to afford independent living, these young men had contributed as much as ninety percent of their benefits to their families, and were thus negatively affected in complex ways that were omitted from statistical reporting about "decreased welfare rolls."

My research involved lengthy field visits, including overnights and weekends at participants' homes, participation in family events, attendance at clinic visits and hospital bedsides, telephone updates, and reading of respondent diaries. I witnessed drug deals, I saw mothers cry for the children they would soon orphan, and I witnessed deaths. I visited shooting galleries, three-generational households where no one was yet thirty, and tenements where children wailed in hunger in front of empty refrigerators, until despairing AIDS-afflicted mothers took to street sex work to feed them; I listened to seropositively mixed couples debating how one partner's HIV might impede pregnancy. I tagged along, listening in and observing and asking questions and challenging interpretations until I felt respondents' realities were as much my own as possible, a process I call "empathic witnessing."

Accidental Versus Chosen Risk

We constantly assess decisions and relationships partly in terms of their perceived risks to others and to ourselves. We cannot extricate this process from the choices we make about how and where we do ethnography. In the United States, inner cities host a higher number of localized, recorded index crimes per capita than more affluent neighborhoods, partly because poor communities draw outsiders who clutter local crime statistics (Simon & Burns 1997). Doing ethnography means being physically present, in this case, in an environment targeted by extraordinary law enforcement efforts to count, catalogue, and prosecute inner-city residents for drug-related offenses and other misdeeds ignored elsewhere (Dunlap, Tourigny & Johnson 2000). Conversations with police officers alerted me to the risks of over-policing. I once engaged an exquisitely polite and genial twenty-seven-year-old African-American police officer in conversation after he stopped me to ask whether I was lost. Since I was on my way to a shooting gallery[8] I hoped to dissuade him from following me. He commented on "preventative" policing practice:

> "We pull 'em in for DUI ["driving under the influence"] or something when we can. They're hot, the young brothers. Sometimes you can tell the way they drive, "leaning"[9] and all, they're looking for trouble. So if you can pull him over and stop him short. . . . You gotta think of it as crime reduction. We profile, so if he looks like he's the type that might be doing drugs or drinking and it's three A.M., well, get him off the streets."

Including "leaning" in profiling exacerbates the social reality of DWB ("driving while black"). It was a style, not an indication of intoxication. Constant and relentless scrutiny of drivers heightens anxieties and general animosity, and increases the likelihood of car chases. The ethnographer then risks facing altercations as driver, passenger, bystander, or unwitting recipient of the anxieties triggered by excessive police zeal.

I always insisted that my passengers carry neither weapons nor drugs.[10] Since police were prone to pulling me over and inquiring about my destination (allegedly, and often sincerely, for my own safety), and because of my justifiable fear that the "right" circumstances could quickly lead to a search, I tried to minimize risk by insisting that young African-American male passengers not sit with their backs to the passenger door. This was to avoid any suggestion that I was being threatened or held against my will. I typically refused to ride in young male participants' cars, partly to reduce police interest, but also as a proxy measure to maintain respect. One day I broke this rule.

Shoot-Out

Little O.G., a major drug distributor, offered me a ride back to his mother's home when my car needed repairs. He always detailed the changing landscape of gang control, advised of particularly risky intersections, and helped take care of me when I was ill. We discussed, but I did not fear, his constant anger about financial worries and his sense of futility. It seemed clear that Little O.G.'s offer to drive reflected our shared destination. I wrote notes while he used a pay phone. He returned saying:

"I gotta make a quick stop, if that's okay. No big deal, right?"

I assented unthinkingly, only vaguely noticing when we entered a neighborhood O.G. had repeatedly warned me to avoid. My discomfort grew when we drove up a garbage-strewn alley, and turned to fear when we drove to within inches of the rear bumper of a truck just as a utility vehicle tucked in behind us, hemming us in. The van door opened in front of us and several set members stood there, armed and looking nervous. Little O.G.'s jaw froze—he was furious. What perhaps began as negligence fast spiraled into the anticipation of disaster.

"We can talk later, O.G., I'm getting out of here."

He looked rather surprised and puzzled:

"You can't go anywhere, you won't be safe."

"Yo! . . . safe? . . . leaving won't be safe? I'm not having that conversation right now. Just waive me through."

I knew someone *might* shoot a white woman running away from a gang leader's car in a back alley in the middle of a drug deal, which is exactly what I planned to do. I also knew a bullet *would* kill me if I were caught in crossfire. Just as shots rang out, I jumped into a window well half-filled with water and disintegrating waste matter. When the dust settled a few minutes later, O.G. came looking for me:

"You okay? You'se all wet and you stink, is you hurt?"

"Well, I'm not dead. Hope you're not too disappointed."

My comment obviously hurt O.G., but at that moment I was past caring. No one died that day; two members of gangs on opposite sides of the transaction were wounded; three were arrested. O.G.'s lieutenant would end up in a wheelchair. And I faced a crisis of faith.

Understanding the Unexplainable

Determining whether I could stay in the field meant understanding these two incidents. While Chuckie Dog's and O.G.'s decisions seemed inexcusable, I knew they hid important lessons. I feared that my own temporary but severe health problems (a partial paralysis resulting from an accident unrelated to my fieldwork) upset the balance of power. Perhaps my obvious vulnerability threatened all of us. I felt guilty that I was somehow responsible for a shoot-out involving two young people I had known for a year, and truly valued.

I had chosen to enter their social domain. Like any tourist, I had tacitly agreed to abide by local rules. Now I needed to assess how much of the underlying structure, the syntax, of local reality I had somehow overlooked. I knew two things: Chuckie Dog had used me to schedule a potentially lethal confrontation. The Mask had used me, or at least, my presence, to solve a problem.

Everything I knew about Little O.G., particularly his fanatical need to control his environment, suggested he dreaded losing face publicly. I guessed mere negligence brought me to the shoot-out, but was he emboldened by the first, strategic, standoff? The Mask had been his lieutenant. Deciding whether to continue with my fieldwork included finding out whether O.G. planned to use this strategy again.

Two more possibilities warranted consideration. I might have become the member of a club I had not asked to join: I knew far more about the links between sets and among gangs than I had a few weeks earlier, and I had walked away unscathed. I had not notified police, and no one attempted to debrief me. Was knowledge the outcome of tests like this? And could I tolerate such tests? Was this research component sustainable?

The scariest possibility was that I had stepped over some invisible line. If a mistake had gotten me into trouble, if my field credibility was eroding, my ethnographic vision would be skewed, and my life, and potentially that of innocent bystanders, were possibly at risk. Breaches needed healing, but warnings needed heeding. If I still had credibility, no one would expect that I tolerate disrespect; if I was no longer credible, bluster was my only hope. I remembered a conversation with Little O.G. about strategy, when he spoke of the power of the number three:

> "People think three's awkward. That's be the point, man. You bring punks together that don't know each other like you be knowin' them, and you'se like, watchin' when they just runnin' off they mouths for each other. It like buy you time and if you'se gonna get mad, you can bite back a bit."

I knew both youths in ways far different from their street knowledge of each other. They would never be friends: although strikingly alike in shared intensity and leadership presence, they nurtured vastly different self-projections: Chuckie Dog deceptively laid back, and Little O.G. always wound up. I had to find out where I stood in both their minds before my presence in violent contexts became "business as usual." If each blamed the other, tensions between them and potentially between sets would exacerbate. Separate conversations would yield incompatible stories, which would need investigation, investigation that could destabilize the field and the different sets of a national gang and possibly trigger violence. Meeting before witnesses would showcase conflicting styles, status, and allegiances. Their drug-dealing antagonism was somewhat tempered by their shared role as AIDS care provider, but none of that ruled out the possibility of all-out war.

I decided to call on the respect they had shown me before and since the incidents, asking them to meet me unescorted. Excluding Little O.G.'s lieutenant, the Mask, was primarily strategic. His allegiances were uncertain; had he sought to solidify his place in Little O.G.'s set by defending him, or to take over by aligning with Chuckie Dog? He was the most vulnerable link; either man saying he lied and set him up might jeopardize his life. Besides, he was still in the hospital after the shoot-out.

I needed a setting I could control, somewhere public and unfamiliar to both young men. For shock effect, I whipped up my own anger and informed Chuckie Dog and Little O.G. by conference call that I would see them fifteen minutes later at a relatively fancy restaurant, adding, "My car won't be there," which suggested that others would be watching. Both arrived just a few minutes late, having met while they circled the block to avoid arriving first. I presided in the small private dining room.

They looked positively astounded as I explained why I had brought them there. Finally, Chuckie Dog blurted,

> "Yo, I wasn't gonna let nuthin' go wrong with you, man. Not never, man. You know this by now. I won't diss you. . . . Ain't nobody else been goin' to my mom's and, like, listenin' to what we'se goin' through. I won't hurt you. And so you bein' there means no bad shit's gonna go down."

I replied:

> "Well, excuse me. But given the situation, shotguns talk louder than words. Besides, if you're not going to "diss" me, maybe not setting me up is a good place to start?"

O.G. piped in:

> "You gotta understand, man, bid'ness be bid'ness. We ain't gonna let you be hurt, coz we likes you and coz that be bad bid'ness. Your bid'ness be AIDS, and I respect that. But my bid'ness be feedin' my family, and takin' care of 'em. And you'se gonna be as safe as the rest'a us, man, but we ain't in your world, you know. We cain't spare time to worry 'bout feelin' for folk till we'se figured out food for folk, man."

Chuckie Dog's voice became wistful as he added:

> "It be nice if we could, man. Shit, we can't even be keepin' family safe, man. My moms done everythin' one moms can do, and it ain't enough, man. When my pops be kilt, I figured out you do what you gotta do and you don't be wastin' time worryin' 'bout folk. I cares 'bout you, doc, but all I can do is what I can do. No mo' than that. I gotta care 'bout getting' through, too."

Conversation over lunch was enlightening primarily because of what remained unsaid. Clearly the events so perturbing to me had not been about me. I struggled to get out of my own experiential way, as someone whose fence-straddling made her oddly safe but also without individuality or value beyond the needs of the moment.

Several more years in the field were to elucidate how, given limited choices and exigent circumstances, strategy is necessarily, and sometimes unforgivingly, immediate. I was obviously right in enforcing rules that allowed me to transcend gang boundaries while protecting myself:[11] ethnography in this setting, like the reality of living there, was hazardous to life and limb. These events forced me to appreciate "risk" as highly contingent upon the viewpoints of those making moment-by-moment decisions. From their perspective, they had simply included me in part of their lives—which was, after all, what I had asked of them.

The Risks of Theory

These moments of risk were first about young men never allowed to be "children." Their life history interviews, and my subsequent enmeshment in their lives, revealed the hurt of seeing parents beaten down and beaten back by racism, effective apartheid, oppression, discrimination, and, eventually, by the compound influence of the context and of their own, increasingly frustrated, responses. These young men had witnessed and memorized enough of the strategies of last recourse necessary to survive a life riddled with problems to ensure that those tactics unavoidably framed their response to fear, challenge, and risk. Scheper-Hughes reminds us that

> In the shantytown, day-to-day moral thinking is guided by a "lifeboat ethics." The central ethical dilemma of the lifeboat concerns the decisions as to whom among the shipwrecked is to be saved when it would spell certain disaster to try saving all. . . . In emergency situations the morality of triage—the rudimentary pragmatics of saving the salvageable—often supersedes other, more aesthetic or more egalitarian ethical principles. (1992:405)

The social sciences provide important clues about why people who see themselves as lacking choices may enact behaviors that impose or inflict risk upon others. Social stratification appreciates the weight of context; social psychology explains how those who have the talents of leadership will lead, in whatever context they find themselves. Bringing these perspectives together highlights why, and how, structural confines focus the direction of their leadership. Chuckie Dog's and Little O.G.'s behavior reflected compound mechanisms of social exclusion erected around the inner cities that house them, which were incorporated within their own biographies and integrated within their own relationship management skills.

Whether or not I stayed in the field, the data I had already accumulated about these events would need analysis. Tackling the problem from both experiential and theoretical ends might improve understanding, and help me evaluate my own strategic decisions without losing precious rapport. Caring about young people who had made me feel threatened was certainly inconvenient. I had to find ways of understanding and working through my feelings of disappointment and victimization in order to extract lessons about what these events meant in a specific context. It is the ethnographer's job to document that reality. How else can we understand, appreciate, witness, and analyze lived experience? Our collective level of responsibility requires that we talk both about strategy and about an epistemology of risk.

As ethnographers we regularly push our negative emotions outward until they flood the people on the periphery of our work, those whom we believe are creating the pain that constrains our respondents' lives. Among students, we find teachers wanting, and periodically loathe principals. If we are studying the experiences of patients, surgeons become our nemeses; among street workers, johns and police officers acquire the same taint. Sometimes, resentment results from witnessing oppression; sometimes it emanates more diffusely from the weight of the burdens of those whose lives we study. Analytic strategies must appreciate that oppressive realities emerge in concentric circles, each one pressing inward toward the center, each experiencing slightly more pressure—and exerting more force in turn, driving the most powerless to the crowded core. We cannot assume that blame lies, even primarily, with the most proximate persons.

This project sheltered me from the most extreme of those impulses to apportion blame. Problems identified at the level of individual people living in conditions of extreme socioeconomic vulnerability certainly require the conjoined insights achievable only by shining analytic lights from multiple vantage points—from social stratification and social psychology, social policy, and ethnic relations. Fundamental questions about a structural environment sustaining oppression are eerily appropriate to policies targeting the poor. Otherwise, analyses claim the "uselessness" of suffering, and thus imply that those who suffer must be pathologically complicit in their suffering. Multiple contexts (especially the defunding of Michigan's General Assistance) forced themselves upon every aspect of my analysis. Thus, the outwardmost circles of accountability resided far away from the center, and certainly not among those youths struggling to survive changes in social policy by establishing power enclaves within particular street gangs.

Back to the Beginning: Keeping the Faith While Surviving the Field

I stayed in the field because I could not leave. These events were pivotal to the project, but also to any subsequent research. They harked back to my sense of myself as an ethnographer involved in a broader, freely chosen, journey toward social justice. Left unaired, they would almost certainly substantially alter anything else I did. Analysis "around the edges" would certainly disappoint me, and inhibit further involvement with similar research projects. Further ethnographies—should I decide to undertake them—would be tainted with the memory of having abandoned a project I cared deeply about, and leave me positioned quite differently with respect to risk. I would become a fearful ethnographer—afraid of undertaking similar research, of encountering similar risk, of enacting similar cowardice. Therefore, I could neither leave nor pretend these critical moments had not occurred, without significantly altering my research directions or my self-perception.

Chuckie Dog and Little O.G. were immersed in a lifestyle born out of necessity, a lifestyle that my particular ethnographic commitment brought me to document. As a result, their risks became my risks . . . and their risk-management strategies compelled me to reflect on the meaning and the management of risk for ethnographers, as an intrinsic part of the mandate we adopt.

Certainly, the risks to my own safety warranted attention—personally, but also because they were sure to significantly alter my relationship to my work and to my data. They also had the potential to modify my capacity to theorize effectively. The genuine anger triggered by a gun pointing at my face was fleeting—but the impact was long-lasting. I was hurt, but also forced to ponder my own behavior. Had I overreached by conducting research while quite significantly disabled, in a cultural environment where requiring, and receiving, physical assistance could trigger shifts in power relations? If the answer was yes, what might that mean for my long-term career?[12] And how significantly would these incidents affect my capacity to understand risk in marginalized communities?

The pivotal moment may have occurred during my confrontation with Chuckie Dog and Little O.G., because it put me back in the driver's seat with respect to the project. I wrote field notes about those two days, from as many temporal and experiential perspectives as I could, because only data can take us back *to* the moment. I then put the notes away, because only distance can give perspective *about* that moment, and because as the project continued to unfold and my relationships with the various participants grew, I knew I was empowered as an ethnographer, valued in the

community for the contributions I was able to make, and able to appreciate those risks as passing moments, rather than driving forces. Balancing
emotion and reason, empathy and knowledge is necessary to do justice to
the complexity of difficult moments.

Implications: Thinking About an Epistemology of Risk

Concern about, rather than evidence of, risk often weighs disproportion-
ately in research design. "Vulnerable ethnography," like war reporting,
requires one to make thoughtful professional choices involving prior knowledge and acceptance of risk. Since participants, like soldiers, do not have the
luxury to absent themselves from the troublesome dimensions of their lives,
I suggest that neither should ethnographers. Sheltering ourselves from elements of our respondents' reality will unavoidably distort our understanding, as the decision to stay away from the front lines would significantly
skew the journalists' reporting. Without a dialogue explicitly detailing the
realities of places and people generally perceived as "dangerous," we too fall
back on rumor, innuendo, and public opinion, entrenching rather than
investigating precisely the urban myths that we purport to explain.

Making informed decisions about risks requires knowledge about, and
sensitivity to, the attributes of the field. The ethnographer needs some
understanding of which risks are avoidable, how, and at what costs.
Extant discourse about risk tends to be tactical and strategic, but strictly
atheoretical. Frequently culled from guidelines designed for interviewers
engaged in quantitative surveys, suggestions given to junior field
researchers—often by ethics committees—typically urge them to stay
away from criminal behavior (ruling out a staggering proportion of
ethnographic research), from drug users under the influence (ruling out
shooting galleries or even families dealing with drug use), from dangerous
places (including entire neighborhoods and probably police ride-alongs),
and from antagonistic people (everywhere). Surely, ethnographers considering those guidelines are ethically bound to engage in thoughtful consideration of their appropriateness in the light of the specific project, the
types of data sought, the setting in which the research is to take place, and
their relationships to participants. Measures such as gradual integration
into some of the riskier elements of the field—contingent upon the building of relatively safe relationships and safeguards, for example—allow
one to exercise control without relinquishing key data.

Staying away from gangs would have excluded one of the most important sources of data for understanding inner-city responses to the con-

verging pressures imposed by AIDS and by welfare "reform"; avoiding substance users would have canceled the entire project, and much other AIDS-related research as well. Practicing ethnography anywhere involves a measure of risk, of emotional attachment, of worry, of loss. For reasons that have to do with poverty, inequity, racism, sexism, deindustrialization, and oppressive social policies, we know that these risks and some others may be greater in inner cities. The capacity to engage in the energy-consuming activities of ethnography in particularly vulnerable communities requires that one bring a degree of psychological comfort and emotional balance to the task. Alertness enough to ensure survival should not become paralysis at the thought of threat, nor should the researcher have blind faith in anyone else's ability or willingness to protect the research setting or oneself. Either possibility could well prove antithetical to survival, literally or intellectually. Either could heighten risk by distracting and isolating the researcher from the participants, for whom the community and its risks are generally not a matter of choice.

We need to assess how our presumptive fears alter the genuine interaction that is presumably at the core of ethnographic understanding, if what we seek is genuinely empathic witnessing. Our capacity to truly understand the participant's point of view—to "own" it in a visceral sense, for it to make intuitive sense—is highly contingent on our ability to keep making the choice to remain open to whatever the day-to-day field experiences may bring. When, and to the extent that, we silence our receptivity out of fear (or mistrust or even concern about loss and grief), we filter our perceptions and therefore mute our understanding. Imposing a distance between our participants and ourselves, and again between what we see and what we choose to feel, may reduce fear . . . but it also erodes insights, understanding, and appreciation. It makes ethnography less than it is meant to be, and disrespects the generous investments participants make in our projects.

We need a collective conversation about risk and the part it plays in our work. Once we disaggregate presumptions of risk from mere geography, we need to talk about how particularly high-risk projects can be managed. Ethnographers who remain committed to researching difficult questions among underprivileged populations can never eradicate risk. Uninformed fear can easily return inexperienced fieldworkers to their long-standing preconceptions. But lost empathy will return our readers to their own biases—something that is obviously not an option. No one is immune, researchers or participants, from the visceral fear that grips us at the sight of the barrel of a gun. Perhaps we should not attempt to eliminate risk.

Better to remember that with genuine threat—and genuine fear—comes the possibility of real empathy.

Notes

* This title is used in memory of Chuckie Dog, whose favorite salutation it was, and who remained a key informant until his death (Tourigny 1998). Names, gang affiliations, and other potentially identifying characteristics have been modified, using credible alternatives derived from the field.
1. Because of complex medical issues hindering my performance of activities of daily living and inhibiting my ability to type during the five years of this project, participants grew accustomed to the ubiquitous presence of a tape recorder; muddled or mumbled passages were reconstructed from memory.
2. A native French speaker who first learned English in Harlem (a predominantly Afro-American New York city neighborhood), I delight in the sounds and expressions of that culture, and am as comfortable in it as in formal English. Over time, that fluency eased many fieldwork tensions unavoidable when a middle-aged white woman works with Afro-American youths in deprived communities.
3. This generic reference applies to all young black males, and particularly to young men who identify with and are known as gang members. The term thus includes but is not limited to members of the national gang known as the Bloods.
4. Ironically, as ethnographic contributions are added to quantitative projects, ethnography's unique demands risk getting lost under the streamlined administrative structure of grant management. In drug research in particular, part-time, junior "fieldworkers" with no design input and little theoretical rationale provide "backup qualitative evidence" to "flesh out" quantitative monitoring by investigators whose background typically lacks any time in the field, and who lack an appreciation of its complexity.
5. A number of researchers report that studying elites involves much higher risks, including possible imprisonment, given the respondents' ability and willingness to take legal recourse should they feel the research misrepresented or otherwise disadvantaged them (Chrisman 1976; Berreman 1991; Gilbert, Tashima & Fishman 1991; Tourigny 1993). Elites are also much less likely to agree to participate in the first place than are people who experience the effects of marginalization (Toth 1993; Scheper-Hughes 1996; Edin 2000).
6. The distinction between primary and auxiliary respondents pertains more to clinical status and to recruitment than to the allocation of research time. While the needs of persons with AIDS predominated as a focus of attention, gaining a full-bodied appreciation of how loved ones met those needs involved considerable time.

7. The welfare provisions known as General Assistance in Michigan had included means-tested eligibility for all adults irrespective of marital status, until a "demonstration project" scheduled to facilitate what would become known as "welfare reform" in the United States significantly curtailed the benefits eligible to young and unemployed single males.

8. Shooting galleries are spaces where illicit drugs are consumed. They are often located in condemned/abandoned housing or, for a fee, in someone's home.

9. At the time of fieldwork, "leaning" (sometimes descriptively called "low-riding") was "cool." Some young men sat so low in the car that only their eyes were visible, through the steering wheel. Leaning is usually done at very low speeds, showcasing (preferably very large) cars and creating speculations about drivers (Majors & Billson 1992).

10. I knew well that this was sometimes futile. Chuckie Dog was one example.

11. I carried no packages for anyone, and only took passengers as a part of research, not in the process of gang activities such as drug or weapons dealing.

12. The disability was surgically corrected several years later.

CHAPTER 10

Reflections on Fieldwork Among Kenyan Heroin Users

Our reflections on fieldwork derive from 2000–2001, when we undertook research on the lives and health needs of women heroin users living in a Kenyan coastal town. Susan had been working there for some years with the Omari Project, a community-based rehabilitation program for heroin users. We had also worked together previously in the Middle East and knew that collaboration suited us. In this earlier study Gillian had been familiar with the setting and led the study. In Kenya, Susan was on home turf and Gillian took more of a supporting role. Susan's involvement with the Omari Project gave her access to heroin users. However, this same involvement meant that she could not appropriately interview health personnel and local healers in the small town on the services they provided for users. Susan therefore carried out the ethnographic work with users while Gillian joined her to interview health personnel of all kinds but also to support and accompany her in the field. The fieldwork was difficult and sensitive. This chapter has two foci: the nature of the awkward spaces encountered and how they were managed on a day-to-day basis; and the role of team ethnography as a joint enterprise where experiences are shared and understanding negotiated through separate but parallel observations.

There can be no doubt that heroin users occupy awkward spaces within Kenyan society. They use an illegal drug and constantly need to raise money to purchase it, which they do through tourist work, sex work, theft, and begging, as well as legitimate activities. Fieldwork involves negotiating access to, hanging around in, and exiting from these socially and physically awkward spaces. It also involves the daily management of strong emotional pressures. Heroin users are often in distress, nearly always require money or other assistance, and sometimes die. We reflect here on the strategies we adopted in our fieldwork with users.

Studies of drug users sometimes employ ethnographic research methods, including participant observation (Power 1995). These methods enable researchers to gain the trust of groups of drug users, to observe their behavior, and to hear how they talk about drugs and join social networks (Moore 1993; Power 1996). We used a range of ethnographic research methods, including informal interviews and participant observation, combined with methods developed by drug researchers, to assess patterns of heroin use. It was possible to negotiate access because Susan was known and trusted as the founder of the Omari Project (Beckerleg, Telfer & Kibwana Sizi 1996). Furthermore, she had acquired some insider status (Beckerleg 1995) as a result of having lived in the area for many years, and as the partner of a well-known local Kenyan. Nevertheless, good access did not always lead to easy fieldwork.

Working in Awkward Spaces

One of the aims of the fieldwork was to understand more about how people use heroin, and how they perceive the risks associated with their lifestyle. The following story tells of how Susan negotiated the opportunity to observe one research participant, F, inject himself. It was important to observe the detail of day-to-day injecting practice, since this had health consequences for the users and the wider community in terms of the risk of Hepatitis C or HIV transmission through unsafe injecting practices. It also provided insights into the developing injecting culture among this group of heroin users (Beckerleg, forthcoming). The case illustrates a number of the dilemmas we faced while working with this community.

One day in the middle of my fieldwork, I got up early with the aim of finding a group of heroin users who would allow me to watch them inject their first daily dose. I knew that many users congregated three times a day (early morning, lunchtime, and sunset) in local *maskani*, meeting places such as street corners, coffee stalls, or juice kiosks, with the aim of finding others to share heroin. *Maskani* are also places for sharing information about drug supplies and for negotiating deals to fence stolen goods or to pool money for purchasing drugs. Most are not used exclusively by heroin users but are neighborhood centers where street food is sold, and where men sit around and exchange news and gossip.

Although my presence in these places initially triggered suspicion, my association with the Omari Project and with some of the users ensured that I was quickly recognized as trustworthy and accepted as part of the scene. I was often approached with requests for money, or asked to buy people food or drinks. In the early evenings, some users, when they had the funds to spare, would also buy me juice or fruit salad and chat about themselves. In these ways I participated in and learned about the lifestyles of the users. The good relationships that I developed, along with knowledge about the daily movements of regulars, allowed me access to the kind of information I wanted to gather for our research project.

It took less than five minutes to walk from my apartment to a place that I knew to be popular with users. I found Z, a user who smoked "cocktails" (heroin mixed with cannabis), selling breakfast snacks on behalf of her mother. I sat down on an old tin can that served as a stool and asked her if she knew where the other users who injected heroin were. She assured me that they would be along soon and, sure enough, within a quarter of an hour about fifteen users had appeared. They huddled together in groups of twos and threes, discussing how much money they had to buy supplies and who might use with whom. I approached some of the users I knew and asked if I could watch them inject. They either denied that they were about to use or said they would be happy to let me watch if I handed over 100 Kenyan Shillings (KSh) (approximately 1.3 American dollars) so that they could buy a sachet of heroin (containing about one tenth of a gram). I was not willing to do this.

Meanwhile, those who smoked heroin had disappeared up nearby alleyways. Next I approached F, who from previous experience I knew to be an exhibitionist. He also had a reputation for being a "heavy junkie." F agreed to let me watch, and explained that he and his friends were about to go and buy supplies, and that I was welcome to follow. Users refer to the street corners where dealers position themselves as "*bases*."[1] F was very open about the base he was going to visit, although other users were often a lot more coy. Buying supplies was one of the most dangerous activities involved in drug use and could lead to police arrest. Visits to the sites where dealers operated also involved additional risks for me. Many of them knew me by sight and knew of my work with the Omari Project. The main dealer in town, whom F and his friends were going to buy from, had already sent me a couple of messages promising that the rehabilitation center would fail. I therefore declined F's offer to follow him.

After about half an hour F reappeared with another user, a woman who could not inject herself. She was very high. Although he had also used, F appeared more or less *compos mentis*. F told me that he had

(continued)

injected his companion with three *vikete* (sachets) of heroin. He had also injected himself with two *vikete* and produced a syringe with specks of blood visible and no cover. When I asked him why he had not let me watch him inject his friend, he replied that he was shy. F still had a piece of string tied around his arm. Specks of blood on both arms indicated that he had had trouble finding a vein. He produced four more *vikete* from his pockets, a plastic bag, and about two or three hundred Kenyan Shillings, enough for at least two more sachets. F told me that he was going to inject again and that I could watch this time if I would give him KSh50 for lunch money. I agreed to pay him after making my observation. He then disappeared into his nearby home to get water. He reappeared after a minute and we went into a derelict, partly built house.

Once heroin has been purchased, users have to find safe places to smoke or inject it. Some take the drug home and use it openly in front of their families or in the privacy of a locked bathroom. Many, however, do not have a home or are forbidden by family members from using heroin in the house. Some users simply enjoy the street scene and prefer to smoke or inject in the company of others, in quiet alleyways, boat shelters, or derelict houses, for example. Such locations for using are referred to as *vyimbo,* and are hidden from nonusers. They also change regularly. Although I already knew of some *vyimbo,* they were unoccupied for much of the time and even if I did happen to find someone in the process of injecting, he or she may not have been willing to let me watch, either because they did not know me or because they were embarrassed by their injecting practices.[2] It was therefore necessary to negotiate opportunities to observe people injecting in *vyimbo* in advance of the event.

The building F took me to was a well-established *chimbo,*[3] one that I passed regularly and always checked, looking though a hole in the masonry to see if there was anybody inside. Usually there was not. F put the plastic bag filled with tap water on the ground, which was strewn with discarded syringes and the papers used to wrap sachets of heroin. He took the syringe from his pocket and assembled it. Next he pierced the plastic bag with the needle, filled the syringe with water and rinsed it out a few times. He disassembled the syringe and blew on it to check that it would not block, put the pieces back together, opened the top, and put in one sachet (*kikete,* singular), sniffing the paper before discarding it. Next he drew a small amount of water into the syringe, checked it for color or pieces of adulterants, and shook it. He examined the veins in his arms and tied the piece of string round his right arm. This time he got the vein first time and pushed the needle in as far as it would go. He drew back the pump and blood-filled about half the syringe. He untied the string and did about four "flushes," whereby he filled the syringe with his own blood and injected himself. Then he sat with the blood-filled syringe in his arm and smoked a cigarette.

A friend of F's arrived with some cannabis that he had bought at F's request. Cigarette papers were produced and F prepared a cocktail of cannabis and heroin. He then did two more flushes of his syringe. F's friend was given first puff of the cocktail. They smoked together, F still with the syringe half-filled with blood sticking out of his arm. After smoking, the voices of both faded away and F started dozing in the way characteristic of heroin users. His friend explained that F was helping him out because he was in withdrawal and felt ill. F said he had one sachet remaining that he was going to smoke in the alleyway shortly. He had already used five sachets that morning, but complained that he had lost one.

As we lapsed into silence, F still had the blood-filled syringe in his arm. His friend began nodding off, and I started to think about getting back to my flat and having breakfast. Watching the injection of heroin left me feeling that I was bearing witness to self-damage and dangerous practices. I was looking forward to finishing this bit of fieldwork. Suddenly F asked me if he had done or said anything wrong. I assured him that he had not, and that I was merely thinking about my breakfast and the cheese I had in the fridge. He was reassured, and added that he liked cheese and wanted some. Abruptly F removed the bloody syringe from his arm and chucked it on the ground at his feet. He rubbed his bleeding vein and commented that he had no white spirit to clean the injection site. He continued to rub his arm with a piece of paper from a discarded schoolbook picked up from the ground. He said we should go as the police knew of the house and might come. I could not resist commenting that the syringe was at his feet. He picked it up and chucked it in the corner, saying it was finished. I gave F the agreed KSh50 and the three of us left the derelict house. F's friend went his way, happy to have had a free smoke, while F and I walked down to my flat making small chat about the tourist season. It was no longer appropriate for me ask questions about his heroin use because we were in a public space dominated by nonusers.

Once heroin has been successfully purchased and injected or smoked, users must turn their attention once again to raising money for the next

(*continued*)

supply. Places such as bars, the beach, the streets, and markets are referred to, by users, as the *kiwanja*,[4] a Swahili word denoting a ground, such as a sports field or plot for a house. At the *kiwanja* petty trading is carried out, scams are deployed, pockets are picked, sex is sold, drugs are dealt, and money begged. *Viwanja* consist of the public places of the town where users mingle with the majority population of nonusers. These are the spaces that users enter when they leave the *maskani* and the *chimbo*, and go "out in the world." As it was my personal rule to not allow users, or indeed any visitors, into the flat, I left F downstairs and went to get some cheese. When I had given it to him we parted company. I went back into the flat, ate my breakfast, and wrote up my notes on my laptop before the details of the morning's events faded from my memory.

Negotiating Awkwardness: Physical, Ethical, and Emotional Strategies

This fieldwork took its toll on Susan, and several strategies were devised to deal with the emotional stress. Fieldtrips were planned to be short and intensive in two- to three-month stints with Gillian arriving, on two out of three trips, toward the end. This provided the opportunity to debrief, share insights, and offer support.

As the research progressed and the services of the Omari Project became better known to users, Susan started avoiding the old town *maskani*, unless she had a specific reason for going there. The space had become too awkward. Attempts to carry out everyday tasks, such as buying freshly baked breakfast foods on a Sunday morning, were met with demands on Susan's time and money. Members of the community as well as users would regularly demand that she help particularly distressed users or that she explain why the Omari Project had not solved the local heroin problem. Even walking through the area involved fending off numerous requests for money and information. Some wanted to engage in long conversations or counseling sessions that were often emotionally and intellectually draining. As far as users, their families, and the wider community were concerned there were *no* weekends or off-duty times. Susan encountered users all over the town. A visit to the local shop or café, or a swim at the beach, might entail lengthy discussions on a range of topics relating to heroin abuse, so that Susan began to feel as though her very identity as an individual with a range of interests and tastes was under threat. On the other hand, that users readily approached her facilitated her fieldwork and made her feel part of the local community.

Users view the entire town as a large *kiwanja*. Susan, who was observing and participating in their world, was constantly required to make judgments about how to interface with users she encountered during their daily business. Although she often felt under pressure from the demands of users, there were also times when she sought out individuals, particularly women, for interviews or to ask about their welfare. However, if she had failed to locate users at their homes or in the *maskani* it was often inappropriate to engage them in conversation or even approach them in the *kiwanja*. Usually users do not want potential customers, such as tourists, to know about their heroin consumption. In any case they are busy earning money and have no time to talk. Hence, if Susan encountered users when they were at work, greetings were sometimes exchanged, while at other times they behaved like strangers.

Users expected Susan to know how to behave, and if she got it wrong cordial relations with individuals would be suspended or broken off permanently. Most users are vulnerable people with low self-esteem whose social skills are impaired by drug use. They can be bad-tempered, irritable, and unreasonable and might become upset if they think they are being slighted, ignored, or refused a request. Thus, a user would meet Susan and ask for money to buy food. If Susan refused but offered to buy food directly, the user might be insulted by the lack of trust and declare the friendship over.

These pressures caused Susan to plan routes through the town that avoided particular places at specific times. Users who "followed" tourists awaited work on particular street corners in the mornings and late afternoons, but not at lunchtimes, for example. It was thus possible, albeit inconvenient, to avoid passing these places when users were likely to be present. On the other hand, it was easy to find individual users, such as F, at the old town *maskani* early in the morning, at lunchtime, or at sunset. Users follow set routines governed by their physical dependence on heroin, and are thus fairly predictable.

While the behavior of users often follows a regular pattern, their key sites shift depending on levels of community control/tolerance. Users must be constantly one step ahead of the police and activists such as the Council of Imams and Preachers. Dealers shift premises or work from different street corners. Sometimes the *maskani* also becomes a *base*. In order to understand the lives of the users and for her personal security, Susan needed to know about these changes. Such knowledge was not difficult to acquire, provided that time was spent on a daily basis talking to users, many of whom were eager to pass on the latest news and to gossip about the drug scene.

The Ethics of Paying Cash

Susan paid F KSh50 lunch money. She agreed to this because she knew that he already had money and had already purchased a considerable amount of heroin. For Susan the issue of paying participants in the study had both ethical and practical dimensions. She was concerned that the money she gave to heroin users would probably be used to buy drugs that would cause further harm to the recipient, or even lead to an overdose. Such concerns are familiar to those who carry out research with illicit drug users (McKegeney 2001; Power 2001).

Furthermore, Susan was operating under the scrutiny of the community and did not want to acquire a reputation for helping young people to use heroin. At the time of observing F, she had received feedback from the police that a woman user, an informer, was saying that Susan gave her money. Indeed, it was true that Susan gave money to users, but in doing so she followed a number of self-imposed rules that she hoped would protect them both. She never gave enough money to buy a sachet of heroin; she tried to buy food rather than handing over cash; or she accompanied ill users to doctors' surgeries or to pharmacies and paid the bill. Nevertheless, on a daily basis Susan handed over small amounts of cash, the price of a plate of beans, to several users. Others were told that she had run out of money or that it was unacceptable for them to beg from her every time they saw her. Some users, such as the woman informer, were extremely persistent, and a few could be a little threatening. Begging is one of the main ways that users raise money, and they knew that Susan was a good bet because she was sympathetic to them, wanted information, and, as a European, certainly had plenty of money. The exception to this policy was A, who worked regular hours as guide and key informant and was therefore paid a wage. His assistance was essential in terms of ensuring our physical safety and social access. We developed this approach after much discussion and itemized it on the research budget as part of the field expenses.

We also frequently invited users to have meals with us that we paid for at small cafés in shacks along the roadside or in town. This was a way of spending time with users and ensuring that they ate more. On one occasion, Gillian asked a café owner to provide chips and a Coke for a user who had said she was hungry and paid for them before leaving. She later heard from the owner, however, that the user had canceled the order and asked for the cash.

Anthropologists carrying out ethnographic studies with users of illicit substances often pay cash as compensation for lost "earnings" when interviews take up a significant part of the users' time (Wiebel 1990; Goldstein et al. 1990). Although this aspect of the research is not often raised in the literature, Fry and Dwyer (2001:1320) have reflected on whether paying a respondent is a breach of ethics and argue that "the task of judging when a payment constitutes undue incentive is a complicated one."[5] Susan handed over money to any of the drug users she knew who begged from her, not just those central to her research. All the women users whom Susan contacted in the town had been recruited to the study by giving verbal consent, although this counted for little given that Susan could not coerce participants to answer her questions. Nonetheless, she chose not to pay directly for information, fearing that it would set up a potentially costly precedent. When Susan was collecting questionnaire data from women users about their reproductive health one woman demanded a cash payment that would permit her to buy a sachet of heroin. After negotiations over several days Susan told her that there was no problem if she did not want to cooperate. Other women had filled in the questionnaire for free, or in exchange for a cup of tea or a snack or for a payment not exceeding KSh50. Gillian did not pay any of the health personnel for their time.

Emotional Space

Susan found it uncomfortable to watch passively as F carried out a dangerous operation that was destroying his life. Similarly, she wished that his friend were not there smoking heroin. As a researcher she could not interfere, and as somebody with training and experience in counseling heroin users she also knew that intervention would not stop the heroin use of either person. In addition, Susan felt in danger of contamination from the exposed, blood-filled syringe and by the blood spilt on the ground. Although she did not come into contact with F's blood, she could not help but worry about the possibility that F might be HIV positive.

Indeed, at several points during the fieldwork, Susan experienced anxiety about the risk of becoming HIV positive through her close contact with users. Such fears are not uncommon to researchers or health staff working in settings with seriously ill people. We therefore decided to purchase a prophylaxis kit for use in the event of a needle-stick injury.[6]

Much academic work omits discussion of the researcher's emotional engagement with and response to his or her subject matter. As part of a reaction to this approach that has emerged over the last couple of decades, Hastrup states, "Fieldwork is situated between autobiography and anthropology. It connects an important personal experience with a general field of knowledge" (1992:117). By the 1970s and 1980s, ideas about the value of empathy and subjectivity were being advocated in the field of illicit drug research. Adler (1990:97) claims, for example, that "the value of fieldwork lies not in how the researchers maintained distance from the data, but rather in how close they came to the phenomena." It was only possible to do this fieldwork by being close to the users and, in particular, the key informant. Such intimate proximity was feasible as a result of the trust that had been developed through Susan's commitment to the Omari Project.

Ethnographic Field Stations and Team Ethnography

When Susan left F she retreated into her rented first-floor flat, our only private space in the town. Although risking accusations of rudeness, it was important to us that nobody should be admitted to the flat. Inside, we were able to write notes and relax without having to deal with the demands of others. But the world of the users was not far away. Because our flat was located in a *kiwanja* (comprising a bar/restaurant, a fish market, taxi stand next to a baobab tree, a kiosk, and shop), we could sometimes hear the voices of individuals we knew calling to tourists just outside the window. Susan became so identified with this *kiwanja* that, when Gillian arrived at the local airport and was not met owing to a mix up, a user from a neighboring town directed her to the bar. A waitress knocked on the door of Susan's flat and informed her that her guest was awaiting her.

In the 1970s and 1980s, researchers working with illicit drug users in the United States developed a field method involving the use of ethnographic field stations. These were fixed spots considered "safe" by visiting users (Weibel 1990; Goldstein et al. 1990). The area outside Susan's flat became an informal ethnographic field station. While the flat remained a private space, users would wait outside, sometimes calling up from beneath the window or occasionally ringing the intercom to ask for money, counseling, conversation, or information about getting admitted into the rehabilitation project. The clear demarcation of a space that was off-limits to users was essential in providing physical and intellectual respite; besides eating and sleeping, this apartment was our main space for writing, reviewing, and discussing data and the events of the day.

Team ethnography (Erickson & Stull 1998) made this difficult fieldwork manageable and enjoyable. Susan undertook the bulk of fieldwork alone with the users, but she was joined by Gillian for two periods during which they worked as a team. Gillian was able to access health professionals and key community members relatively quickly because Susan was already established in the town. The people she wanted to interview in the hospital and clinics generally knew of the Omari Project. Gillian carried out her interviews in English, with a Swahili interpreter, or in Arabic, depending on the respondent, and wrote them up in the flat on the laptop the same day. Only then would she and Susan discuss the interview within the more general context of the study. This rule of no discussion of data until the interviews were written up was important since Susan had often had prior encounters with these respondents and premature discussion might have biased Gillian's interpretation of the interviews. Field notes were also shared, and we each had our own sets. Being part of a team meant that we were able to debrief and reflect together as well as providing mutual support for each other. This was a valuable way of managing what was otherwise a very challenging set of fieldwork conditions.

Employing a Key Informant

Estimating the number of users and documenting patterns of use required a good knowledge of the whole town, including districts unknown to Susan. Once located, however, many heroin users would be reluctant to speak to a foreign researcher about their illegal drug use. After trials with several users, A emerged as a suitable "research assistant" and team member. As a former dealer, native of the town, and long-term user, he had good knowledge of heroin-using networks. He was interested in Susan's work because he was considering detoxification and rehabilitation through the residential center that was due to open shortly. He also had "superior communication skills" and was both reliable and willing to take on the responsibilities associated with our work (Wiebel 1990:9). A met all the desired criteria.

After several ad hoc work sessions during which A located users, introduced Susan, and vouched for her good intentions, a pattern was established where he reported for work between 9 and 10 A.M. daily. Visits to different parts of town ensued, with the aim of locating "hidden" women users. At lunchtime Susan paid him KSh100 and he went to buy heroin and use it at home. In the afternoon a similar routine was followed, with payment at sunset. Over time, his work role developed so that he also acted as a combined bodyguard and key informant for Susan, and for Gillian during her visits. A made the decisions about what was and was not safe, and movement around town involved trusting in his ability and judgment. He also took on some of the functions of a peer educator by stopping any user he knew on the street and explaining that a residential rehabilitation center was opening soon. In addition, he directed Susan to talk with and provide counseling to users he thought were particularly vulnerable.

Over a period of about six weeks Susan was able to build up estimates of the numbers of heroin users in the town and had acquired extensive knowledge about their patterns of use and daily routines. The users were also given information about the proposed treatment services that were to be part of the Omari Project and, having been introduced, could approach Susan more easily for information and counseling. A's drug use was reduced and became less chaotic, the regular use of two sachets being considerably less than the five to six sachets that he reported using several months previously. When the residential program opened he was among the first clients admitted.

Conclusion

More than a decade ago Adler (1990:97) advocated casting off the "shackles of the classical approach and striving for subjectivity and involvement" in research with drug users. More recently, Power (2001:335) has called for "a more imaginative and flexible qualitative research" into illicit drug use, a robust approach that goes beyond questionnaires and allows for triangulation of results, thereby complementing more quantitative approaches. Studies of drug use clearly benefit from close interaction between researchers and users—but we should not be coy about the trials and tribulations of such difficult work. Although fieldwork of this kind can be emotionally taxing, its results are rich and rewarding. The purpose of this chapter has been to share some of the more difficult and less often discussed problems associated with work of this kind. As such it shows how carrying out participant observation requires a willingness to inhabit awkward spaces for long enough to convey the texture and timbre of peoples' lives. By analyzing these awkward spaces we hope to enhance understandings about how difficult, dangerous, and delicate fieldwork is done while also contributing to knowledge about the world of heroin users on the Kenyan coast.

Acknowledgments

We would like to dedicate this chapter to A, the local research assistant who was so essential to this research and who died, drug free, in 2003, aged thirty-one years. He unstintingly shared his sensitive understanding of the world of users and kept us safe. The research was funded by the UK Economic and Social Research Council (Grant number R000238392).

Notes

1. "Base" has become a Swahili loan word derived from the English.
2. This embarrassment or shame concerning injecting practices is well documented by researchers working with injecting drug users from a wide range of cultural backgrounds (Lockley 1995).
3. *Chimbo* is the singular form of *vyimbo*. Its literal meaning in Swahili is "hole."
4. The plural of this term is *viwanja*.
5. "A core principle of peak guidelines in Australia and other countries is that the provision of financial incentive to respondents will constitute a breach of ethics where it is sufficient enough to render consent involuntary. In practice, the task of judging when a payment constitutes undue incentive is a complicated one for which there are no clear guidelines" (Fry & Dwyer 2001:1320).
6. The prophylaxis kit was a course of tablets that should be taken after coming into high-risk contact with somebody who was HIV positive. The tablets reduce the chances of sero-conversion to being HIV positive. Susan took the course of tablets once, after fearing that she had scratched her hand with a syringe recently used by a heroin injector. However, a doctor advised her that a scratch of this kind would be very unlikely to transmit HIV.

John M. Coggeshall

CHAPTER 11

Closed Doors

Ethical Issues with Prison Ethnography

Every teacher's first day of class is a memorable experience, and mine was no exception. As I nosed my car into the visitor's parking lot that morning, I was filled with the same doubts and fears that grip other new college instructors. I glanced up at the low brick building guarded by the national and state flags and took a deep breath. The morning sun sparkled off the fresh dew on the grass and the barbed wire along the perimeter fence. My first teaching job was at a medium-security prison, and my first class consisted of sixteen male residents.

Teaching university courses inside a prison presented unique and challenging opportunities for fieldwork. This experience also introduced me to a field situation that requires the reconceptualization of some standard ethical decisions and practices often taken for granted by anthropologists. In general, the nature of the institutional setting itself and the complexity of social relationships inside make prisons different from most other ethnographic field situations.

Fieldwork for this study was conducted in two medium-security Illinois state correctional centers between 1984 and 1986. Hired to teach university-level anthropology courses, I presented three classes over four semesters to a total of forty-four adult inmates serving sentences of varying lengths and representing a range of ethnic identities characteristic of the overall prison population. On a typical visit I spent between five and eight hours in the prison. While there I also recorded observations and conducted interviews with administrators, guards, staff, and inmates. Both staff and inmates knew I was doing research, and the latter encouraged me to "use" them as informants. Conversations were held before and after classes and during meals and other breaks. I also corresponded with a student inmate both before and after his release; his comments and insights have proven invaluable.

Prisons as Fieldsites

Prisons provide special places to test the limits and types of ethical decisions in anthropological fieldwork (e.g., Waldram 1998). Goffman (1961:xiii), one of the first to study such places, termed them "total institutions," places of residence and work where a large number of like-situated individuals, cut off from the wider society for an appreciable period of time, together lead an enclosed, formally administered round of life. While more recent scholarship, reviewed by Rhodes (2001), has critiqued Goffman's classic characterization, it remains true that prisons do not resemble most field situations. First, various categories of authority restrain inmates' social interaction into a regimented series of activities. This allows for easier administrative control (Goffman 1961:74, 78) but creates possible conditions for exploitation, particularly through the misuse of information (e.g., ethnographic data), by either guards or inmates. Residents remain isolated from society against their will for a relatively long time, and this deprivation often leads to anger or resentment, directed against the omnipresent staff or innocent bystanders.

Because of the clear social dichotomy in prisons (Goffman 1961:7), anthropologists may need to decide with which group to identify, for it becomes difficult to remain completely neutral. As Appell (1978:3) notes, field situations involving conflicting identities and roles typically abound, and anthropologists in any field situation must often choose which role to occupy. To conduct fieldwork in such a situation, one might manipulate, disguise, or contextualize identities (Punch 1986:41), but such behavior is sometimes dismissed as unethical (Cassell 1980:35). As anthropologists, we are expected to be completely open about our goals and purposes as well as about ourselves (AAA Code of Ethics 1998).

The ethical dilemmas I faced in prison research stem directly from the nature of the institution and its occupants. In most field situations, levels of knowledge and degrees of truth help establish Geertz's familiar "webs of significance" (1973:5). In prison, however, these same webs ensnare the unwary, for facts, rumors, and lies might become mechanisms for controlling or harming others. Moreover, some informants from other "outside" fieldsites have become my friends; in prison, my informants were convicted felons, creating a social and moral ambiguity between us. Some of these ethical dilemmas I reconciled, but others I did not. From all of them, though, I gained a greater understanding of the challenges facing fieldworkers in closed field situations, and a deeper awareness of the ambiguity of fieldwork itself.

Life Behind Bars

Externally, the prisons in which I taught resemble junior college campuses. One glaring difference, of course, is the perimeter's double row of fencing topped by fearsome-looking barbed wire. Both prisons had been built in the early 1980s from the same design and looked virtually identical. After passing through a series of nine locked doors in an administration building, one enters the central courtyard. Surrounding the long, narrow concrete courtyard are various buildings, including the commissary, gymnasium, clinic, education and vocational-training building, and chapel. Long, wide concrete walkways stretch from one end of the commissary in three directions. Inmate housing units are located toward the ends of these walkways.

The front line of command and regulation of order in prison consists of the guards. Guards consider their job to be like any other, and most merely "put in their time and go home," as one mentioned. However, long periods of monotonous repetition and paperwork contrast with the realization that one's life is constantly in jeopardy.[1] Generally, guards' attitudes toward their charges, shaped in part by their attitude toward work, are those of disinterest, disdain, and occasional hostility. Most guards are from rural communities in the surrounding area, communities with a long-standing antipathy toward urban dwellers in general and African-Americans in particular.

Adding to the guards' resentment are their assumptions about the "easy life" of the inmates, who are entirely supported at taxpayer expense. Guards resent that state-provided, "nutritious" food (which they also eat) and modern recreational facilities (to which they also have access) are provided to the inmates. Perhaps most of all, guards resent the educational benefits allowed to the residents. "These guys don't realize how lucky they have it," a young guard once told me. All this resentment reinforces the guards' negative perception of the inmates.

Guards use this resentment as a very effective social control mechanism. As primary interpreters of prison regulations, guards have the power to enforce or relax rules at their discretion. As Goffman (1961) noted, the fear of, or direct imposition of, hierarchical authority at arbitrary times assures that inmates will be constantly surveyed and judged. Moreover, by arbitrarily enforcing or relaxing rules, guards keep inmates constantly unsure of their every behavior, and this uncertainty contributes to a sense of powerlessness. Through time, inmates learn a range of protective measures in order to achieve varied ends, each ultimately involving control over their lives and dignity. One solution is for inmates to beg for favors that the guards would normally perform as part of their duties. You must adopt a "pleading type of attitude," an African-American inmate noted.

My most chilling personal experience in prison highlights this same attitude. One spring evening, I escorted an older inmate back to his housing unit for nightly lock-down. Upon my return to the Education Building in the now-vacant courtyard, I found the door locked with my jacket, lecture materials, and that day's field observation notes still inside. Immediately I turned to the only two people present—two young white guards. I approached them and requested, in a friendly manner, if they would mind unlocking the building so I could retrieve my property. Although I wore "professional" clothes and my ID badge, and although we were of the same "race," they both stared at me wordlessly. A second time I entreated them, in a more humble manner, to unlock the building. This time, one asked into his walkie-talkie if the Education Building had already been secured: "ten-four [affirmative]!" came the response. For a third time I pleaded, this time unwittingly staring downward, shuffling my feet, begging them to open the building, and apologizing for being so much trouble. One guard spoke again into his walkie-talkie, asking the officer on duty to bring the keys back to unlock the building. While the captain unlocked the door, I continued to apologize profusely. I grabbed my books and left as quickly as I could. That next week, I related my experience to the inmates waiting for class to begin. Suddenly the reality of my suppliant behavior dawned on me, and I could feel the hair on the back of my neck rise as a young African-American inmate stated bluntly: "Now you know what we go through every day."

Specific inmate qualities that are respected, and indeed essential, include keeping one's thoughts to oneself while maintaining a facade of humor and deference with the guards. Such condescending behaviors and attitudes not only disturb African-Americans but also irritate racist white inmates, who may be forced to deal this way with black guards. More important, this degrading behavior becomes all the more humiliating given the values placed on dominance and dignity in prisoner culture.

Adding to inmate uncertainty, guards may shift demeanor at any time from a joking to a serious manner, and inmates must learn to predict and read these mood shifts. For example, during an institution-wide search, I overheard a guard tell an inmate clerk behind the commissary counter that the shelf nooks behind him looked suspiciously capable of hiding contraband. The inmate responded jokingly about hiding material until he heard the guard's stern voice and saw his impassive face. The inmate immediately shifted to a docile, plaintive tone, claiming that he knew nothing and only worked there. In order to exist successfully, inmates must appear to acknowledge to guards that the latter have total control.

Inmates retaliate against their perceived oppression through an intricate variety of means. For example, at each prison they have use of a complete law library, which allows them to challenge the institution on legal grounds. Another way of active retaliation is through violence. I was told by an older inmate that younger inmates actually become more violent when they first arrive in prison than they had been on the street, and a few never seem to adjust to the reality of prison life. Violence is their way of maintaining dignity.

As prisoners acculturate to a life of incarceration, they learn that serious violence rarely accomplishes much. Older inmates learn more subtle but equally effective ways of control. "You learn to balance the illusion" of personal independence versus institutional control, one inmate told me. For example, inmates may react deliberately slowly to guards' commands. Inmates may also retaliate by showing exaggerated deference to guards. Guards view this behavior as humorous and tolerable, while inmates see a deeper layer of meaning.

More direct and perhaps more necessary means of safeguarding one's dignity also exist. Inmates have commented numerous times about the importance of forming "cliques" or "associations" (see Davidson 1983). In order to maintain these associations, inmates must learn what information can be shared with guards, what can be shared only with other inmates, what should be revealed only to one's associates, and what should be kept only to oneself. One inmate compared these degrees of secrecy to those between guards, officers, and administrators. Indeed, it seems as if various levels of hidden information coexist in prison settings. Prisoners keep information from guards (such as smuggling operations), guards from officers (such as minor rule infractions), and officers from administrators (such as paperwork bungles).

Another major vector of inmate influence is *through* the guards. The prison's front line of control and defense is also its most vulnerable. Despite official proscriptions, some guards socialize informally with the inmates. They may share the same hobbies or prejudices, or even come from the same region. Consequently, friendships develop, and these friendships may be enhanced or manipulated. Ingenuous guards might then overlook additional infractions, eventually perhaps smuggling drugs or money to their inmate friends, thus further incriminating themselves. What starts as a small favor may end as a sizable and grave commitment.

Reciprocal social ties also develop in other ways. Naive guards may commit or overlook a minor infraction, which clever inmates then threaten to report or use to their advantage. Other inmates with inside or outside connections may attract greedy guards with the promise of extra cash, drugs, or sex. Having committed an infraction, a guard then becomes bait for inmate blackmail or a target for further "favors." Once trapped in this extortion web, the guard or staff member cannot escape easily, and some may not even wish to if they feel sorry for, or friendly toward, the inmate.

These entrapped guards provide inmates with data that may potentially embarrass another guard, harm a reputation, or damage an employment record. With this clandestine information, clever inmates maintain their dignity and gain numerous benefits as well.

Ethical Challenges in Prison Fieldwork

The complicated web of social relationships and cultural rules inside prisons creates unusual research conditions for anthropologists. While I had gradually become aware of the cultural complexity of social life in prison, it took a relatively long time for me to realize how this unique field situation influenced ethical concerns. My eyes were opened one evening in class.

During the semester, I had been teaching American Culture, both at a large public university and in a prison. For both of my classes I had planned to teach ethnographic methods and then assign a field project on a subculture in American society, so the students could apply their classroom skills. The university class did this, but the prison class did not.

When I first mentioned the class project, many inmates were quite excited about the possibility of collecting inside information. The more we discussed negative aspects of the idea, however, the more concerned I became. In fact, my suspicions were aroused by the overly vigorous objections raised by some inmates to my eventual proposal for a substitute assignment. One concern first raised by an inmate in class was that ultimately there could be no truly "safe" topics for research. The enclosed nature of the total institution, where all residents live together under each other's watchful eye, automatically transformed anthropological fieldwork into another form of unwelcome surveillance. I had naively hoped inmates might examine their athletic clubs or civic organizations, and they offered such groups as examples. However, as I came to realize, all topics carried the potential for exploitation, not only by other inmates but also by guards or administrators. The danger lay not only in the research itself but also in the misappropriation of the research process.

Such endangerment stems from the field situation itself. Participant observation of most bureaucracies typically requires the permission and active cooperation of all categories of informants, who continually interact with each other in a mutually respectful manner, even if bearing alternative cultural perspectives. However, in total institutions, the categories of supervisors, staff, and residents coexist in mutual disrespect, distrust, or outright hatred of one another. While one level (e.g., the administration) may give official permission for research, another level (e.g., the guards) may offer only indifferent support. "Informants" (as controlled, restricted prisoners), on the other hand, have no inherent rights to avoid observation by researchers (Wax 1982:40, note 4; Waldram 1998: 239–240), although they can refuse to be interviewed. Fieldwork in prison thus becomes a delicate act of diplomacy between sparring factions, a condition many anthropologists might find inhospitable to research.

These tiers of authoritative control, linked to one another through indifferent tolerance or respectful caution, drastically alter the field situation. Collecting information across levels potentially threatens the jobs and lives of nearly everyone. Officially, guards cannot socialize with inmates; to do so (even for the purposes of the most innocuous research) requires the breaking of formal administrative regulations. Should inmates use unofficial channels of socialization with guards, the fact of fraternization, once disclosed, might harm the inmate or guard. The latter could be fired, reprimanded, or even given a more dangerous assignment, while the inmate could suffer punishment ranging from "accidental" administrative paperwork bungles to a transfer to a harsher institution. Unlike many other field situations, merely cooperating in the ethnographic research process places informants at high risk.

A related ethical concern involves the potential loss or theft of information. While in most field situations theft of information is highly unlikely (although see Fetterman 1983), the structural situation of prison life places outside researchers in a more precarious position. Field notes could be stolen and "ransom" sought by inmates, who could then use the information to their own advantage to threaten or bribe their fellows or guards. Likewise, guards could confiscate field notes as contraband, particularly if they felt the data compromised their safety or criticized their efforts. Guards could then use this "intelligence" to embarrass or coerce more vulnerable inmates.[2] Because of the ultimate lack of security behind bars, a fundamental ethical issue then becomes the legitimacy of conducting fieldwork in a situation where the researcher cannot reasonably guarantee informant anonymity or protection from harm—although these conditions are also similar in certain other field situations.

Ethical ethnographers might safeguard their data as much as possible by removing their materials from the prison context, as I did every day. However, since total institutions limit access to the outside, sensitive or critical information collected internally must be "smuggled" out by researchers. In this case, notes become contraband and subject to possible inspection or confiscation by guards, negating any prior agreements to protect informants. This ethical dilemma thus might create criminals of well-intentioned researchers, who technically violate prison rules and perhaps endanger guards or inmates through these security lapses. I constantly worried about the potential theft of my field notes, for example, and always kept them in a virtually illegible scrawl, transcribing them away from the prison the next day. One time, a guard specifically asked me what I was writing down, and I nervously replied in an ambiguous manner that I was writing descriptions of prison life. Other times, I was required to open my briefcase upon leaving prison, and always feared that my field notes would be confiscated; they never were, but the potential for this to happen was there.

One way to avoid theft or confiscation of my material was to allow inmates to do the research for me, just as many fieldworkers enlist local assistants to help them document a wider range of informants. One inmate, in fact, enthusiastically volunteered to conduct a large number of interviews about homoerotic behavior.[3] My inmate assistant mailed the interviews to me, along with two unpublished manuscripts he asked me to edit for him (which I did). While I trusted his confidentiality, I still remained a little concerned about the potential theft or misuse of the information before it left the prison.

Inmate researchers also face theft or confiscation of their notes by guards or fellow prisoners, for they lack any official security at all, for either their person or their possessions. Just as inmates can be stopped and searched at any time by any guard, so too can the cells be "shaken down" at any time, without the occupant's presence or permission. To punish a recalcitrant inmate unofficially, or merely to reassert a damaged ego, a guard has the potential power to take or to view an inmate's "illegal" materials at will. In this way, information collected by prisoners about others behind bars tentatively remains "public" property until taken from the institution.

Perhaps the most serious ethical question about doing research behind bars relates to the legitimacy of collecting material at all. Inside prisons, the manipulation of information becomes the *sine qua non* for controlling people. Simply by collecting data, ethnographers contribute to this subsystem of potential manipulation and control.

Clear divisions in levels of authority also exacerbate the potential for misuse of the research process in a prison setting. Guards and/or administrators might commission or blackmail their inmate friends, perhaps enrolled as students in a class, to collect information surreptitiously from other inmates, increasing the underground network of snitches. Inmate ethnography then becomes a tool for the subordination of others (see Feldman 1991:12, in Rhodes 2001:73); in prison, these potential networks of covert intelligence add a more chilling emic meaning to the term "informant."

It is important to note that in such cases of theft or manipulation, the unwitting researcher may follow all appropriate ethical guidelines for collecting information suggested in the AAA Code of Ethics (1998). However, the nature of the field situation itself sometimes transforms the ethical meaning of the research process. In a social context where normal conditions involve multiple levels of coercive authority and complicated layers of identity manipulation, access to knowledge of others becomes a powerful weapon, one that can be extremely dangerous in the wrong hands.

In a prison, just as staff may attempt to wrest or coerce information from internal or external investigators, so might inmates. Again, the collection of field data contains a deeper level of meaning and a virtually inescapable potential for abuse. For example, prisoners could bribe, blackmail, or hire others (their fellow prisoners or guard associates) to collect apparently innocuous ethnographic data to further their own ends. Gangs could spy on other gangs in order to dominate illegal trade, or inmates could eavesdrop on guards or administrators in order to obtain potentially damaging gossip, all under the guise of "legitimate" fieldwork.

Even outside researchers might not escape potential manipulation by inmates. Through friendship ties between prisoners and ethnographer, for example, an outsider could be urged to collect data about a particular group of inmates, ideally to add a more complete picture of prison life, but in reality fulfilling the hidden agenda of a gang. Some inmates have complete knowledge of prisoner culture, a depth usually denied to the outsider (although see Davidson 1983). Because of this difference in cultural awareness, the fundamental reasons for collecting information, as well as the information itself, take on alternative meanings, depending on who ultimately guides the research. Studies of bureaucracies or hierarchical organizations would undoubtedly offer similar challenges.

Another ethical dilemma in prison research develops as an outcome of manipulation: the misuse of trust. Mutual trust between informant and fieldworker is expected and normal, but in prison trust varies in degree and context. Thoroughly acculturated and successful convicts maintain a facade of aloofness and indifference while controlling and manipulating information about themselves and others. Thus, an ethnographer might trust the information received from a convict, but not the informants' reasons for confiding that information. For example, a young African-American man once intimated to me that a socially prominent [in prison] Anglo-American man was not the male he pretended to be; in other words, that he was a passive homosexual.[4] Was this innocent gossip for my amusement, an honest and trustworthy statement of fact, or an attempt to vilify a racial opponent? While some deception may be a normal part of life (and maybe even of certain types of field situations, as Punch [1986:41] contends), the masks worn inside prison often disguise people and motivations on a more fundamental level and for more sinister purposes.

The very real possibility of data manipulation by some informants to harm others is, of course, not restricted to research in prisons. However, what makes fieldwork in such places ethically more difficult is that bribery and manipulation of others and the masking of oneself form crucial parts of the expected cultural value system. In fact, an essential method of survival is to establish a debtor relationship with someone else, to acquire contraband, sex, power, or information. Thus, when an ethnographer offers to trade friendship (or other gifts) for knowledge, in most field situations a morally acceptable reciprocal relationship develops between researcher and informant (Wax 1982:45). This relationship assumes a particular ambiguity in prison settings, where tensions between the need to maintain a social distance and the desire to establish closer relationships are intensified. Again, this dilemma is not uncommon in many field situations (e.g., Fetterman 1983:215), but it does take on another dimension in prison fieldwork. For example, one of my students, also a casual informant, once asked me to smuggle a personal letter out of prison for him, a violation of prison regulations but a means to avoid the scrutiny of the guards, who have the right to read all nonlegal outgoing mail. I refused this "simple" request, but felt slightly guilty for not helping my student. To this day, I have no idea whether or not I was being manipulated.

Fieldwork inside total institutions requires a careful restructuring and redefining of informant relationships often taken for granted by anthropologists working under different conditions. Recall my inmate student/friend who had offered to collect information on homoerotic behavior. In addition to the friendship we had developed in prison, we had also agreed that, as partial compensation for his fieldwork, I would purchase and send him a book of contemporary short stories (which I did), for he wanted to be a professional writer. About a year after his release, he also asked for a letter of recommendation for graduate school, which I also gladly provided. However, at the time, I wondered why else he might have been collecting this information, with whom he may have shared it, and what else he might eventually ask me to do. About seven years after his release, we shared a beer at a national anthropological meeting, and I realized I never had a reason to doubt his ethical integrity.

Inside total institutions, the social groups dichotomize because of the need for hierarchical authority (Goffman 1961). Thus, at least two sides develop, and it becomes increasingly challenging for the ethnographer to maintain ties to both. Guards knew that I spoke with the inmates as human beings and as students, and I distinctly felt several times that this made me more of an outsider in their eyes, and that they treated me accordingly. Likewise, inmates noticed how the guards interacted with me. Thus, I was always careful to maintain my social distance from the guards, by joking about them with the inmates, by not cutting into the cafeteria line between inmates (as guards did), and occasionally sitting with the inmates at dinner. Inside a prison, in fact, this social division takes on a life or death meaning, for a mistake in judgment or a leak of information may jeopardize a human life (see Jacobs 1977:215–229, in Rhodes 2001:72). While formal neutrality is optimal for obtaining a complete view (Gilmore 1991:222) or for the continued flow of information, in prison this may be virtually impossible.

For me, social neutrality was challenging but not impossible; moral neutrality, however, was more difficult. Despite temptations it is often difficult to empathize exclusively with either inmates or guards (e.g., compare Fleisher 1989 and Davidson 1983) because both groups potentially challenge the moral sensitivities of fieldworkers (Thomas 1993:46–47, in Rhodes 2001:73). Principal informants who are guards may be racists or homophobes, deliberately ridiculing inmates in order to inflate their own self-esteem. Numerous times, for example, I maintained an impassive expression as I overheard racial or homosexual jokes in order to maintain rapport with guards.

Inmates may present even greater moral dilemmas for ethnographers. Some of my students, for example, were convicted murderers or rapists. During my prison-teaching tenure, I tried to remain unaware of inmate histories in order to evaluate them as fairly as possible as students and to interact with them on a friendly basis as possible informants. Occasionally, however, I was told more details through the prison grapevine. For example, I discovered that one of the best prison students I ever had had been sentenced to multiple life terms for random, racially motivated murders in a

Midwestern city. At another institution, during a casual after-class discussion, I discovered that an inmate informant had graduated from my high school's rival institution, and that we had even attended the same undergraduate college for several years. Unlike most field situations faced by anthropologists, informants and friends were thus also convicted felons.

Inside total institutions like prisons, the varied layers of oppression and control may require fieldworkers to readjust their moral definitions about "good" informants, or may cause them to remain more socially, emotionally, or psychologically aloof from field relationships. For ethnographers in prison or similar situations, these personal compromises may be discomforting, difficult, or even impossible (see Rhodes 2001:76).

A final ethical issue relates to the psychological stresses inevitably encountered by the researcher, as well as the people living or working within the prison system. Again, the effects of psychological stress are evident in other field situations (Fetterman 1983:221), but are intensified by the social structure in prisons. Indifference, antagonism, and hatred between categories of informants, along with the moral ambiguity of befriending convicted murderers or dictatorial guards, created many uncomfortable situations for me. Furthermore, most researchers are unaccustomed to seeing some of their informants deliberately mistreat or ridicule other informants in the ethnographer's presence. I distinctly remember the awkwardness I experienced when I passed one of my students leaving prison under guard escort; the man wore leg manacles and handcuffs, which were fastened to his waist by another chain. To ease our mutual discomfort, he joked: "I have a good excuse for missing class tonight!"

By the time I was completing my final semester teaching in a prison, even the smell of the evening meal wafting across the prison courtyard caused me to feel queasy, for it immediately brought to mind all the layers of oppression, hatred, and ambivalence behind the walls. One spring evening, in fact, I distinctly remember my feeling of relief when leaving my fieldsite. Unlike many ethnographers, homesickness did not repel me from my fieldsite; instead, it was the site itself and the social relations within that repelled me.

Conclusion

While my time teaching in prisons was certainly valuable in terms of data collection, and my maturation as a fieldworker, I have not returned and have little desire to do so. The delicate balancing of mutually antagonistic social groups and the stress over conducting research under varied levels of secrecy, rumor, and gossip offered challenges to me as no subsequent field-site ever has. I found it depressing to see my inmate students mistreated and dehumanized by racist or indifferent guards, and yet I often walked in fear among those same inmate students. I also befriended men convicted of multiple murders, rapes, and drug dealing, creating morally ambiguous relationships that continually troubled me. While the awkward spaces and uncomfortable relationships in prison taught me much as an anthropologist, they also created significant ethical dilemmas, some of which I could never resolve. Others may also find fieldwork in prison or similar institutions to be a valuable experience. Be prepared, however, for the challenges that lie behind closed doors.

Acknowledgments

A much briefer version of this paper was first presented at the Society for Applied Anthropology meetings in Charleston, South Carolina, in March 1991. Comments from the session's participants were appreciated. Kirsten Harken and Brian Bodine, graduate students in Clemson's Applied Sociology program, updated some references. I also appreciate the editorial comments from Donna Arnold, Lisa Faulkenberry, Kate Gavounas, Holly Norton, Cindy Roper, and Candace Vickery. The views expressed in this paper, however, are mine.

Notes

1. See Fleisher (1989) for the guards' views about the very real dangers they face.
2. See Waldram (1998:242–243) for a similar dilemma.
3. My research interest at the time; see Coggeshall (1991).
4. See Coggeshall (1991) for the social implications of this role inside prison.

Gary Robinson

CHAPTER 12

Living in Sheds

Suicide, Friendship, and Research Among the Tiwi

W. Lloyd Warner's *A Black Civilization* appends a brief autobiography of his chief informant and friend, a Murngin[1] man called Mahkarolla (1969:467ff). This is followed by Warner's account of a canoe voyage in which he and Mahkarolla had feared losing their lives. Warner, Mahkarolla, and some Murngin comrades are in two dugout canoes, pitched and tossed in a wild sea, unable to turn to make for calm water. Warner curses the storm. He wants to turn back and cries, "What shall we do?" Mahkarolla is silent, head bowed. Warner keeps calling out, then shouts abuse at his friend before falling silent with the rest. After finding land, Mahkarolla says that he could not respond, because he was crying; he was frightened his friend might die. Warner is ashamed.

Warner juxtaposes this story with a brief account of his departure. In Darwin, Warner mingles with other whites on a ship, which Mahkarolla is not allowed to board. Mahkarolla remains silent as Warner calls to him. Warner hurries to the end of the boat, cries out; Mahkarolla waves, crying, then lowers his head. Like the canoe voyage, "Our parting now had death in it, too, because it was certain we would never see each other again" (490).

Mahkarolla had protected and nurtured his friend throughout their relationship; just as he might have lost him to the storm, he was to lose him to white society for good. Warner's rage in the boat—for which he felt such shame—was itself a reaction to evidence of separateness, the fact that he was, for all their closeness, a white man who spoke harshly and swore, like any other. At that moment, he failed to live up to the ideal that he had invested in Mahkarolla. No doubt they had forgiven each other these differences many times before. In telling his own story, Mahkarolla had said of the white men, "Sometimes they swear at you, but inside they are all right" (479). This separateness forces itself on Warner again at their parting, when the moment was out of reach, just like Mahkarolla, disappearing in a crowd at the wharf. Despite the intimacies of their relationship, Warner does not further reflect on it; his was, he says, a study of the society, not the man (467). He presents their separation as the effect of external forces, the crowd, the boat, which leave Mahkarolla crying on the dock, with Warner, the white man, waving, again calling out (490).

What is the relationship between Warner's testament to Mahkarolla and his objective, systemic analysis of Murngin society? Mahkarolla's presence stamps Warner's famous work. However, only this suggestive, largely implied analysis of the relationship between the two men and its role in the creation of the impersonal objectivity of the systemic analysis of Mahkarolla's society is evident in the text.

The formation of ties of dependence and reciprocity between researcher and subjects, the researcher's incorporation into social groups, and the sometimes gut-wrenching sundering of ties as he or she disengages from research subjects constitute largely unexamined terrain in analyses of ethnographic fieldwork. One may simply not know what to do with the fact of one's dependence on others, nor how it can be made meaningful to a professional audience; those disciplines that push us to obscure the arbitrary forces of our own lives within the analytical view of the "other" do so not without a touch of shame. A challenge for anthropology is to systematically reflect on the human relationships underpinning research, as a basis for development of its methods as a human science.

Hungarian-born ethno-psychoanalyst Georges Devereux (1967) drew a parallel between what psychoanalysis refers to as countertransference—the analyst's unconscious emotional response to the "other"—and the establishment of method in the social sciences. The emotional impacts of undertaking ethnographic research are, potentially, a crucial source of insight. Devereux is mainly interested in the emotional shock of witnessing unfamiliar practices: ritual mutilation like subincision, sexual practices, extreme interpersonal violence, seemingly self-destructive alcohol consumption—the things that "others" do, which ethnographers must understand if not as "normal," then as meaningful. For the ethnographer, writing about other cultures often entails explaining practices that in one's own world would be highly anxiety-arousing, untolerated, or repressed.

Devereux' own self-understanding resembled that of the professional clinician, in that he took the social detachment of the observer more or less for granted. However, the emotional impact of observed difference, the trauma of witnessing conflict, violence, or death, for example, needs to be understood in terms of the observer's own involvement in the actions of others: the forbidden desires, fears, rage, and childishness, the sense of responsibility for others, the enmeshment in their daily lives. Ethnography presupposes the capacity to form relationships that are interpreted at least partly in terms of local idioms of relating. How does one relate? As a brother or sister? As a child to an adult? As a friend or colleague? This is too often passed over as an incidental aspect of incorporation into a new social group as participant observer. What is the significance of these emotional relationships for one's intellectual grasp of the field? In recounting research to a detached public audience, explanation becomes interwoven with rationalization: the emotional meanings of such involvement are difficult to reconstruct and are all too often suppressed. Wisps of human shame inhabit the expert account—as Warner tried to show. "Participant observation" is not simply a research technique: it rests on the human capacity to form relationships, and it entails a struggle to maintain some degree of reflexive distance without violating those relationships.

Beginning with Suicide

Late in 1985 I commenced fieldwork on Melville Island in Australia's Northern Territory, in a community of around four hundred Tiwi persons.[2] I intended to study the life of Tiwi adolescents, in an ethnography informed by a reading of psychoanalytic anthropology. On arrival, I lived by myself in a tin shed that had been used as quarters for visiting contractors and that had the advantages of shower, kitchen with appliances, and a number of beds. One or two men in their twenties began to show some interest in me and I soon found myself in regular contact with a group of young men and adolescent boys, listening to their stories in the shed and accompanying them around the community, day and night. I wanted to be involved, to hear their stories, to learn about anger and fighting, sex, dreams, swearing and teasing, their relations with their families and with one another.

As I became more familiar to these youths and young men, individual motives for making contact with me, or for using the space that was created around me, were expressed in sometimes competitive, sometimes curious, demands for response. The more extroverted boys were overtly assertive and competitive; more withdrawn or reserved boys showed their interest indirectly, sometimes in angry reactions to exclusion from the group. As an older non-Tiwi man who was always available, who listened and played along with their talk and intrigues, and who tolerated their silences, I provided a context within which a range of possibilities emerged for individuals as well as for small groups or self-styled "gangs."

Young boys came in and out, usually in groups to drink tea and eat damper, to "talk stories," and to sleep on the beds. Older men in their twenties would also visit, often in pairs, usually to drink tea and to talk.

I slowly became aware of the many layers of communication within ordinary interaction; it was sometimes like being caught in tides running in many directions at once. Tiwi seem to achieve highly individualized communication within groups. They individualistically demand or expect recognition while also showing a capacity for interpersonal intimacy in settings where the collectivity appears to override individual motive. These communication settings are very rich. They can also be disconcerting for persons whose culture favors one-to-one interactions over diffusely structured group processes.

A man in his late twenties became a regular guest at these gatherings, usually visiting with a younger companion. His first unaccompanied visit was driven by some anxiety. "Everyone," he said, was at a discotheque at the club, at which alcohol was available. He was afraid of being drawn to follow, and thus to breach the conditions of his court-imposed bond, which (after many court appearances and lengthening prison sentences) had become a critical issue for him. He was heavily dependent on the company of a group of younger men who, like him, were serving noncustodial sentences. I was not fully aware at the time that his visits, his frank discussions about fighting, drinking, and prison, his references to the deaths of his parents, and his talk of years of sexual abstinence signaled a rapid intensification of emotional investment in our relationship.

I had expressed an interest in dreams. A youth reported a dream. The older Tiwi man, whose name was Seahorse, immediately followed this with a dream of his own. Seahorse's dream included vivid reference to me and to the preceding nights at my place (Robinson 1992:118).[3] It began with a representation of dialogue between the dreamer, myself, and some other youths the night before and can be summarized as follows: We were talking, then I yawn and he yawns. The dreamer leaves then returns, having, he thought, forgotten his key. He calls out my name from the dark outside. In response, I say, "Nothing here," then tell him I had seen another man take the key. He goes to his room, unlocks it, to find the other, younger Tiwi man naked in the room with a Tiwi woman. She invites him in. Instead of saying no, he says yes straight away, strips off, and joins the other, and they have simultaneous sex with her. "We was saying dirty things to her (in Tiwi language) and she say dirty things to us (in English)." The other man calls the dreamer's name; the dreamer explains his name and the name of the other Tiwi man to the girl, telling her that the other man is horse "dreaming." She says, "I get the picture."

Afterward he said, "Good dream, eh?" and asked whether it would be published one day.

Seahorse reported this dream and two others over the following weeks, along with stories about his personal history: the sexual dilemmas that had led to rejection of his betrothed, his "promised wife," some years before and left him sexually abstinent for the seven years since his mother's death; and years of violent conflict and frequent criminal offending, which had led to numerous periods of imprisonment. In his early teens he had been placed in juvenile detention for attempting to shoot a brother-in-law. His wild behavior intensified in his later teens after his father's death and again in his early twenties after his mother's death.

In the first part of the dream related above, the dreamer called my name and I rejected his overture; at the end of the dream, his wish for acknowledgment is realized when the other man calls his nickname, "Seahorse," and he explains its meaning to the girl. This nickname was in fact an amalgam of his patrilineal totem, or "dreaming," seagull, and the other man's horse "dreaming."[4] At the same time, the invocation of "horse" (as another man's "dreaming," or father) may have been an echo of ambivalence toward his own father. The woman was "wrong" for him (i.e., an inappropriate partner for him) but "right" for me and the other man.[5] Seahorse had by that time been fairly open in talking about his father's death, but avoided reference to the later death of his mother. Thus, with its combination of sexual content, allusions to incest, and references to paternal symbolisms, this dream seemed to refer to many of Seahorse's sources of conflict and anxiety; it also seemed to locate me within them.

In psychoanalytic terms, this first dream was a transference dream, which made me the object of the informant's unconscious preoccupations (see Le Vine 1981). The dream was simultaneously the commencement of something real and something unsettling in my relationship with Seahorse. The overtly sexual content almost certainly produced some anxiety in each of us. The interaction between transference and countertransference that played itself out over the coming months was, like the meanings of the dream itself, never fully explored in direct dialogue during the remainder of our contact.

Confronted with the complex demands and wishes expressed in Seahorse's dreams and stories and his need for contact, I was anxious that I did not have any answers. Even so, our meetings, and his contribution to storytelling and dream-reporting, continued until I left. When a rowdy bunch of youths ran away from school in Darwin and took advantage of my place as somewhere to be, I allowed them to take center stage, although Seahorse and the older men continued to visit. The older men led the storytelling, when the younger group let them. During the last three weeks of my stay, the challenge of Seahorse's introspection was somewhat displaced by my interest in the boys' dream-telling and their ever-present concerns with sex, teasing, fighting, gambling, and sorcery.

This visit to the island had been a short three-month stay to set up for an extended period of fieldwork. When I returned from Sydney eight months later, I believed that I understood some of what had happened between myself, Seahorse, and the other youths, and that I had a chance of reestablishing the dialogue with him, while continuing my involvement with the boys and other members of the community. The boys vigorously took over where they had left off, and a number of them moved in to share the shack with me. The most energetic was Seahorse's nephew, his elder half-sister's son, who wanted me, his "big brother" to support him in his quest for excitement, his sexual conquests, and his evasion of responsible involvement in his family group. At the same time, Seahorse had returned to drinking, and was a much more sporadic and unpredictable visitor.

On my return, Seahorse and his brothers recounted how they had visited an elderly "father" on Croker Island. The three brothers had taken turns having sex with a girl there. However, far from liberating Seahorse, this had led him to fight with his brothers. He told a number of stories that idealized the place but also pointed to diffuse sources of anxiety and threat. He dreamt, while there, about being home, driving too fast, and losing control of the car. He crashed near a pandanus tree (*pandanus spiralis*) next to the house in which he had lived with his parents from birth and lost his arm. Two days later he spoke about "being made [into a clever man]" by a clever man (i.e., medicine man) who sucked blood from one's arm; tying pandanus fronds around the arm would prevent too much blood loss. Pandanus was also his matrilineal "skin" group[6]: maternal symbolism was thus interwoven with images of self-mutilation and flight to the protective mother. He also reported that he had been shown the lair of a powerful devil who lived at a secret place on Croker—in fact, there were strong associations between this "lair" and the house of his birth a few hundred meters away. He told of waking in fright as a child in that house, and being quieted by his father; he said that his father was a clever man with power over devils. During this period of rising anxiety, with its echoes of childhood fears, Seahorse's *aminijeti*[7] brothers became increasingly impatient with his clinging dependence on them.

Not long after my return, a female patrilateral cross-cousin of Seahorse died, and he was led by his brothers to perform an active role in the funeral as "widower." This experience unsettled him through its powerful resonances with his mother's death. He visited at night with some urgency, becoming increasingly preoccupied with the stories of devils, retelling in detail the story of the destructive devil on Croker. One evening after work related to the funeral, Seahorse arrived at my house, drunk, to tell me important stories about his mother's death. These accounts were, I later learned, driven by denials about his own conduct at the time (she had been hospitalized for some weeks after an accident, which caused her death; during this time he did not visit her). His *aminijeti* brother tried in vain to leave him there talking with me. I did not want the drunk and argumentative men to stay and offered to escort the two of them toward the village. The brother tried to leave us, and Seahorse was torn between following him and his beer or staying with me. I was undecided, then smiled and walked on.

Seahorse said that he wasn't smiling, wasn't happy; that he was in a bad mood. He then flew into a rage at me on the road and said, "You white cunts think you're smart! You think you know everything! But you're not serious! You don't know our ways." He had earlier said, half-jokingly, that he would kill his *aminijeti*. Now, enraged, he said he would kill me, too. He then backed off in terror. I said what I could to calm him, and he started to cry; he held me and cried out repeatedly to his mother, sobbing, "Mama, Mama!" into my shoulder. He later pretended that he had been crying for the recently deceased cousin and had called out for his mother by mistake.

Some days after the incident on the road, there were reports of a conflict between Seahorse and his younger brother at home. A couple of days later still he committed a break-in at the community store. The morning before he was due for interview by the police, he committed suicide.

After his body was found, his younger half-brother came to get me at the shed. As we hurried down to the health center, where a large crowd was gathering, he kept repeating over and over that Seahorse had been looking for me the night before, but that I wasn't home. At that moment I knew only too well what *hadn't* happened. But what *had* happened? What had happened to blind us to this ultimate possibility, even though we had heard the threats? What had determined the fluctuations in closeness and distance between Seahorse and myself, limiting our readiness to confront the difficult themes in our relationship?

Relationship and Understanding

There had been clear resonances between Seahorse and myself during my first visit. As a newcomer, I wanted to learn as much as I could about life history and questions of identity and conflict. I was, in a way, dependent and immature, without an identity, struggling to remake myself, to have myself "made" by the Tiwi experience. It was my presence as outsider trying to get in that was of use to Seahorse at the beginning. It provided a framework for him, for his unusual introversion and self-reflection; I was able to listen, free of ambivalent and conflictual histories, and my shed offered a protective social space outside of the compulsions of conflict within his residential group. However, in a sense, my shed was like an extension of prison, which had also shielded him from the dramatic conflicts at home without helping to solve them.

Seahorse's crisis opened up anxieties that neither of us had the means to fully deal with. He was subconsciously preoccupied with the past, if not obviously with death, and later with an underlying fear of futility. As a researcher, I wanted to be drawn into many relationships, to know about everything going on; I felt the need to ration the time I spent on various activities and with various people. At times, I chose others over Seahorse. For example, I sometimes chose his nephew's dramatic confrontations, his exuberance, his wild sexual adventurousness, and his readiness to defy his own fears, over Seahorse's anxious retreats, his sexual stalemate, his fears, and his social isolation. At the same time, through his sensitivity to rejection—and through his drinking—Seahorse himself subconsciously created limits on what sorts of relationships could coexist in his life.

My understanding of this man's death, and of the symbolisms produced in the dreams, stories, and actions leading up to it, is largely retrospective. Even so, at the time I had a sense of the central themes in Seahorse's preoccupations. Feelings of guilt and responsibility—his largely toward his deceased parents, mine partly toward him—and anxieties about failure had characterized our interactions before his death. My sense of failure lay, first, in my inability to recognize that suicide had, by this time, become a possibility for him and, second, in the knowledge that I had not responded to him when it mattered. His sense of failure may have been related to the hope he had, for a time, invested in me, but that had remained unrealized; this was a reflection of a sense of failure to say goodbye to his parents, especially his mother, whom he had refused to see as she lay dying in hospital.

My notes later revealed that Seahorse's suicidal intent had begun to crystallize in the days and weeks before his death. These messages were dispersed in his stories and pronouncements, hidden, perhaps, to keep them from himself as much as from me. His evasion of me during the last days of his crisis seems now to have been linked to an idealization of me as unapproachable—perhaps because his drinking and fighting so dramatically contrasted with the self-control he had shown during my earlier visit. I may have unwittingly confirmed this idealization (and thus his shame) as my social interests widened, amid the many demands now made on me by others participating in my research. Thus I sat in the shed, talking about the break-and-enter with the teenage boys (one of whom had been an accomplice to the robbery), but did not seek Seahorse out the next day.

I have generally felt that my actions toward Seahorse, including my inactivity and nonresponse at certain times, were based on a sense of what was possible and tolerable between us. However, the questions remain: Did I abandon him? In some senses, perhaps I did. Could I have achieved and then tolerated a closer relationship with him? In the circumstances, I doubt it. Did I feel that he could not be helped? I do not know. At some points during fieldwork, the critical questions are less about research or professional responsibility, and more about the human ambiguity of our personal ties and responsibilities to others. There are times when the researcher cannot be a researcher. To think "research" at such moments may be to evade the emotional meaning of these interactions. The ethnographer is vested with neither a higher moral authority, nor omniscience about the cause and meaning of many of the things that happen in the field. Even these questions came long after the event: at the time I was struggling under the emotional impact of Seahorse's death, taking shelter in action as the community prepared for his funeral.

Events have meaning as communications. The decisive communicative moment between Seahorse and myself may well have been during the confrontation on the road, although I did not know how to pursue it with him or his brother. That event needed interpretation in terms of Seahorse's inability to mourn his mother. It had been preceded by urgent, elaborate tales of visits to see his mother on her deathbed and watching her die in hospital, both of which he had failed to do. Apparent rejection by me during this moment of vulnerability—perhaps suggested by my smile—produced sudden rage and the threat to kill me *too*. Like his *aminijeti* brother, I had appeared unwilling to listen to these urgent misrepresentations. From my perspective, however, I had simply wanted to hand over the querulously drunk, angrily rambling man to the responsibility of others.

At the time I noted with uneasy gratitude that Seahorse's acts of apology for his rage (both at the time and later, as he recounted the events to his family) were a kind of resistance to further communication. They may have been an attempt to exonerate me of any responsibility I might have felt for him. His wish for my forgiveness masked a retreat, while I was transfixed by my inability to provide an appropriate "analytical" response and by anxiety about forcing a discussion that I could not control. At one level, I had idealized him as a potential dialogue partner, but—during the last visits—had also sought to exclude the bits of him that did not conform to this ideal—the erratic, resistant bits of the person enmeshed in drinking and fighting, or the person too ready to take flight from me and from my interest in talk.

Self-critical awareness of these themes does not give one control over them. While accumulated experience in a complex cross-cultural setting may mean that the ethnographer is a little more willing to risk interpretation, slightly better prepared to recognize and respond to particular events, deep insights are not necessarily available in the midst of important and intense interactions with research participants in the field. In order to understand what I refer to as Seahorse's idealization of me, I had first to deal with a tendency, common among ethnographers perhaps, to deny the possibility that my otherness, my "whiteness," was always present as a potentially distancing or inhibiting factor for the people I was working with. Projections based on the ballast of social difference and habits of blame readily infuse interaction at crisis points. The always latent burden of imputed aggression and guilt on either side only *appears* to vanish when the ethnographer feels accepted, "one of the gang," an adopted member of a kinship group or family. In this case, acceptance and, more important, trust momentarily broke down between two people at the one's perceived rejection of the expectations of the other. Seahorse, drunk, had reacted to something in my demeanor, my smile, my wish to deflect him at that moment; I was trying to evade his aggressiveness and drinking and did not see the urgency of his need at the time.

Relationship, Responsibility, and Expectation

The idea of "relationships" based on trust and obligation is central to human concern and to ethnographic practice. It can also be an oppressive idea, suggesting a sometimes intolerable degree of responsibility for the other, a life and death responsibility that no party can reasonably accept, but to which most of us commit ourselves, on all sorts of grounds—be they parenthood, marriage, friendship, even professional relationship. Strategies for limiting responsibility for others, making individuals responsible for themselves, and rejecting others' attempts to become overly responsible for us are elaborated in all cultures.

Among the Tiwi, struggles over blame and responsibility are often played out through threats to others, damage to property, threats of self-harm, and overt self-neglect. The unhappy person may in effect challenge others to abandon him to his fate, and sometimes those others must do so, by resisting his demands and coercions. The ethnographer may have many experiences of "misplaced worry" about others in the context of the emotional demands of everyday life combined with the additional demands of research. This is perhaps particularly so in a cultural setting where acts of bravado, personal risk–taking, and overt suicide threats are frequent occurrences, as they are among the Tiwi (see Robinson 1995).

In reaction to Seahorse's suicide, I withdrew. The Tiwi boys and their families, on the other had, drew closer together, becoming watchful and solicitous, not letting anyone be alone. Boys moved into the shed to keep us company. And I soon realized that I was trying to move out. I was no longer satisfied with the once self-sufficient social scene at my place. Leaving the shed was a painful process, however. Seahorse's nephew had invested a great deal of energy in our bachelor life. I can still see his reaction as I broke up our household; slashing at his leg with a knife, in agitation (without breaking the skin), then avoiding me for a couple of days, only to become a frequent visitor at my new place. In the two or three years after we stopped sharing the shed, he plunged into volatile relationships with women, and then into four or five years of violence and imprisonment. Our life in the shed had temporarily helped stave off some of those potentials. For me, Seahorse's death and the breakup of our household produced a kind of anxious suspension of my own self-image as a "researcher" with the power to understand the relationships surrounding me and my work.

Biography, Anxiety, and Method

"In the field," as in life, we often make selfish, not merely self-interested, choices. Participant observation, our primary methodological technique, requires that we consciously try to divide ourselves, while simultaneously and paradoxically struggling to avoid such a division. Ethnographers may wrestle with their own preconceptions about, and preferences for, research participants whose input promises success—who seem to offer understandings of the research project that could eventually sustain intellectual products for the public domain, visions of "culture," "system," or "society," or, in Warner's case, "civilization"—against those whose contributions seem of implicitly lesser value.

When, as researchers, we equate objectivity with the need to eliminate overt moral judgment of others, we are often acting to obscure the moral preferences that underpin our visions of our subjects and our subjects' worlds. In gathering the material for these visions, we consciously and subconsciously encourage forms of dependence between ourselves and our "informants" while also rejecting uncomfortable levels of dependency. The subsequent intellectualization, the "cleaning up" of our researcher enterprise for print or presentation, often disguises the fact that, even when highly responsive to what others put before us in the field, we unknowingly make choices about relationships that are, in some respects, narcissistic, self-gratifying, and defensive. Looking back, it can be hard for us to accept our researcher selves "warts and all," just as it may have been hard to accept our informants and their demands. However, unless we are able to accept the full range of our engagements with our research participants—as Warner sought to do, with his admission of shame at his own "hardness" and swearing—our understanding of what went on in the field will remain only partial.

The "choices" we make as researchers, independently of their intellectual justifications, reflect the working out of themes in our own biographies. This trajectory does not discount insightful engagement with others; in fact, it is the source of the ethnographer's power to be able to persist through many renegotiations of relationship. It provides the tenacity and positive desire to engage that pushes us simultaneously toward both independence and meaningful relationship with others. This desire is reciprocated by others, whose response opens pathways to some relationships while reducing the sustainability of others. The ethnographer's engagement in relationship-building from a position of dependence distinguishes the ethnographic situation from that of many other disciplines; reactions to and denials of this motivated dependence—in assertions of competence, detachment, or independence—are part of the countertransference response, that is to say, the researcher's response to emotionally charged interaction with others.

Any formal research apparatus provides a rationale for the ordering of time and relationships in ways foreign to the lifeworlds in which the research occurs. While I was living in the shed with the youths, visited by men like Seahorse, method seemed no more nor less than emotional survival: the attempt to understand extraordinary interactions and my own reactions to them. I was not prepared for this aspect of fieldwork, and wonder if indeed such preparation is at all possible.

The absence of pre-given institutional markers of social distance (such as a formal work day, opening times, or the trappings of a distinct professional role) differentiates the work of much anthropology from the practices of clinical medicine, psychology, psychotherapy, or other professions. These are normally differentiated from the everyday through all sorts of mechanisms, rules, and informal understandings that constitute a kind of self-protective methodological apparatus. The institutionalized, rule-bound, methodology-driven professional, however, would be a dysfunctional person in the relationship settings described above, and would be seen by the Tiwi as such—unless he or she had sufficient maturity to become personally involved and abandon the safety of professional disciplinary armor.

Ethnographers work at the other end of the methodological spectrum. Participant observation requires flexible adaptation to noninstitutional patterns of communication, to messy, ambiguous relationships that exist, at least partly, as unexpressed wishes in the researcher's own mind. However, to the extent that ethnographic methods partially mirror the communicative patterns of everyday life and assume ordinary patterns of reciprocity and response, the ethnographer's very flexibility constitutes a barrier to some kinds of methodical work, as he or she becomes hostage to social demands and unpredictable trajectories within the group being researched.

The ethnographer's professional armor is much weaker and potentially more unstable: it is partly created through relationships established in the field—for example, incorporation in social networks, the assumption of an ascribed "identity"—and in the management of those relationships according to the purposes of researching "culture," or a similar overarching idea that justifies both professional purpose and social distance to some degree. However, ethnographic armor is only really consolidated and strengthened with written elaboration after the fact: this is, for many ethnographers, the time when "method" is *invented* out of the muddiness of field experience.

For Devereux, the methods of the social and behavioral sciences are projective systems enabling reduction and containment of anxiety. The researcher's analytical apparatus helps to preserve emotional distance and detachment, often at the cost of failure to recognize the unconscious determinants of interaction with others. The researcher's objectivity entails both the consolidation of a view of the "other" and the establishment of the researcher's professional, public self in a dialectical process. Through a process of self-objectification, the researcher deals not only with intellectual problems of research, but with the anxieties aroused in the ethnographic encounter, and with the fact of his or her separation from it. Theory (or its absence) is already an integration of the self; it conditions observation in terms of the imagined futures of finished work. It helps to extract the researcher from the indeterminate futures of lived involvement.

To return to the beginning: Warner's testament to Mahkarolla and his account of their painful separation gives a glimpse of this process. Warner (1969:467) suggested that the *ultimate* objectivity of his account of his relationship with Mahkarolla was based on recognition, rather than denial, of the nature of his emotional engagement with the other. This acknowledgment presents an apparently sharp contrast to the kind of objectivity evident in his systemic analysis of Murngin society.

While it can be argued that the risks of emotional involvement are always present in ethnographic research to some degree, they are not always decisive for the intellectual outcome. This account has considered an ethnographic extreme, in which the researcher plunges into an exotic world, intent on engaging open-endedly with difficult areas of social life—in my case, the conflicts and troubles of adolescence—in which ready-made frameworks or paradigms for interpretation are not at hand. The objectivity, always partial, that comes with the recognition and analysis of emotional engagement rests on processes of self-maturation in respect of potentially dislocating social involvement and rupture. At these extremes, the maturation implied by living with, and working through, challenging relationships cannot be forced. It takes time, and cannot be achieved solely by emotional and intellectual effort in the field: the effort must be continued beyond the point of separation.

Notes

1. "Murngin" is the term Warner used to describe peoples of Northeast Arnhem Land in the Northern Territory, now usually called *Yolngu* people.
2. The Tiwi are the original inhabitants and today's legal traditional owners of Bathurst and Melville Islands, which lie just to the north of Darwin, capital of the Northern Territory. For an account of the Tiwi social system and some recent social adaptations see Hart, Pilling, and Goodale (1986).
3. See also a short outline of the case in Robinson 1997. Seahorse is referred to here as "Goldfinger."
4. In Aboriginal Australia, the term "dreaming" has been coined to refer to the totemic symbols with which Aboriginal persons identify. They do not have any literal association with dreams, although they represent personal symbolisms that may appear or be mentioned in an individual's dreams, as in this case. Among the Tiwi, one's "dreaming" is patrilineally transmitted, and may be an animal or bird, a spirit, or an object, and is always associated with a distinctive dance, performed by persons identified with that "dreaming" at mortuary rites and other ceremonial occasions.
5. I had been incorporated in Tiwi relations as the maternal "uncle" of Seahorse; the other man in the dream was my "brother." Seahorse pointed out

that our relationship to the woman was "right," his "wrong," i.e., not acceptable, incestuous. Tiwi society is based on a system of exogamous matrilineal clans, called *imunga*. All Tiwi and some non-Tiwi persons are accorded status of kin by putative descent based on clan membership and/or marriage. For an explanation of Tiwi kinship see Goodale (1972).

6. Tiwi society is organized into matrilineal exogamous clans referred to colloquially as "skin groups" or sometimes "tribes"; these are named after birds, fish, insects, features of the landscape, the sun or moon, or similar (see Goodale 1972).

7. Patrilineally related "brother" with a common paternal grandfather, almost always a member of a person's landowning group of "countrymen" (see Hart, Pilling & Goodale 1986).

Graham Harvey

CHAPTER 13

Performing and Constructing Research as Guesthood in the Study of Religions

Serendipity, relationships, and intrigue are significant but underrated inspirations and foundations in research and the discourses that arise from research. Equally, anxieties, misunderstanding, partiality, and advocacy are among the obstacles met by researchers either "in the field" or when attempting to communicate the results and significance of research to colleagues, peers, students, and the wider community. Sometimes, too, such experiences turn out not to be purely private and individual, but to resonate with wider trends and currents. This chapter reflects on challenges encountered in the process of research in religious studies, a subject whose developing understandings of and approaches to fieldwork have often emerged in dialogues with other ethnological disciplines.

Without rehearsing the whole history of the study of religions as a discipline, it is useful to note some matters that provide a backdrop and foundation to the discipline's interest in field research. The common origins myth of the subject suggests that it arose in opposition to theology as a way of studying religions that is only partly located in academia. Theology is the attempt by expert insiders to a religion, usually Christianity, to improve the understanding and practice of their religion. In contrast, religious studies scholars attempt to research and discuss the phenomena of religions as they are presented by religious texts, people, places, and occasions. Scholars of religions are not the only academics who study religious phenomena, but they tend to see their discipline as uniquely placed to engage with *all* rather than only some of the phenomena that might be considered "religious." Religious studies inherits much from philologists and other scholars of literature as well as benefiting greatly from the work of ethnographers on social movements and cultural complexes. Religious studies scholars are also interested in philosophies and theologies arising among and having a bearing upon activities of importance to religious people. While others might share some of these interests, religious studies attempts to view the full picture that emerges from bringing all these perspectives together.

While theologians have only recently engaged in something like fieldwork (when they began to be interested in the activities and views of marginalized communities), the phenomenological foundation of religious studies immediately called for engagement with lived realities. Thus, the trajectory and pursuit of religious studies may cast interesting light on some of the academic debates about methods and positions in all academic subjects. This is all the more so because religious studies typically engages with communities and matters that call for, and sometimes insist on, participation, engagement, commitment, and enthusiasm. That is, religions proffer an immediate and almost inescapable challenge to the kind of objectivity often required by and of academics.[1] This essay discusses my own journey among scholars and practitioners of religions as a reflection on my discipline's various negotiations of the stresses and strains of doing fieldwork among those who do not always value the positions, perspectives, and methods central to academia.

These reflections are rooted in the shifting sands of religious studies' (and academia's) struggle between the twin temptations of objectivity and subjectivity—clearly a precarious place to attempt to put down roots. In conclusion I suggest that such (and perhaps all) dichotomies hinder the acquisition of knowledge, prevent understanding, and, especially, disable the continuous process of debate that is, perhaps, the distinguishing characteristic of the academic project. I argue here that the practice of participant observation as a method for conducting fieldwork often reenshrines the dichotomies it seems to challenge, and thus requires contestation. Another possibility, that of guesthood, has been available all along and has been offered by those among and with whom field research takes place, specifically indigenous peoples.

Participation and Observation

At the heart of the matter are conflicting understandings about what participant observation, as one of the primary ethnographic methods, might actually mean. A brief and contestable summary of some of these understandings serves as a prelude to later discussion of examples from religious studies practice.

In the twentieth century, field research rapidly replaced what had seemed entirely acceptable to the previous century's social scientists, namely, distant reflection on the collated narratives of travelers, missionaries, and colonial officers (among others). The underlying understanding of research continued, for a while, to be the attempt to achieve an objective, universally acceptable presentation of the facts. Thus, participant observation began as a refinement of more distant kinds of observation. It arose from the understanding that it was necessary, for example, to join in ceremonies rather than just interview participants after the event. Postcolonialist, feminist, and queer studies have been central to the various provocations of reflection that have led to more dialogical and engaged versions of participant observation.

As one part of a widespread challenge to the whole notion of objectivity, it is immediately obvious, for example, that those undertaking research in their own communities must necessarily conceive of matters differently from those "outsider" researchers who fear or even vilify the possibility of "going native." If anthropologists have settled the issue in their own discipline, scholarship about religions continues to be fraught. If "insider" views of religion become acceptable, it seems necessary to accept theology into the fold. How will we deal with the opposite move to the one by which trained "outsider" observers became methodological participants? That is, can academia accept as critical scholarship research done by participants who observe their own community and even themselves? This question became clear to me most recently in examining a doctoral thesis (Sollis 2002) that applied Riet Bons-Storm's theological approach (1984) to research that also calls itself "participant observation," meaning insiderly reflection and dialogue, wherein participants learn to observe for academic purposes.

There is one final introductory matter of some importance to my argument that indigenous knowledges, protocols, and performances may contribute significantly to more ethical and valuable academic research. Alongside postcolonial theorists of various kinds, indigenous scholars (e.g. Weaver 1998; Deloria 1998; Smith 1999) and broader indigenous communities make it clear that academic researchers are not—and never have been—detached or uninvolved; in fact, social scientists frequently engage with matters, and communities, that demand they take clear ethical and political positions. Some indigenous and nonindigenous postcolonialist writers argue, for example, that if researchers fail to challenge colonialism, then they cannot claim to be detached from it; instead they might even benefit from it while their work acts to reinforce Western structures of power. There are at least three positions available for social researchers within this framework: as supporters of explicitly colonialist agendas, as passive beneficiaries of colonialism, or as writers and thinkers *against* colonial hegemony. Other positions are available, however, especially given that each of these positions is complicated by individual entanglements in the messy realities of everyday life.

I propose here that by adopting a position of "guesthood," researchers can engage more fully with the communities they are researching. While embracing the role of "guest" cannot solve all the problems associated with doing ethnography, it can provide an ethical and respectful position from which to face these challenges.

Shifting Engagements: Encountering Indigeneity

Following on from my doctoral study of names and naming in ancient Jewish and early Christian texts (Harvey 1996), my research focus shifted to the field of contemporary Paganisms.[2] I was drawn away from the study of historical texts, where it seemed easier to be "objective" (or at least detached), and initiated into the world of fieldwork by an emergent scholarly interest in Paganism as it is currently being practiced in Europe, North America, and elsewhere. I began to reconnect with the Druids and other Pagans I had met through my participation in the Stonehenge Peoples Free Festival and related events since 1976.[3] These explorations resulted not only in a book (Harvey 1997), but also in a personal "coming home," my own "coming out" as a Pagan (see Harvey 1999).

In contrast to Tanya Luhrmann (1989), who explicitly removes herself from the taint of "insiderly" or "native" experience during research among magical practitioners in London, I celebrate a more messy situatedness. In common with many other ethnographers (including Devereux [1967]; Jules-Rosette [1978]; Eilberg-Schwartz [1989], Young and Goulet [1994]; Medicine [2001]; Spickard, Landres & McGuire 2002; Blain [2002]; Wallis [2003]), I consider it vital to be open to the possibility of being changed, finding that those with whom we dialogue know more than we do about important matters, and welcoming the opportunity to revise lifeways and thought patterns. Participant observation (of any kind) necessitates at least some complicity in performing acts of local significance. Pagan groups, for example, regularly celebrate seasonal festivals by forming a circle of participants in which there are not supposed to be any separate, distant observers (although sometimes people do step out of the circle to take photographs). In that position, the participant observer is performatively indistinguishable from any other participant. Furthermore, since these events do not (always) privilege interiority, belief, ideology, intellectual assent, or understanding, to participate at all may make everyone full members of the group of celebrants.

Religious studies scholars, like others, have debated the benefits and problems of insiderly and outsiderly status (see McCutcheon 1999). Scholarly engagement with Paganism furthers these debates by encouraging serious reflection on dialogical, experiential, queer, and reflexive approaches (see Blain 2002; Wallis 2003; and Blain, Ezzy & Harvey 2004). Reflexivity requires that academics consider whether criticisms they make of those they research might also (or more particularly) be aimed at academia itself. Accusations have been leveled at New Agers, Pagans, and some other white religionists that their practice of "shamanism" appropriates in inappropriate ways from indigenous people. Far from being respectful guests receiving gifts of knowledge and performative styles from willing indigenous donors, Western shamans are frequently accused of being thoroughly colonialist. However, many of these people have actually learned their craft from academics of various kinds, and it is important to question whether scholars are any less colonialist in their appropriation of knowledge and skills (see, for example, Welch 2002; Harvey 2003; Wallis 2003). My initiatory realization of the depths of antipathy toward academic researchers (including those whose observation is conducted through participation) occurred at a conference hosted by St. John's University, Newfoundland, but located on the reserve of the Conne River band of the Mi'kmaq Nation.

Having gone to talk about Pagan shamans, I stayed on for the powwow that followed the conference (a significant event in the return of this band to traditional ways). At lunch one day I asked people surrounding a vacant chair if I could join them. They said, "Are you an anthro?" Uncertainly but honestly I said that I was not, and was thus welcomed with the joke, "Good, because we eat anthros." During and after an entertaining meal I was made aware of the depths of antipathy toward those who engage in "hit and run" research (Biolsi & Zimmerman 1997; see also Smith 1999): visitors who ask lots of questions, gain access to otherwise restricted ceremonies and private lives, and then leave to write the book that will establish a reputation and career. Too often the erstwhile hosts of these participant observers gain nothing. Worse, some hosts find themselves disenfranchised by such "experts," who later claim the authority to comment on the "authenticity" of the community and its practices, sometimes with the result that yet more land, property, or knowledge is lost.

My thinking about research methodologies has been significantly inspired and influenced by later realizations and reflections about the protocols, performance, and passions of encounters between potential hosts and guests. At Conne River I received real and welcome hospitality, despite some of the tensions associated with academic research. I also noticed ceremonial and other occasions when particular visitors were made welcome in particular ways (especially elders, veterans, drum groups, and spiritual leaders). I was given a gift and told how it had come to the donor (an encouragement, I later understood, to pass the gift on in the future). I spent time by a sacred fire and could not fail to notice continuous and easy gift-giving. However, as Vine Deloria (1997) notes, such generous hospitality is commonplace among indigenous peoples and does not indicate acceptance or validation of a person as a researcher, or of their research. The importance of the reciprocal move, not of hospitality but of guesthood, among indigenous communities was made more evident to me in a further, serendipitous, journey. Or rather, what is made clear in initiatory guest-making protocols and procedures is that a reciprocal relationship between hosts and guests is frequently offered by generous indigenous hosts.

As a condition of co-publishing my book on Paganism (1997), Wakefield Press insisted on my doing an "author tour" of Australia. This seemed like an ideal opportunity for me to meet with some Aboriginal people. As a Pagan, I was concerned to show respect to the ancestral traditions in other lands. As an academic, I was beginning to make contact with scholars (many of them indigenous) who were interested in contemporary indigenous religions. In the central Australian town of Alice Springs I met with Aboriginal teachers and others who guided me to reflect on how I, as a European, might show appropriate respect to local ancestors and lands. I also encountered a second group of indigenous people in Alice Springs, a community who led me into another new phase of research.

Maori in Alice

There are now Maori in many countries of the world. Quite a few of them meet regularly with other Maori, often to maintain and develop traditional cultural and spiritual practices. In Alice Springs, to my surprise, I met a small Maori group who gather regularly to learn and perform songs and dances from their homelands. I was intrigued by how a spirituality so rooted in the forests, mountains, and seas of New Zealand might be celebrated in Australia's central desert. I encountered this group after visiting local churches and the mosque, where I had been asking clergy about their relationships to sacred places as defined within local Aboriginal law, or dreaming. More than once I had been told that it was irrelevant and uninteresting. Places of worship required planning permission, but, I was told, nobody had ever asked Aboriginal elders or owners for their permission.

Before I had an opportunity to ask a similar question of Alice's Maori community, I was told that there would be a meeting that evening, in which I could participate as a guest, in a small building near a sports ground. Apparently, these Maori had previously approached Aboriginal elders and asked permission to construct a meeting place of their own. The reported reply continues to impress me: "We know you are also indigenous people, but if we give you permission to plant a tree, you might plant a forest. So, we will watch you for a while." This response seems to have been accepted as entirely appropriate (and as insightful given the importance of forest trees to Maori). Thus, when this Maori diaspora greeted ancestors and elders in their borrowed building, they first acknowledged the priority and prestige of local Aboriginal Australians. They celebrated Maori culture but sought ways to enhance Aboriginal prestige and thereby demonstrated what it means for Maori to be respectful guests. The knowledge of this foundational encounter between two indigenous peoples (and its resonant contrasts with my own encounters) made my first experience of Maori protocols for meeting and greeting so much more profound.

Researching Indigeneity

I have long been impressed by an article on Maori religion by a Maori scholar, Paka Tawhai (1988). I consider it important not only, or even primarily, as a statement about Maoritanga (Maori culture) but even more as an insightful model of scholarly approaches to and discourses about religions. Although Tawhai had died by the time I tried to contact him to invite a contribution to a book about indigenous religions (Harvey 2000a), Peter Mataira, a Maori colleague of his, responded to my enquiry and thus initiated a valuable collaboration and friendship. To date, Mataira has written chapters (2000, 2001) for two books in which I have been involved, and has introduced me to his friends, family, and wider community. Two additional research interests emerged for me out of these new relationships. One was a desire to see what was happening among contemporary indigenous religionists. It was obvious, for example, that many Maori continue to sing songs, tell stories, and engage in ceremonies that would be familiar to their ancestors, even as they identify as Christians, or Sai Baba devotees, or Rastafari, and so on.

Second, and not surprisingly, given that my introduction to Maori was in Australia, I am also interested in "indigenous diasporas," indigenous peoples living by choice or otherwise outside the lands to which they belong. The notion of an "indigenous diaspora" challenges preconceptions about the temporal and spatial fixity or boundedness of indigeneity (cf. Thompson 2001) and can also be used to explore various indigenous responses to land loss, for example, loss of control over local resources, and loss of access to places of particular cultural or religious significance. Too many social researchers continue to be interested in indigenous religions only in an attempt to uncover their "original," usually precontact, form. Although the habit of using such constructions to theorize about the earliest religions of humanity is now less common than it once was, it is not entirely dead. In contrast, it seems to me more valuable, both to academia and to indigenous communities, to dialogue about contemporary concerns, issues, and activities. Certainly I have found that introducing my own interests in these topics leads to visible relief and immediate discussion of mutual interests. I have benefited greatly from the generosity of indigenous hosts and colleagues and, as a result, my primary purpose here is to show how indigenous, and in particular Maori, protocols of meeting and greeting provide models or paradigms from which social researchers can learn much about ethical research methods.

Participant observation opened the gates to experiential and dialogical modes of scholarship that began to move beyond assumptions of pure objectivity toward a greater recognition of the subjective aspects of social research. Contained within this methodology, however, is the fear of, or desire for, "going native," becoming an "insider" rather than an (allegedly) objective scholar. Some scholars assume that "participant observation" should cease with the formal conclusion of fieldwork. Happily, the insider/outsider dichotomy that supports this understanding is contested by recent experiential and dialogical modes of research and reflection that have emerged from the fieldwork process itself. "Guesthood," for example, is not just a temporary method, nor is it collapsible into one side or the other of the old dichotomies (insider/outsider, subjective/objective, participant/observer, scholar/native, etc.).

Based on my experience of research among a Maori community in London, I want to show how the idea of "guesthood" challenges such dichotomies, thereby constituting a third position from which to engage in research with indigenous communities. While arising from and recognizing indigenous sovereignty, agency, and empowerment, becoming a "guest" insistently puts the researcher into relational encounters requiring ethical behaviors that are simultaneously vital and vitalizing for academia and for our hosts. Although "participant observers" are always guests in the weak sense that they research among others, "guesthood" carries the stronger implication of a more complete, participative, relationship that changes people.

Many communities have protocols for meeting and greeting. While some religions make "conversion" the priority, thus attempting to change "outsiders" into "insiders," Maori encounters with visitors have led to the evolution of ceremonies offering richer choices to those who are potential enemies and potential guests. Uncertainties are not collapsed immediately but faced and considered in the hope of developing more mutually fruitful relationships. And that is precisely the situation that confronts researchers today: will we be enemies or guests? This claim may be more clear on discussion of the Maori approach to this issue. It is important that I acknowledge that, far from attempting a description that could be universally applicable, I write from my experience as guest, *manuhiri*, of particular communities. I will refer, in particular, to the present elaboration of *marae* protocols among a group of Maori living in London, Ngati Ranana.[4]

Marae Protocols

In weekly gatherings, Ngati Ranana meet in central London to practice songs accompanied by posture and movement for cultural performances.[5] Their meetings also engage them in protocols of considerable importance to Maori everywhere. These usually occur in a complex labeled a *marae*, which comprises an open space, the *marae atea*, and a meeting house, *whare nui*. While the house (especially when elaborately carved) may attract considerable attention, the *marae atea* space in front of it is vitally important, as it is full of potential and creative power. In London, a room on one floor of New Zealand's embassy forms both *marae atea* and *whare nui*. Along with other Maori and guests, Ngati Ranana also meet less regularly at Hinemihi, an ancestral *whare nui* (treated as the current form of the female ancestor, Hinemihi) rebuilt on the grounds of Clandon House near Guildford (fig. 13.1), and restored initially through the efforts of Maori Battalion troops and later by Maori from Aotearoa New Zealand and Ngati Ranana (see Gallup 1987; Hooper-Greenhill 2000).

For the purpose of this discussion it is precisely the presence of visitors that is important. Were the majority of Ngati Ranana to be elsewhere on a particular Wednesday night, someone would be around in case visitors arrived, whether they be Maori recently arrived from Aotearoa, officials of the High Commission, academics, media,

Figure 13.1   Ngati Ranana, London's Maori club, at Hinemihi. Photo: author

researchers, or whoever. All such visits are facilitated not as consumerist spectacle, but in the protocols that form and maintain relationships, especially those of hosts and guests. Such protocols recognize (and further establish) the priority of the local hosts. Such places are considered living members of particular local kinship groups (see Harvey 2000b). They are ancestors of the local humans who might receive visitors in order to host or confront them.

At Clandon House, the Hinemihi *marae atea* is not demarcated from the grass lawns, but those who use it know where the boundaries are. Similarly, in the embassy in London, regular visitors and hosts know which room is treated differently from other rooms—for one thing, it is only entered after the removal of shoes. Those who do not yet know the protocols are expected to follow and learn by doing. Someone will always suggest the removal of shoes, the putting aside of burdens, attentive silence, or whatever the moment and place require. Additional lessons about expectations, behaviors, and Maori culture are learned from the familiarity of more intimate introductions and longer acquaintance. It is, of course, important that Hinemihi, even though she is a long way from her original home, remains an honored ancestor, and that the embassy is New Zealand territory and therefore subject to the ramifications of the Treaty of Waitangi (see Orange 1987; Brookfield 1999).[6]

The visitor (myself, for example) approaches the *marae* respectfully and waits with other visitors as one or more senior women call in welcome. Visitors are invited forward into an arena full of potential and seething with possibilities. Even a first-time visitor will probably sense that the welcome is to those both seen and unseen. Even if only one person appears to step forward, a community moves with them—because the ancestors and those yet to be born are always present with (or in, or as) the current generation. This is not a question of belief, private thoughts, or desires: it is a fact to be acknowledged that each person is one form of the presence of all that the ancestors did and bequeathed.

Rugby fans will recognize a further element of encounters between locals and visitors: the *haka*. This posture song makes a powerful point, one that I have so far misrepresented in this discussion. It is not as "visitors" that people come to a *marae*. Even when it is Maori who are encountering Maori, there is still something more fraught happening than hosts merely greeting visitors. The encounter is between locals and strangers. On the one hand there are those who belong and know the land and the ancestors, whose right to stand there derives from being "bound in specific and palpable ways, to the expressive earth" (Abram 1996:139). They are *tangata whenua*, local or indigenous people. On the other hand there are those who might in fact be enemies. The protocol thus provides for the possibility of conflict. In part the *haka* says, "If you want to fight, we honor your bravery, and we are ready for you, let us be worthy opponents." It ends with an offering that determines all that should happen next. The offering is not forced into the potential recipient's hands but placed in front of them so they may choose to receive or to reject it. To accept the gift is to accept guesthood. To reject it is to maintain an oppositional relationship, to offer confrontation.[7] As Viveiros de Castro (1999) and Chernela (2001) make abundantly clear, even enmity is relational. Research based on "guesthood," however, requires a different kind of relationship.

For those who accept guesthood, the next steps of *marae* protocol involve presenting and listening to speeches in which relationships are created or enhanced. Some guests and hosts discover mutual ancestors and thus closer kinship, responsibilities, and rights. Greater intimacy follows as hosts invite guests to *hongi*, sharing breath together while pressing noses. Entry into the *whare nui* initiates an even greater intimacy, made evident, for example, by the carved mouths and vaginas on most *whare nui* doors. Inside the *whare nui* debate takes place. It is no longer appropriate to arouse the possibility of conflict, but it is expected that differences will be clarified and expressed, and solutions sought. This social intimacy is further consolidated by later sharing a meal in a neighboring *whare kai*, food house or dining room.[8] In the past, those who chose to be enemies were also confronted by the possibility that instead of eating with local people, one group might eat or be eaten by the other.[9] I have yet to witness what would happen today if visitors chose to enact enemyhood instead of guesthood.

The above summarizes some of what is standard in encounters between Maori hosts and their visitors. Necessity requires that Ngati Ranana do things slightly differently. Although food is eaten in another room, the meeting room collapses functions of *marae atea* and *whare nui*. Even at Hinemihi, Maori have to negotiate the use of a place that is perceived very differently by other interested parties (e.g., tourists). Consideration of who is local and who is guest when Maori greet Europeans in London or Clandon further demonstrates the multifaceted and multilayered entanglements of these events. Since words like "syncretistic" and "traditional" continue to be used in religious studies in ways that dismiss the continuing evolution of indigenous worldviews and lifeways, the sovereignty of my hosts demands that I challenge the notion that their spirituality is inauthentic just because it is different from that of their precontact or early contact ancestors.

Ngati Ranana are not engaging in nostalgic role playing when they adapt the protocols of *marae* to a room in an embassy on the opposite side of the globe from their *turangawaewae* (standing places). Their European guests are not (necessarily) appropriating from them when they perform *haka* and *poi* songs. They are all continuing what their ancestors began: the encounter between people who might find that, even if ancestry separates them, place and time unite them. Indeed, such encounters themselves significantly contributed to the evolution of these protocols and environments. The presence of increased numbers of potential enemies /guests— especially ones with new metal tools—both required and enabled the elaboration of structures in which to perform the protocols of meeting and greeting. Carving skills, for example, further asserted the sovereignty of locals confronted by colonizing settlers.

Conclusion: Negotiating Awkward Relationships

The injustices of colonial histories have resulted in significant ongoing power differentials between many indigenous and nonindigenous communities around the world. It is not surprising, therefore, that "academic research," long associated with the dominance of "Western" cultures in the minds of those who have been the objects of study, now carries some degree of stigma based on the contributions, actual and perceived, of its practitioners to the colonial project.

My own research negotiations have led me to conceive of what many social scientists (whether interpreters of texts or ethnographers of communities) do as entirely relational. Some relationships are dysfunctional, colonial, oppressive, and detrimental to the goal of increased understanding. Rather than finding my discipline's typically phenomenological approaches to be entirely empowering and enlightening (for researcher or researched), I have instead found copious evidence of their complicity in dualistic systems that are too often colonialist (e.g., in denigrating contemporary religious movements).[10]

My work has been a series of emerging and evolving contests with the norms of alleged objectivity that continue to diminish research conducted dialogically, experientially, and to the benefit of researched communities.[11] In my various encounters with Pagans, indigenous peoples, and various other religionists, I have found that there is a position that is neither "native" nor "objective observer": that of guest. The experience and participation of guests are necessary to some performances/rituals and certainly challenge the dichotomy that can continue to embed researchers in dysfunctional encounters.

Guesthood means that researchers need not choose between objectivity and subjectivity, but may challenge such a dichotomy. Dialogical and reflexive modes of conducting research (including the practice of participant observation) have initiated and empowered such challenges. The struggle, however, is incomplete. "Guesthood" is not simply a poetic label for what participant observers do by necessity. It is perfectly possible, after all, to observe participatively and then retreat into claims of superior objectivity (or "critical thinking") that dismiss the power of insiderly experience and knowledge. Researchers are neither insiders nor outsiders, but are always participants in processes of change.

Too often such scholars have ignored the formative protocols in which they might have negotiated a turning from being strangers to being guests. Too often, they have made themselves and all future researchers enemies (as indicated by my dinner companions at Conne River, and by Linda Smith's 1999 eloquent call to "decolonize research"). Just as a visitor to a *marae* might head straight for the alluring carved meeting house without waiting for the call to become guests by careful stages and negotiation, some researchers have headed for that which is attractively "other," strange and unknown. But it is in the slowly diminishing space and, concomitantly, in the increasing intimacy between host and guest, researched and researcher, knower and seeker, that empowering and vital understanding may be achieved. Guesthood is not available from a distance or to those who *demand* entry, but to those who acknowledge and respect the prestige of their hosts.

The demonstration of respect in some form of return, reciprocation, conversation, and even, perhaps, collaboration (but see Beit-Hallahmi 2001) demands further and continuous consideration. After the commonplace collaborations of research (in which researchers gain much from local informants and/or coresearchers) are complete, the researcher might be expected to collaborate with the community rather than with those who, for example, wish to restrict indigenous rights over land and hunting, or over the interpretation and even (re-)possession of ancestral artifacts. Guesthood entails negotiations about the prestige, *mana* in the Maori context, of all concerned. These take place (metaphorically or otherwise) inside the *whare nui*, where debate proceeds differently because of what occurred on the *marae*. The moment for being an enemy is past, vigorous debate is rooted in the realistic recognition of both differences and similarities of hosts and guests. Researchers as guests do not have to agree, need not become insiders or "go native," but they can be required to defend their understandings to their hosts. In short, guesthood does not replicate the old dichotomies, but neither does it resolve all the uncertainties and ambiguities of research altogether.

If participant observation has been compromised, in religious studies at least, by the continuing polemical call to be "objective" and "scientific" against being or becoming "insiders" or "natives," guesthood suggests an alternative. It is, finally, not enough for academic researchers to participate only as a temporary means of observing (as if that just required a little training to make it properly academic). Guesthood demands that researchers seek a common ground that recognizes the priority and even the prestige of local hosts. Hutton (2003) suggests that

> the biggest question that hangs over modern Western scholarship [is] whether it is, in fact, the work of a particular tribal culture, committed to its own, subjectively effective, views of the cosmos, or whether it has the responsibility for creating some kind of universal explanatory structure for all humanity. The historic problem is that it is actually designed to be the former, and is struggling to be the latter.

However this dilemma is resolved, guesthood recognizes the fact that academic researchers are full participants in one tribe that is inescapably engaged with many others, each of which have their own sovereign and valuable needs and desires. And if we cannot defend what has seemed normative in our tribe then we should be ready to change and provoke change.

Notes

1. It is important to note that religious studies scholars are among those who have most vigorously debated such claims and encouragements to objectivity.
2. These are spiritualities centered on the celebration of nature that often claim to revive pre-Christian religious traditions. See Harvey (1997) and Hume (1997).
3. A series of alternative and/or countercultural events valuably discussed by McKay (1996, 1998).
4. While this is the name of one performance group and may be translated as "London's Maori Club," it can also refer to all Maori living in London, *Ranana*.
5. One part of their repertoire is available on the CD that accompanies Ralls-MacLeod and Harvey (2001).
6. An excellent guide to the customs and protocols of *marae* is provided by Hiwi and Pat Tauroa (1986); this might well be expanded by reference to information in Cleve Barlow's invaluable discussion (1991) of "key concepts in Maori culture," and imaginatively encountered in the true-to-life fiction of Patricia Grace (e.g., 1987:26–30).
7. Thomas's contribution (1991) to the vast debate about "gifts," generated especially by Mauss (1954), underlies this suggestion that reciprocity is not the only possible meaning or outcome of any offering of gifts.
8. The dynamics of such acts are mediated, however, by *tapu* (taboo) regulations (see Mataira 2000); examples include the stricture that invocations or prayers must precede eating, and that particular local etiquette is followed.
9. Debates about cannibalism are also fraught, but ancestral cannibalism is part of the popular knowledge of contemporary Maoridom, as represented in the film *Once Were Warriors*.
10. This is not to undermine important advances such as those of Cox (1998), who argues for a refinement of religious studies' phenomenology that would make it more respectful, or the critique offered by Flood (1999), who challenges a style of phenomenology that actually ignores the historical and local variations in religions in favor of constructing something more abstract and, in the end, theological.
11. Examples of such diminishment are not hard to find in discussions of new religions and indigenous religions.

PART III MULTI-SITED ENGAGEMENTS

CHAPTER 14

Not Quite at Home

Field Envy and New Age Ethnographic Dis-ease

ORGANIC FARM, OCTOBER 2000

Twelve people assemble inside the hexagonal "Temple of All Faiths." In the anteroom, we take off our shoes then grab prayer mats and giant pillows. In the temple proper, the Aboriginal elder, G, is sitting cross-legged opposite the door, a small possum-skin pouch and a wooden staff with emu feathers beside him. He doesn't speak but nods at each person as they enter . . . to my discomfort the others remind him that I'm an anthropologist, although I don't think he hears them over the ringing of his mobile phone.

On the wall above his head there is a quilt with symbols (Christian cross, Arabic crescent, Yin and Yang) . . . a stained-glass skylight and an assortment of oil burners provide the only light. The room smells like sandalwood. We sit in a large semicircle facing G. His wife and her sister sit on either side of him like acolytes. I try to sit cross-legged on the pillow, as I imagine you are supposed to do, but my knees crack and I slide off.

My field notes from the event described above conclude with the reflection that this was "one of the most ridiculous experiences of my life." I would like to think that such a response to fieldwork does not make me a bad anthropologist, but I am wary of admitting my ambivalence to colleagues nonetheless. After all, ethnographic fieldwork is what anthropologists do (Stocking 1992:13), and many continue to believe that personalizing field accounts with angst-ridden "confessional tales" (Van Maanen 1988:73) risks undermining the validity of the ethnographic endeavor (Howell 1990). If negative experiences in the field *are* discussed, they are usually treated as essential experiences, grist for the ethnographic mill (e.g., Briggs 1970).[1]

I cannot help feeling that this lack of public discussion about the sometimes frustrating, embarrassing, tiresome, and awkward aspects of ethnography is unfortunate. Those anthropologists whose fieldwork, for whatever reason, does not meet disciplinary ideals of holistic, or "thick," ethnographic description may feel a profound sense of failure.[2] The promotion of the "ethnographic method" as if it were a single, well-understood, methodology—one that primarily relies on participant observation—also elides the miscellany of techniques that are carried out under the rubric of "fieldwork."[3]

In this chapter, I explore some of the methodological and personal anxieties I experienced when researching the use of Australian Aboriginal culture as an inspiration and tool for "New Age" self-expression.[4] At the root of this ethnographic anxiety was the difficulty I had in reconciling a nontraditional and unbounded ethnographic subject with traditional expectations of participant observation. My field experiences of chatting on the Internet, browsing Aboriginal souvenir shops, and learning tribal dancing at New Age workshops seemed exemplary in their engagement with a modish "multi-sited ethnography" (Marcus 1998). Without culture shock, amusing linguistic misunderstandings, or exotic diseases, however, it did not feel like the "real thing." Ethnography may not be what it used to be, but sometimes it is difficult to know what it should be.

What's in a Name? Anthropology and Identity

Over the last twenty years, anthropology has found its traditional subject matter—localized "cultures"—increasingly eclipsed by mobile sociocultural practices. Metcalf (2001:165) identifies Appadurai's elaboration (1990, 1996) of a range of cultural "landscapes" as a watershed in attempts to move beyond objectified cultures to grapple with a world characterized by the transnational and the transitory. Accompanying this transformation of the anthropological subject has been an increased focus on the implications of global disjuncture for ethnography and its construction of "the field" (see Auge 1995; Clifford 1997a; Marcus 1998). Indeed, as Metcalf (2001:165) observes, it is now rare to find a graduate student whose project does not involve global process and disjuncture in some way.

However, while notions of culture and its relationship to place have been dramatically revised, ethnographic method has not yet caught up with its subject matter (Hastrup & Fog Olwig 1997:4). Although Marcus (1998) promotes "multi-sited ethnography" as a way of investigating culturally connected, but geographically dispersed, phenomena, he is less clear about how such investigations will take place in the field. As Clifford (1997a:57) has noted, there is a difference between the concept of mult-sited ethnography and its implied practice of multilocale fieldwork; where the former recognizes the many locations of culture, the latter requires field study in many locations. This raises unresolved questions about whether one should spend less time in each site, and whether this implies forgoing some of the depth often considered the main strength of ethnographic fieldwork. Nor is it clear if one should apply the same criteria for "good" fieldwork in traditional ethnography to multi-sited ethnography.

In any case, despite the effort spent moving the ethnographic imagination into "shifting locations" (Gupta & Ferguson 1997b) and "nonplaces" (Auge 1995), most models of fieldwork still evoke the ethnographer's entry into a discrete "field" to commence a "profound engagement in a community's life" (Weiner 1995:6). Second only to the fervent exhortation that anthropologists should do fieldwork is the command that long-term participant observation should remain the archetypal anthropological practice (Hastrup & Hervik 1994:3).[5] This assumed lengthy cohabitation also dovetails with another of anthropology's regulative ideals: that fieldworkers build a special rapport with their informants (Marcus 1998:127). Stocking (1992:14) has observed that traditional fieldwork methods have always been inconsistently taught, if at all. Hence, the few principles that *are* taught acquire the force of moral injunctions.

In the absence of other distinguishing features, many anthropologists also seem to feel that the discipline's identity should be tied to the methodology associated with anthropology since Malinowski landed in the Trobriand Islands almost a century ago (e.g., Austin-Broos 1998:295; Mac-Clancy 1997).[6] Even Marcus shies away from endorsing a "thinner" model of ethnography by suggesting that field study, although framed by a "multi-sited imaginary," should for the moment remain a "site-specific, intensively investigated and inhabited scene of fieldwork" (1998:15). Fieldwork that does not fit disciplinary norms—or worse still, anthropological projects without any field component—can be marginalized, the suggestion being that they are "not really anthropology." Indeed, Stocking (1992:14) suggests that without the "initiation" of long-term participant observation, one's career choices in anthropology may be restricted.

Into the Field

In the shadow of the heroic ethnographer, I set out to do my fieldwork. Prior to my unsatisfying attempts at "real" fieldwork, I had thought little about its role as a marker of disciplinary identity. I simply assumed it was what one did: one goes into the field, collects data, and then writes it up. However, my experience of the field was one of incoherence and fragmentation. It did not resemble the archetypal fieldwork I had read about, nor was it the rite-of-passage into the ethnographic fraternity that I had expected. Most of the markers of "real" fieldwork—and of anthropological identity—were missing: I did not learn a new language, rarely had to leave home, and did not become immersed in a "community."[7]

Nor was it clear where the field began and ended. The project was a continuation of my nonprofessional observations of the way many Australians look to indigenous cultures as exemplars of spirituality, naturalness, and belonging.[8] Everywhere I looked there were bookshelves stuffed with Aboriginal wisdom for "the present day," and everywhere I turned I met individuals who were convinced they had had a profound experience with Aboriginal people or cultures. At parties, people told me about their life-changing meetings with Aboriginal elders when on holiday in Arnhem Land. My flatmates told me that their tattoos and eyebrow piercings were "tribal" and recommended courses that would teach me about "living with nature." Yet when I read one of the popular New Age books on Aboriginal cultures, Lawlor's *Voices of the First Day: Awakening in the Aboriginal Dreamtime* (1991), it seemed a work of fantasy, full of ridiculous misinformation. I wondered what was happening here. What do people hope to gain when "borrowing" from other cultures, and what are the consequences?

A natural starting point for this study was the spiritualized consumer goods that first drew my interest: the Dreamtime tarot decks, Earth Mother greeting cards, didjeridu relaxation tapes, and the notorious *Mutant Message Down Under* (Morgan 1994).[9] All offer the consumer a commodified version of Aboriginal spirituality as an ingredient for self-transformation. The *Oracle of the Dreamtime* (1998), a widely available set of divinatory cards, exemplifies the packaging of culture as a tool for personal growth. Ordered from an online New Age shop—my virtual purchase epitomizing New Age cultural consumption—the "Oracle" arrived at my house in a shiny box containing "Dreaming cards" designed by "six Aboriginal artists." Accompanying and explaining the cards was a book of Aboriginal myths compiled by a non-Aboriginal spiritual healer, Donni Hakanson, and the Aboriginal storyteller Francis Firebrace. The accompanying myths and instructions described how the reader could lay out the cards, tarot-style, and access "ancient" Aboriginal wisdom to ease the problems of modernity.

The plethora of New Age consumer "stuff" and its representations of indigenous cultures seemed highly amenable to analysis, and perhaps this should have been enough. Unfortunately, the nebulous field of cultural borrowing did not seem very amenable to the participant observation I had envisaged as the core of my study. That I wanted to do a field study at all was as much a product of my desire to make the research seem "anthropological" as it was to get better data than that found in the liner notes of didjeridu and whale-song CDs.

Where the Natives Are

Primed by ethnographic field manuals, I initially planned to spend one or two years in the field collecting data. However, "the field" turned out to be elusive—neither located in one place nor commensurate with any delimited community. Scattered here and there, in practices, attitudes, and consumer commodities, New Age cultural borrowing seemed "everywhere and nowhere" (Pink 2000:114); the number of places I could physically inhabit for study were limited. This led to a paralyzing methodological uncertainty, and, in the absence of a "bounded-island entity" (Stocking 1992:367) in which to do "real" fieldwork, I was tempted to abandon the project altogether. It was only the many New Age commodities with Aboriginal themes, and the vociferous Aboriginal and academic complaints that such commodification was cultural appropriation, which reassured me that there was something worth pursuing "out there."

My difficulty in identifying an ethnographic locus arose partly from the diverse range of practices and beliefs that come under the New Age label. Although the New Age is often described as a new religious and/or social movement, self-ascribed group identity is often lacking.[10] Nor do most participants necessarily believe in the millennial change that gave the phenomenon its name (Heelas 1996:16). At best, the common pattern of drifting from one New Age activity to the next can be described as a form of "intentionality" (Helliwell 1996:128), one in which participants carry out similar, but independent, projects of self-development. Almost everyone I know—academics, friends, and family alike—have consulted alternative health practitioners, attended yoga classes, or read a self-help book. These people are not "New Agers"; they are individuals who like some aspects of New Age philosophy and whose commitment to it as an identity may not extend beyond owning a dream-catcher.[11] The individualistic pursuit of self-fulfillment, spiritual or otherwise, could even be described as symptomatic of Western modernity (Lasch 1984).

If the New Age was hard to pin down as a fieldsite, so was my subfield of intercultural borrowing. My reading of critics such as Julie Marcus (1991) and Grossman and Cuthbert (1998) suggested that the New Age was a sociocultural agent that actively appropriated indigenous culture: a group of Westerners cannibalizing indigenous wisdom to fill the spiritual void of technological modernity. I set out intending to study this "group," but they proved hard to find. Although an airbrushed Aboriginal artifact may be evidence of the commodification of Aboriginality and spirituality, it does not in itself constitute a fieldwork site. As Fog Olwig (1997:33–34) has noted:

> It is difficult for the anthropologist to get at the natives' point of view, when the natives' universe is made up of a wide variety of resources of worldwide dimension, and when it is not embedded in particular places where anthropological fieldwork may be carried out.

This can be particularly troublesome when one does not really know who the natives are or where they live. Although the spiritual and political beliefs I was interested in sometimes find expression in the production and consumption of spiritual commodities, often they do not. Even people who attended New Age events could seem unconnected to any larger community of belief: I often found myself a more regular presence at workshops on Aboriginal spirituality than many of the other participants, for example.

My preconceptions about what makes for "real" fieldwork probably presented a greater problem than the ineffable nature of the subject matter itself. In planning the fieldwork, I had assumed that places for intensive participant observation would just be there. The "field" that I had read about in fieldwork manuals and ethnographies always seems clearly defined—if not by location then by cultural markers such as ethnicity. In contrast, my field seemed hopelessly fragmented, even illusory. Although all fieldworkers make personal and pragmatic choices that limit their research focus, this process is rarely documented in published ethnography. Neophyte fieldworkers therefore have few examples of how to reduce the complexities of social phenomena into manageable ethnographic projects.

This uncertainty about the boundaries of the field became a source of considerable anxiety as I fretted over the project's validity. With no village to visit, no community center in which to ask questions, I delayed the field study by vacillating over where to begin. Unwilling to commit time and funding by traveling to the "wrong" places, and unsure which ethnographic tools were appropriate, I almost certainly missed out on a number of potentially rewarding research opportunities.

Imagining the Field

Marcus's (1998:90) description of multi-sited ethnography was helpful in suggesting an approach that looked beyond bounded cultures to "chains, paths, threads, conjunctions or juxtapositions of locations." Equally instructive was Strauss's (2000) description of the movement of yoga from India to the West and back again. Strauss (2000:169–171) proposed that the amorphous and ephemeral "spheres of activity" in which yoga was practiced could be understood as "matrixes," a concept taken from mathematics that describes an intersection of "vectors," multidimensional flows of ideas, practices, objects, and actors. Although neither schema was necessarily directly applicable to my field, such hermeneutic metaphors are useful for imagining and explaining messy social realities.

More important, I realized that the absence of an obvious location for long-term fieldwork, or a community of people wearing "I Am a New Age Appropriator" t-shirts, was itself a significant clue to understanding the New Age and cultural borrowing. I came to think of the multiplicity of therapeutic practices and ideas described as New Age as part of a pervasive discourse of spiritualized self-help and healing rather than as a concrete social or religious entity (Heelas 1996). Had I been able to find a specific site in which to work I may have continued to think of the New Age as a culture or religious community. Instead, the focus on a pervasive field of attitudes and related practices clarified the existence of a broad cross-section of people for whom indigenous cultures are a source of authentic difference and "naturalness" that act as an auto-critique of "Western" secular materialism (Bowman 1995). For many settler-Australians, internalizing the Aboriginal connection to land also helps them feel more at home in a nation-state with an unresolved colonial heritage. One nonindigenous Australian at a spiritual workshop claimed that a personal understanding of Aboriginal spirituality is vital if nonindigenes are to live in Australia. Similarly, a participant at an Aboriginal-organized Reconciliation camp told me:

> If we can get the people together, get some kind of political agreement and maybe a treaty, then society as a whole will be a whole lot healthier. How can we heal ourselves, or feel any kind of kinship with the land . . . when we have this sick society? We have to listen to the elders, listen to what the Aboriginal people are trying to teach us.

For many "New Agers" and political activists alike, Aboriginal wisdom and spirituality offer a way to both "heal the nation" and "heal the self"; they represent a means of both critiquing technological modernity and saving it from itself (Gelder & Jacobs 1998:2). This interest in Aboriginal cultures could be expressed in a variety of ways; while some "hyper-spectacularised and hyper spiritualised" (Grossman & Cuthbert 1997:49) representations of Aboriginality are of little practical benefit to Aboriginal people, the desire for personal fulfillment and social change among non-Aboriginal seekers can lead to active political engagement. The belief in an indigenous other, whose wisdom should be embraced by nonindigenes if they are to become better, healthier people, can be as evident at political rallies for Aboriginal self-empowerment as in the instruction booklet to my *Oracle of the Dreamtime* tarot cards. As Pfeil has observed (1995:210):

> Once you get beyond the academic left and academic feminism . . . much if not most of the "politics" that still gets "waged by the post-sixties left" . . . is . . . in crucial ways indissolubly commingled with New Age inflections, assumptions, and key terms.

Similarly, the focus in anti-appropriation discourses on a monolithic, neocolonial New Age that steals from oppressed indigenes (e.g., Lattas 1990; Grossman & Cuthbert 1998) has tended to obscure Aboriginal discourses about spirituality that complement and overlap with New Age discourses. My experience of working with urban Aboriginal people has indicated that many believe Aboriginal culture to be inherently spiritual, peaceful, and environmentally responsible (see also Swain 1992). Aboriginal participants told me that by recontacting this Aboriginal heritage and spirituality they could heal their mental and emotional hurts just as nonindigenous people had told me that learning about Aboriginal spirituality was crucial to both their personal healing and that of the Australian nation.

Doing Multi-sited Fieldwork
(There's No Place Like Home)

Even when one is armed with a nifty concept like multisited ethnography, the most appropriate methods or locations for fieldwork are not always obvious. In practice, the fragmented nature of my subject made fieldwork a mess of formal interviews, participant observation, and idle conversation. There seemed little more than a kind of "thematic resonance" (Clifford 1997:58), and my own presence, to link each tour group, seminar, and crystal shop. This field existed somewhere in my imagination; it required me to seek out images of indigenous spirituality, and examples of their mobilization for the use of personal or social transformation, wherever they could be found. Particularly useful were the longer festivals and workshops promoting the idea of Aboriginality as a means to personal enlightenment and/or healing. These events were often the only physical interactions between the New Age and Aboriginality, and offered a rare opportunity for participant observation and penetration into an otherwise intangible sociocultural universe (Handelman 1990:9; Parkin 1996:xviii).

Nevertheless, despite deciding that multisited ethnography offered me a workable field strategy, the absence of traditional markers for good ethnography remained a source of angst. In particular, I had nagging doubts about the depth of my multisite, multilocale field. Whatever the problems of site-specific ethnography, immersion in a limited number of field locations does offer the comfort of ongoing, day-to-day observations. In contrast, many fragments of fieldwork made my ethnography seem broad but thin; I potentially had hundreds of "minisites." Most festivals, workshops, and seminars that link Aboriginality and the New Age are single events organized by individual entrepreneurs. Such events can be frustratingly ephemeral, hard to track, and easy to miss. When I did track down events they were often prohibitively expensive and their organizers unreliable.[12] An advertised tour would be endlessly postponed in the search for more customers; a promised festival or workshop canceled due to poor organization, financial problems, or lack of interest. Consequently, I often had to rely on participant descriptions of past events. These accounts could provide useful information but were of questionable reliability.

My concerns about ethnographic depth were exacerbated by the difficulty of maintaining long-term relationships with participants. The phrase "participant observation" implies face-to-face contact, with the fieldworker becoming a participant in the lives of the people under study. However, although I had only to walk a hundred meters from home to the nearest crystal shop to see "my field," my informants—garnered through personal contacts, attendance at events, and perusal of Web-logs—were scattered around the globe and were rarely accessible or amenable to repeated interaction.

Even when I physically encountered potential informants, the highly scripted, timetabled, and repetitive nature of most New Age workshops and seminars thwarted my attempts to cultivate them. The high cost of attendance also made participants reluctant to waste time with anthropologists (see Mulcock 2001). Like many New Age events, Aboriginal spirituality workshops typically took the form of lectures, with the audience (including myself) passive recipients of instruction about indigenous spirituality and living with nature. Active participation and interaction were usually limited to mass rituals: group meditation, offerings to a "sacred fire," silent prayer to the spirits of the earth. Then everyone would go home.[13] My attempts to chronicle these experiences were also hindered by the reflective and spiritual atmosphere of such events; cameras were commonly banned and note-taking or conspicuous observation was discouraged. To not fully partake of the experience—to appear to be an observer rather than participant—could be perceived as inappropriate or threatening.

The limited opportunities for physical interaction and day-to-day observation restricted the study in a number of ways, most notably by creating a certain shallowness of knowledge about my subjects. For example, nonindigenous participants at events celebrating Aboriginal spirituality often knew of Aboriginal objections to the New Age book *Mutant Message Down Under*, and were aware that they were vulnerable to accusations of cultural appropriation. Because of this, I suspected (but often lacked confirming evidence) that many nonindigenous people tailored their interview responses to make themselves appear culturally sensitive. Similarly, some Aboriginal entrepreneurs or spiritual healers were hesitant about identifying the origins of a particular practice or belief if it seemed to have been "borrowed" from the dominant culture (and therefore open to accusations of inauthenticity). Although I was aware of the partiality of the selves presented in interview situations, I frequently lacked the material to confidently chart the gap between what people say and what they do. Perhaps, as Weiner (1995:6) claims, this kind of analysis really does require long-term interaction with an individual and their social context.

On a more personal note, my attempts at ethnographic rapport were not helped by my own uneasiness about New Age beliefs. Much of the time I felt uncomfortable participating in "spiritual" activities and avoided those I knew would be especially confronting. Although I thought a good anthropologist should be as tolerant of New Age spirituality as of traditional Aboriginal beliefs, I also struggled to maintain a relativist stance toward practices that seemed, to me, hopelessly silly and politically suspect. When, for example, a non-Aboriginal farmer told me that a ring of exotic trees was an ancient spiritual gathering site—one that the "Dreamtime spirits" had entrusted to him rather than to the local Aboriginal people—I struggled to suppress my skepticism and scorn.[14]

Although Narayan (1993) has pointed out that neither ethnographic researchers nor their subjects live within the borders of a single culture, membership in the same "society" or "culture" can feel like a license to judge. This is particularly the case when, like many anthropologists, my instinct was to support the (critical) "indigenous position" against the interests of settler Australians (Morton 1997). I tried hard to not let my political sympathies and squeamishness about spirituality interfere with the study but worried that my ambivalent feelings about my research subjects were unprofessional.

Despite these concerns, few of the methodological difficulties presented by my fragmented subject were insurmountable. My main problem was the feeling that these sporadic field encounters were a poor substitute for the "real thing," particularly when I had to regularly abandon the field for the study of newspapers, government papers, land claim transcripts, and tourist literature. When one is doing ethnography away from home, newspapers and television are often considered part of fieldwork; reading a newspaper at home, however, has little ethnographic cachet. Nevertheless, textual sources displayed a range of otherwise inaccessible attitudes about Aboriginal culture and spirituality. Virtual interaction could also be substituted for physical interaction: the telephone, fax, and e-mail could be used to seek out new contacts or conduct interviews. Some Websites even allowed participation in online rituals or membership in a global spiritual community. Although I was uncertain about the status of e-mail as a fieldwork technique, electronic communication was part of the normal daily experience of my subjects and myself alike. The use of electronic communication technology is itself a socially mediated experience, and notwithstanding the claims of many fieldworkers for the primacy of physical interaction (e.g., Hastrup & Hervik 1994:3), observable social actions and interactions are carried out in virtual spaces.

Participant life histories, used in concert with informal interviews, also partially ameliorated the lack of long-term observation; they provided me with valuable contextual material and insights into participant worldviews, and fostered a sense of trust and intimacy. In any case, despite the irregularity of field events, there were other opportunities for participant observation, although these tended to be an uneasy mix of pseudo-friendship and surveillance. Rather than studying people in a distant field, I shared a socioeconomic background and language with many of the research participants. My interviews took place in local cafés and pubs and often had a social atmosphere.

More disquieting, although ultimately useful, was that I occasionally found the field following me home as I bumped into interviewees at the market or in the dry cleaners. Although I tried to maintain a distinction between research meetings and social meetings, this was not always possible. What at the time seemed like casual conversation could retrospectively be transformed into data; such post-hoc fieldwork frequently proved more useful than formal interviews because of the participant's relative lack of self-consciousness. This informal fieldwork seemed the closest thing to "real" ethnography: uncovering "the inevitable slippages between language, assertion, contestation and avowed knowledge through long-term observation" (Weiner 1995:6). It also felt like spying.[15] Although aware of my research, few people understood how much of what they did and said outside of interview and workshop settings could be included in my study.

Reflections on Ethnographic Failure; Or, What's the Deal with Ethnography Anyway?

My field dilemmas were both methodological and conceptual. The nature of the field itself often hindered the collection of data necessary for a traditional ethnographic account of the ways nonindigenous people borrow or buy aspects of indigenous cultures. The spaces in which people celebrated or appropriated Aboriginal spirituality were ephemeral, hard to track, and expensive to visit. Participants were wary of anthropological scrutiny, particularly if they felt it could leave them open to accusations of cultural exploitation or inauthenticity. What is more, almost every aspect of the New Age experience—including the obsession with spirituality and the desire to get in touch with the inner indigene—was not, and never will be, my idea of fun. Even when I could find the field, I did not much like it. I persisted because I am stubborn and because by the time I realized how fraught my fieldwork would be I had already done too much and progressed too far.

Nevertheless, the very lack of an obvious location for participant observation, which initially had made me feel ethnographically inadequate, ultimately proved intrinsic to the subject and thus crucial to its study. That I was unable to find an obvious fieldsite was largely due to the fact that the New Age "spiritual supermarket" (Wallis 1985) of religious techniques and ideologies is not confined to a community of religious believers but is a significant part of Australian life. My movement from site to site reflected the common intermingling of New Age ideologies and assumptions with a range of spiritual and political commitments. Had I found a New Age or Aboriginal community in which to stay, the pervasive mainstream desire to be personally reconciled with Aboriginal land and culture may not have been as apparent. Conversely, had I undertaken an armchair study of New Age texts, I may have missed the complexity of individual interactions with

New Age ideas. It was in large part the very awkwardness of my field, rather than my own conceptual efforts, that shaped my investigation.

The question of depth versus breadth in my fieldwork remained unresolved. Whether it mattered is something else again. Apart from my concern that I was doing something other than classical ethnography, it is hard to gauge the effect of limited informant relationships on the study. Although I still suffer from field envy when speaking to colleagues with more traditional ethnographic projects, I am not sure whether "deep" long-term observation would have told me much more about the global commodification of indigenous cultures. How useful is the intimate study of a handful of individuals when investigating a broad cultural phenomenon in a large and mega-diverse society? In any case, it is now a truism that ethnographic truth is inevitably partial. The nature of social enquiry means that indigenous cultural knowledge, no matter how it was gathered, is transformed when recreated as academic discourse. Classical fieldwork does not guarantee a more complete or truthful representation of reality than short-term fieldwork or textual studies, making even a decades-long study potentially as partial or plagued by misrepresentation as one composed of short visits.

When "the field" is no longer a field but a shop, a café, an office building, or an Internet chatroom, the way we think about fieldwork needs to be revised (although my multisited experiences make me wary of proposing any particular model of fieldwork as the new paradigm for anthropology). The multiplicity of cultural formations and possible approaches to the study of such sites means that the methods used to chart different cultural phenomena will vary according to circumstance. Not every research plan or planned fieldsite will work out. Neither does the apparent absence of conditions for long-term ethnography necessarily mean that meaningful anthropological study cannot take place. Every field, regardless of its location and degree of boundedness, inevitably presents specific opportunities and limitations that will determine what is possible or useful.

The issue then is not how we should construct the field, although this is of continuing interest. It is more that the shifting locations and subjects of anthropology can no longer be contained within a single model of long-term participant observation. This problem is all the more pressing when one realizes that even classical ethnography was remarkably ineffable as a methodological practice. As Stocking (1992:14) has observed, "an epistemological ideology of cultural immersion justifies a methodological practice that at some point becomes a matter of sink or swim." This being the case, perhaps we should stop writing of ethnography as if it were a single, unambiguous methodology.

One of the consequences of regarding a particular form of fieldwork as metonymic for anthropology is the sense of professional failure sometimes experienced by those unable to meet an often unattainable ideal. There were many practical challenges that arose from studying a nebulous cultural phenomenon, but what I found most vexing was my inability to reconcile my experience of the field with expectations of what comprises good or real ethnography (and thus anthropology). When forced to rely for my research on consumer commodities and e-mail rather than participant observation and long-term residence I felt inauthentic, fraudulent. Without a clear guide as to what quality of data is appropriate for multi-sited fieldwork, and with the touchstones of the ethnographic method absent from my field, I was unsure if I was sinking or swimming. Ultimately these tensions were productive in that they made me think more about *why* I could not find a representative island of the New Age. In this sense both the fieldwork itself and its many failures were vital to the project. Nonetheless, I often wished I had chosen another topic.

Elevating the method of participant observation to "totemic status" (Morton 1999:252) also has implications for the type of anthropological knowledge that is produced. Despite endless discussions about the way the field is constructed (e.g., Gupta & Ferguson 1997a; Amit 2000a), relatively few anthropologists publicly question the practice of fieldwork itself. Nor do many publish their field failures: mentions of the messiness and incoherence of field notes, and the frustrations and failures of fieldwork, are commonly suppressed in seamless accounts of somewhere, and someone, else.

If anthropology is to take advantage of—rather than taking offense at—the common interests and methodologies of sociology and cultural studies, we need to reassess the many ways cultural landscapes can be charted. This should include a more realistic description of the relationship between complex and open-ended social life and the production of ethnographic data and theory. Such discussions might even imagine an anthropology that does not rely so heavily on participant observation for the study of cultural processes. If fieldwork cannot be truthfully described as a single methodology, and if it provides no guarantee of a better study, then perhaps its status as the defining feature of anthropology is of questionable value. Certainly I would have felt greater confidence as a researcher had I not been preoccupied by the search for ethnographic situations that would approximate those I had read about—less for the sake of a good study than to ensure I was validated as a "real" anthropologist.

Notes

1. Corsino 1987 is a rare example of a fieldworker honestly describing the effects of his personal relationships on his study's efficacy.
2. "Thick description," the elucidation of all possible meanings of a social behavior beyond the merely phenomenological (Geertz 1973), has become emblematic of the ethnographer's task.
3. The common anthropological tendency to conflate "fieldwork," "ethnography," and "participant observation" suggests that "real" fieldwork necessarily consists of participant observation.
4. For the sake of convenience I use the term "New Age" to describe a range of alternative therapies and spiritual practices; however, few people identify with this tag or fit easily into a coherent "New Age" category.
5. Medium- to long-term fieldwork remains the norm for the most recent generation of anthropologists. Jolly & Jamieson (2001:14) report that sixty-four percent of their sample of doctoral candidates in Australian universities had completed, or expected to complete, between thirteen and thirty-one months in the field. A further twenty-two percent planned to spend at least a year in the field. Similarly, the American Anthropological Association's 1997 survey of Ph.D. candidates found an average field time of twelve to thirty months (http://www.aasnet.org/surveys/97survey.htm).
6. Stocking's (1992) comparison of Malinowski, the archetypal fieldworker, to the Greek hero Jason is suggestive of the heroic status of the fieldworker and the mythologizing of fieldwork.
7. Colleagues have often asked what Aboriginal "community" or New Age "group" I was working/living with.
8. Romantic depictions of indigeneity exist alongside negative or ambivalent representations of Aboriginal people; however, there is no space here for comment on the contradictory dynamics of aversion and longing in the Australian imaginary (see Gelder & Jacobs 1998).
9. Morgan's book (1994) recounts an American woman's trip across the Western Desert with a tribe of previously unknown Aboriginal people whom she calls "the real people." The "real people" purportedly asked Morgan to transmit their message of wisdom to the world. Although Morgan's book was a bestseller, many Aboriginal and academic critics branded it an exploitative fiction (e.g., Griffith 1996). A Western Australian Aboriginal corporation, Dumbartung, also mounted a worldwide campaign to halt the book's publication (Dumbartung Aboriginal Corporation1995).
10. Heelas (1996:38, note 1) estimates, for example, that only five to ten per cent of "New Agers" are members of any New Age organization.
11. The dream-catcher has become a ubiquitous symbol of the New Age and is modeled on an indigenous North American tradition. It consists of a regular web woven around a circular frame and is usually decorated with strips of leather and feathers, among other things. According to popular understanding, dream-catchers are designed to hang above the bed, from where

they are said to channel good dreams and trap or deflect negative ones. Many people with New Age interests also use them for decoration and personal adornment.

12. This is potentially a problem for any multisited ethnography but was a particular issue in the study of commercial events. A ten-day spiritual tour of Central Australia was comparable to the cost of doing conventional fieldwork for several months (around AUS$2500–$3000). To some members of funding committees, my participation in a commercial tour group seemed like an expensive university-funded holiday.

13. There were usually opportunities for conversation after workshops, but these interviews rarely led to long-term "rapport" with informants.

14. This was also a problem for several of my colleagues, who were amused or bemused by workshops with New Age titles like "Spiritual Unity of the Tribes" or "Aboriginal Philosophy Week." Many critics of the "appropriation" of Aboriginality also promote a discourse of disapproval rather than the balanced analysis of this distinct cultural phenomenon (e.g., Marcus 1991; Griffith 1996; Grossman & Cuthbert 1998).

15. Many social researchers I know believe that intermingled personal and professional relationships are inevitable and therefore largely irrelevant as an ethical issue. Others have been deeply perturbed by feelings of "spying."

CHAPTER 15

Multi-sited Transnational Ethnography and the Shifting Construction of Fieldwork

In this essay, I explore issues of anthropological practice in the increasingly deterritorialized social reality of the late-capitalist world, in which a fieldworker must negotiate her way between the limits of ethnographic method and transnational spaces. As Akhil Gupta and James Ferguson (1997b) outline, the disciplinary origin of anthropology as a "field science" has led to much of its theoretical and methodological development being centered around the assumption of a well-defined physical site as the appropriate focus for ethnographic fieldwork. Rapid globalization has disrupted this and other associated fundamental assumptions. Increased mobility in the late twentieth century made it difficult to find what were traditionally thought of as suitable locations for ethnographic fieldwork. Current social conditions also require anthropologists to view geographic mobility, transcultural contact, and fluid identities as an integral part of human experience, and to question any naive notions of cultural authenticity and static identity (Appadurai 1990; Hannerz 1996; Clifford 1997a; Ong 1997).

My research on the homemaking practices of Japanese housewives in the United States involves an attempt to look at domestic space as the intersection of the global and the local, and also to examine the implications of corporate-driven transnational mobility on the wives of Japanese businessmen. *Kaigai chuuzai*, an assignment, or the state of being assigned, to a remote, overseas post, has become a significant experience for employees at all levels of Japanese corporations with international business interests (Hamada 1992). As these corporations steadily increased their direct investment in the United States between the late 1970s and the 1990s, the *kaigai chuuzai* of experienced Japanese workers and managers facilitated the transplanting of production know-how and ensured the high efficiency of their U.S. operations. The transnational migration of corporate Japanese is thus an integral part of the globalizing Japanese economy and its progressively decentralized mode of operation in the global market. At the same time, the ideology of Japaneseness and corporate solidarity may be threatened by the direct encounter with foreign "others." Therefore, transnational Japanese corporations face a dilemma: they need workers who are international enough to function well in a foreign environment, but not so cosmopolitan that they lose their steadfast loyalty to their companies and their country of origin.

Japanese women's domestic labor becomes a key to managing the contradictory requirements of a globalizing economy and the maintenance of Japanese cultural identity. Outside the physical boundary of the nation and away from well-established institutions of corporate socialization, "Japanese" domestic spaces become the primary location of identity-maintenance for expatriate Japanese workers. Middle-class Japanese women are responsible, as wives and mothers, for the construction of "home" and for cultural reproduction within this domestic space (e.g., Lebra 1984; Imamura 1987; Iwao 1993). Transnational Japanese corporations take advantage of this ideology of feminine domesticity as a means of ensuring the productivity of their expatriate workers. In fact, many Japanese employers require that the wives of their expatriate workers accompany their husbands to their foreign stations, and urge them to fulfill their "female duties" by creating a restful "Japanese" home abroad. At the same time, my research has shown that women also reflect on and renegotiate their own femaleness and Japaneseness as a result of their transnational experience.

In his discussion of multi-sited ethnography, George Marcus (1995) analyzes the productivity of multi-sited fieldwork, and encourages anthropologists to test the limits of ethnographic method by moving beyond the reified notions of the "global" versus the "local" and producing an ethnography "in and of the world system," or an ethnography of a cultural formation in the world system that also leads to the understanding of the system itself. He suggests several ways of structuring multisited fieldwork that involve the following: 1) the movement of people; 2) the circulation of material objects—commodities, gifts, money, works of art, and intellectual property; 3) the circulation of signs, symbols, and metaphors; 4) the plot, story, or allegory; 5) the life history or biography of a specific person or a group of people; 6) the conflict; and 7) the strategically situated (single-site) ethnography that focuses on the interaction between the local subjects and the world system (1995:106–111).

All these research strategies have two things in common. First, they follow the transnational flows of people, things, activities, and events that are configured by the forces of global capitalism to reveal something critical about the workings of the system itself. Second, they are based on the awareness that the workings of the system are visible "in the everyday consciousness and actions of subjects' lives," and reject the assumption that "local knowledge" is constructed merely in a single, geographically bounded site (Marcus 1995:111–112).

My ethnographic project, best characterized as a string of strategically situated single-site ethnographies that loosely follow the movement of Japanese capital in the United States and focus on a particular occupational class, takes Marcus' lead by assuming that local knowledge is constructed in multiple sites. Japan's transnational capitalism has led to varied interests in the United States over time, and I anticipated that the associated demand for women's domestic management may have undergone parallel changes. In order to test this hypothesis I found it necessary to conduct field research in more than one expatriate Japanese community. As a result, I selected three U.S. cities with distinctive expatriate communities: a Midwestern city that I call Centerville (a pseudonym), the greater New York area, and North Carolina "Research Triangle," the area between Raleigh, Durham, and Chapel Hill that is targeted by the state for technology-intensive economic development. My primary informants were married Japanese women who accompanied their husbands on their corporate job assignments in these cities. I interviewed more than one hundred of these Japanese women, and worked closely with several key informants and their circles of friends in three research sites.

Despite rising interest in alternative ethnographic methods that respond to the changing circumstances of our fieldwork, many ethnographers who undertake research in nonconventional sites continue to experience the tension that comes with disregarding deeply internalized disciplinary norms. As James Clifford (1997a: 58) notes, for example, anthropological fieldwork continues to be "seen as a spatial practice of intensive dwelling"; the unconventional ethnographer may also feel driven to create the alibi of exoticism and distance in her field study in order to conform to older conventions. My multisited ethnographic fieldwork in the United States defies the anthropological construction of "places" as a site of academic investigation. It required methodological modifications, which in turn had consequences for the kind of data that I was able to gather. The proximity of my own cultural background to that of my informants also made it necessary for us to negotiate our working relationships in different ways to the dominant trope of anthropologist–other. Finally, questions also arose regarding my own ambivalence toward the "nontraditional" aspects of my fieldwork and my desire for professional credibility.

Pragmatic Concerns

Whether we follow the flow of people, goods, information, or capital, multisited research multiplies the logistical difficulties of any ethnographic fieldwork. As all experienced fieldworkers know, setting oneself up in a new research location costs much money, time, and energy. When an ethnographer starts fieldwork, she has to have a place to live and work, a means of transportation, and enough knowledge to get around. She also has to get to know key people in the social groups of interest and develop rapport with them. In addition, some fieldwork situations may require extensive negotiations with local authorities to obtain research permission. Sometimes navigating through complex political divisions or learning multiple languages or dialects is essential for fieldwork. With much multisited fieldwork, all this has to be done several times over.

Multisited fieldwork can be extremely expensive, and financing it, particularly if one has to maintain two residences (one in the "field" and one "at home"), is potentially very difficult. The fact that I needed a substantial amount of funding to do my multisited research in the United States immediately cut down the number of available grants. To make matters worse, I found few funding sources for which I was eligible to apply. Many funding sources for anthropologists were not available to me, partly because my research location was in the United States and partly because I was not a U.S. citizen. I found that many research grants were intended for "area studies" and required a geographical "fix" (e.g., studying the "Japanese" in Japan) that effectively excluded transnational research like my own. In the end, I found only two funding sources that would even consider funding a non–U.S. citizen to undertake multisited fieldwork for a doctorate in a U.S. institution.

The familiarity of my fieldsites comes first among the reasons why my research diverged from more conventional definitions of the "field." I wanted to work in middle-class American suburbs, on the streets of New York City, and in corporate offices, all of which lack the exoticism of locations more "typical" for anthropological studies. My own anxiety about doing fieldwork in familiar middle-class America, long excluded as an appropriate site for anthropological research, made the start-up phases of multisited fieldwork particularly painful. In any field situation, we struggle in the first few months to get the project going in an unfamiliar place, without knowing where we are going, whom we are meeting, what we are getting into. In a distant, exotic place, though, we have the assurance that everything we do—from asking for a direction to the village chief's house, to negotiating prices at a local market—is a legitimate part of fieldwork.

In my own case, it seemed that all I did in the first few weeks in two field-sites was to make phone calls and to go shopping (to set up my field office and residence)! The problem of this "telephone and shop" phase was that none of the things I was doing appeared to be proper field activities. I also felt an immense psychological pressure to get my supposedly "easy" field project in American suburbia going in the shortest possible time.

While the physical location of my field research was middle-class America, the groups of people with whom I worked were not of those places. Rather, my respondents were expatriate Japanese who resided temporarily in the United States and whose social and cultural lives crossed borders daily. This "misalignment" between the people with whom I worked and the places in which I worked appears to have had a surprisingly jarring effect on the traditional construction of the anthropological field (Gupta & Ferguson 1997a). I continue to feel this sense of misalignment whenever I am asked to identify the geographical "area" of my research. Although I worked in U.S. cities, my research was centered in a particular ethnoscape (Appadurai 1991) within those cities. It was not designed to produce knowledge about "American" cities from the point of view of local players. My expatriate Japanese informants are part of a "tribe" that is outside its natural habitat, a situation that challenges several taken-for-granted anthropological assumptions. One anonymous reviewer of an article I submitted for publication went so far as to state that to document Japanese behavior in an unfamiliar place "will not be a good way to study Japanese culture." While this critique entirely misses the point of conducting transnational multisited research, it also demonstrates the anthropological tendency to look for a perfect match between geography and culture.

Fluid Communities

Expatriate Japanese all over the United States form local social groups of a sort, with tight social networks, certain shared beliefs, and a degree of collective consciousness. People temporarily join these communities of transnational displacement until they return to Japan or move on to another foreign assignment. Thus, they are communities "in transit," lacking both the stability over time and the definable physical and social boundaries of a village community (see Malkki 1997; Passaro 1997). Expatriate Japanese communities in the United States are elusive communities without a "center"—either in the form of a "village plaza," where one can go to meet everybody, or in the form of a visible community organization. The closest things to community centers are the Japanese grocery stores, where Japanese wives shop for specialty food items and rent Japanese videos almost every day.

The expatriate corporate workers I met, and their families, often seemed to be less interested in building relationships in their temporary homes abroad than in maintaining their social ties back home in Japan. It is perhaps related to this "transient" mentality that, as some of my informants pointed out, relatively little community-building took place beyond a circle of friends and colleagues with whom they form a series of closed cliques. Expatriate community organizations do exist, yet these are either too exclusive (e.g., members-only social clubs, or the parents' association, which expatriates without school-age children could not join) or too business-oriented (aimed at male corporate employees) to become gravitational centers for the expatriate community at large. Religious or political institutions, which might have been important "centers" in other diasporic and immigrant communities, had very small memberships among expatriate corporate Japanese, and thus played only very limited roles.

Expatriate Japanese communities also lacked designated "village elders" to whom an anthropologist could attach herself. Each community had "important people," such as high-ranking executives and their wives or long-term residents whose social status "officially" allowed them a certain amount of influence over a segment of expatriate communities, but in reality, the hierarchical relationships between these individuals and other members of the expatriate community were ambiguous and subject to contestation. The constant movement of people in and out of any given expatriate community also made it difficult for key individuals to develop or exercise control over its social relations across an extended period of time.

My "field" was placeless, also because the social networks of Japanese corporate wives were usually not geographically determined. Expatriate Japanese in the United States tend to live in upper-middle-class suburbs around large cities, and although there were identifiable areas where these families were concentrated in the cities I worked in, the density of households was too low to create a sense of community in most neighborhoods. The car-centered nature of American suburban life also contributed to a lack of neighborliness, as people drove in and out of their garages without many opportunities to casually interact with their neighbors. In addition, Japanese wives tended to build their friendship networks on more personal criteria than physical proximity: in their minds, the match between two people's ages, family compositions, interests, tastes, and lifestyles was of utmost importance in selecting friends (cf. Motoyama 1995). When I asked my informants how they met other Japanese wives, a few common answers emerged: at the English classes or hobby practices, through common friends, or at their children's school. Even when expatriate wives became friendly with their neighbors, their initial encounter tended to occur away from their homes. Once I managed to "locate" my potential informants, and tap into their social networks, I had to come to terms with the spatial and temporal ephemerality of my field.

At the homes of my research participants, surrounded by ceaseless Japanese chattering and the imported Japanese videos running in the background, I used to get caught in a strange sensation of not quite knowing where I was. The place—an indistinct-looking house in a middle-class American suburb—and the scene—an afternoon gathering of Japanese mothers and assorted children—clashed and collided. The disparity between the place and the space became even more visible when I went out with my informants to public places, like a shopping mall. It was as though we were moving around, contained in a bubble of our own atmosphere in a deep sea, with strange creatures swimming around us, completely incompatible and incommunicative with our kind.

Temporality

It was not only space but also time which structured and punctuated my informants' lives: my "field" vanished daily at 6 P.M. sharp. The house where we were gathering had to be turned over to another function, for the tired husband of our hostess would soon return home, expecting a hot meal and a restful evening. It was like one of those dramatic scene changes in *kabuki* theater, in which a whole set turns upside down and disappears into the basement, to make way for the new set that emerges out of the bottom of the stage. In fifteen minutes or less, all the traces of the daytime gathering were gone, children's toys and books put away, dirty coffee cups washed, the cost of lunch and afternoon sweets squared away, the mothers and children in their cars and on their way home. Until the next lunch date, or another trip to the mall, my "field" dissipated into thin air. I thought often of a Japanese proverb, *youchi asagake*, or "strike by night, run in the morning," or in this case, *hiruuchi yuugake* (strike by noon, run in the evening).

I wondered whether these "hit-and-run" encounters constituted "real fieldwork." As a soon-to-be professional academic, I also feared that I would gain less academic capital without the alibi of coresidence and cultural immersion (Gupta & Ferguson 1997a; Marcus 1998). Being a transnational multisited fieldworker thus meant for me the constant questioning of my own fieldwork choice, anxiety over the question of authority (Clifford 1983), and self-doubt about the validity of the knowledge that this form of fieldwork was going to produce.

Networking

Japanese expatriate communities around the United States are close-knit, meaning that "everyone knows everyone else's business," as many of my informants would put it. Members of these communities are very cautious, even skeptical, of outsiders, and entry usually requires some sort of introduction by an already-recognized member (not unlike gaining membership to a prestigious country club). The study populations in my three research locations were independent of one another, which meant that I had to develop new research networks in each location through a lengthy and often stressful process.

New York was the hardest place to get my fieldwork going. I had no local lead to begin with, and when I arrived in my fieldsite and began to call every expatriate Japanese organization I could think of, I found them to be extremely challenging to work with. Many of them had an official front person—a public relations manager, for example—whose job is to screen and guard against unwanted outsiders penetrating their organization. I was often politely but decisively brushed off, referred to other organizations, denied information, and even discouraged from doing my research altogether. It was partly the "big city" mentality that got in my way, but it also reminded me of living in Japan, where personal introduction is everything.

The only organization that was open to my research was *Nihonjinkai*, a grass-roots group of Japanese Americans in and around New York that also included some expatriate Japanese members. Although I met a few Japanese corporate wives through *Nihonjinkai*, I was still unable to enter this exclusive expatriate Japanese community. This in itself is an interesting commentary on the relationship between the expatriate corporate Japanese and Japanese-American community. There was marked tension, for example, in and around *Nihonjinkai*, which was started by Japanese immigrants who settled around New York before World War II and had been organized by their descendants and more recently arrived immigrants. However, since the 1980s, the growing number and public status of expatriate corporate Japanese began to overshadow the Japanese-American community so that some members of *Nihonjinkai* expressed concern that the organization would be "taken over" by the corporate Japanese. This tension also reveals different attitudes among expatriate corporate Japanese and Japanese Americans toward "outsiders." To expatriate corporate Japanese, I, a graduate student from a U.S. university with no known ties to the Japanese corporate world, was a suspicious outsider, while the community of Japanese Americans and more recent immigrants accepted me with little resistance.

In the end, the answer was back home. Realizing that the great majority of expatriate Japanese in New York came from the Tokyo headquarters of their respective companies, I decided that I needed to work my way in from the other side of the Pacific Ocean. My only "business" contact in Tokyo was, unfortunately, my father, who had worked in the corporate world for more than forty years and had an extensive professional network. I say "unfortunately" not simply because of the "professional-personal" boundary issues: I was aware that accepting his assistance would draw me into a web of obligation-driven relationships, worst of all, with the very man whose obliging and imposing ways I had, for a long time, shied away from. My anxieties were later realized, when my father gave me a number of tasks on behalf of those individuals who had helped me get connected in New York. These included attending a dinner my father set up with some of those contacts, gathering and translating college application material for one of their daughters, and offering to be a tour guide. As the Japanese saying goes, "there is nothing more expensive than a free gift."

Aside from my ambivalence about incurring social obligation, this strategy was amazingly effective. A few days after I talked with my father about finding contacts in the New York area, he faxed me a list of five individuals—all expatriate managers of major Japanese corporations—who were "more than happy" to help me with my research "in any way possible." Two of them called me before I even had the chance to call them, offering their assistance and asking for the details of my research needs. This incident also gave me an insight into the "Tokyo-centered" worldview of expatriate Japanese workers, who were physically here in the United States, but psychologically "always facing Tokyo," as one of my informants put it. Some of the informants I got to know through this network were high-ranking managers of prominent U.S. subsidiaries who were unlikely to give time to research that did not promise any immediate benefits to their businesses. Although I eventually developed my own local network, I would not have been able to gain access to these informants without the "Tokyo" connection.

Partial Knowledge?

Field research among mobile and fluid transnational populations is an operation in "scenes" and "spaces"—rather than "sites" or "places"—that exist only as they are "practiced by people's active occupation, their movements through and around [them]" (Clifford 1997a:54). When one's informants themselves are constantly negotiating their social spaces and traversing multiple scenes, the more traditional method of intensive coresidence is often impossible or ineffective. In this field of operation, the ethnographer's mode of existence also becomes transient, as she travels around and slips in and out of her "field" along with her informants. In response to such changed conditions Clifford (1997a:55–58) offers "deep hanging out" as an alternative method to traditional "dwelling." This approach enables the ethnographer to share certain aspects, segments, or scenes of her informants' hybrid lives in socially defined time and space. While ethnographic knowledge has always been "partial," the question still remains as to whether this alternative method produces knowledge of people's lives that is as thick and as intimate as what comes from traditional participant observation.

Recognizing the worldliness of contemporary Japanese, their global consciousness, and their participation in transnational capitalism, I knew that it would be duplicitous to view or represent them as some kind of culturally unique, homogeneous group. Living with an expatriate Japanese family was also not a feasible option. Nuclear families, the living arrangement of most of my expatriate informants, are private sanctuaries in Japanese culture, closed to intrusions by "outsiders," except on some special occasions. Housing a stranger without appropriate social or professional connection was almost unheard of in contemporary middle-class households (see, for example, Kondo 1990; Rosenberger 1994). There was no financial incentive to expatriate Japanese families in subletting out a room, either, since their housing was subsidized by their employers.

It struck me one day that, in fact, the way I "knew" my informants was no different than the way they "knew" each other. The thought was prompted by a comment that I overheard one day in Kawagoe-san's living room. One of her friends remarked to another that she had never seen the other woman's home, although they had grown very friendly with each other at Kawagoe-san's. The members of this group of Japanese women were good friends and shared a lot of time together during the week. But at the end of the day they each went home, their associations not always reaching into their individual domiciles. If the relationships among my research subjects were themselves fluid and temporary, then it would be artificial and arbitrary to create a coresidency situation for the sake of anthropological tradition. Although the nature of ethnographic data gathered under these fleeting situations is in some ways different from what I might have been able to learn in a more conventional field-work setting, it is representative of the domain I was working in.

No fieldworker is able to "know" her informants' lives in their totality. Even if we manage to move in with an informant's family and follow them around day in and day out, we are, to paraphrase Clifford Geertz, always listening in on a conversation that started before we arrived and that will continue after we have left. I am aware that, by not spending twenty-four hours a day with my informants (if such an approach is, or ever has been, possible), I missed the opportunity to directly observe their interactions at home and to gain knowledge of private family matters that would not be discussed outside the home. My data on expatriate Japanese family life primarily came from the verbal accounts of Japanese wives, particularly from a dozen key informants. The few occasions where I observed family inter-action were in public places, on social occasions, or in prearranged visits to their homes. This would have been problematic if my ultimate research goal was to generate a composite picture of expatriate family life, but, given my research questions, which were centered on the subjective expe-riences and views of corporate wives and the relationships among the women, the nature of my interactions proved most appropriate.

I felt that other sources of information, such as interviews and casual conversations with husbands, comments from mental health profession-als, published materials, and the few direct observations I was able to make, provided sufficient points of cross-reference. Perhaps my Japanese origin had more advantages in this particular fieldwork setting than in some others, because my data collection depended so much on "talking" with my informants, on understanding subtle verbal nuance and nonver-bal signals. And, although I do not wish to pose as an all-knowing native anthropologist, I often sensed that my female gender and Japaneseness had something to do with the sincerity and candidness of my Japanese informants. Many female informants seemed to find it more comfortable, for example, to speak to another Japanese woman than to a foreign and/or male investigator. Middle-aged informants with grown-up chil-dren often took fatherly/motherly interests in my success in the United States. In fact, I was often overwhelmed by the weight of stories I heard, as my informants expressed profound feelings and poured out memories of very significant events in their lives.

Being a "free agent," without a residential affiliation to any particular family, also had its advantages. As in any fieldwork situation, the complicated *ningen kankei* (human relationships) of expatriate communities may have meant that having a strong affiliation with a certain household could have limited my social mobility as a researcher. People would be more cautious and selective about what they could or could not tell me; some people may have even declined to talk to me at all, if they did not get along with my hosts. At the same time, I would have been obligated to respect my host family's social status, and would have had to refrain from contacting people with whom they did not feel comfortable. My neutrality was also important to those informants who had strong concerns regarding confidentiality. They knew full well that once a story got into an expatriate rumor mill, there was no knowing where it might end up (see Mori & Saike 1997). For this reason, my informants often found it easier to speak candidly to an unattached anthropologist than to their friends within the expatriate community.

The connection that I managed to establish and maintain with many of my female informants was not the natural outcome of our affinity as "Japanese women," but the result of constant negotiation and reflection. It was certainly convenient that I spoke Japanese fluently and was familiar with cultural idioms, and being a woman did make it easier for me to "fit in" to what were primarily homosocial situations. However, my Japaneseness and femaleness were less than unambiguous, as my informants and I found out, and we had to work out our differences and similarities through the course of my fieldwork. When a female "Japanese" anthropologist is beginning fieldwork among Japanese housewives, she has as much work to do as any other anthropologist, in order to negotiate and establish good working relationships with her informants (Narayan 1993). In some ways, the process may sound easier for the reasons I have just discussed; but in other ways it was also quite complicated, often for the very same reasons.

Locating Myself

When I started my fieldwork in Centerville, I had the hardest time making my potential informants understand that it was an important part of my fieldwork to "play" (or *asobu*) with them. I used to hang out at Kawagoe-san's house, spending long afternoons "playing" with Japanese wives and their children. Kawagoe-san and her friends understood that I was a graduate student, and that I was staying in Centerville for several months for my field research. They also understood that I was interested in them as "study subjects," and that I wanted eventually to interview them about their experiences in the United States. But the concept of "participant observation" or "informal interaction" seemed to completely escape them. In the beginning, when I showed up at Kawagoe-san's place for an afternoon of sitting around and talking, they'd ask politely, "How is your study going, Sawa-san? You are getting away from your work to join us this afternoon?" I tried, in vain, to explain that it was part of my "work" to be there. But in my informants' minds, Kawagoe-san's home was a realm of "play," so it did not make much sense to say that I was there to "work."

A couple of months after I started visiting Kawagoe-san and her friends, they began to talk about how funny it was that I could actually be "working," while I was doing nothing but "playing" with them. Then, one of the women exclaimed, "Ah, I understand, Sawa-san is an *asobinin*!" An *asobinin* means literally a person who plays, or a loafer without recognizable and honest means of making a living. They may be gamblers, "wise guys," or someone rich enough to not need a job. The livelihood of an *asobinin* is play, instead of work. *Asobinin*'s marginality also serves as a symbol of resistance against social norms and restrictions, slipping in and out of two social milieus. Thus, the reference to *asobinin* made two moves of signification in one stroke, identifying me as someone who played professionally, and also as someone who defied Japanese social conventions in her professional play.

The *asobinin* discussion summarized the differences these corporate wives perceived between myself, "playing" as I worked toward my professional qualification, and their own lives, which are closely tied to domestic concerns, even in their play. These differences had to be verbalized, in part, because of our similarities, because I was simultaneously like them and unlike them. My physical appearance was one example. For anthropologists who conduct field research among phenotypically distant others, "going native" may be an alluring prospect, a wild fantasy of fieldwork. Similarity in physical appearance may, in contrast, prove threatening to the anthropologist's self. Dorinne Kondo, a Japanese-American anthropologist who is physically indistinguishable from the Japanese among whom she worked, struggled with the sense of blurred self–other boundaries during her fieldwork in Tokyo (Kondo 1990). My field situation has some similarities with Kondo's experience, in the sense that I, too, could look like a "Japanese wife." However, the similarities between myself and my informants went a little deeper than our skin color.

My habitus was also very similar to that of the Japanese corporate wives I worked with. Having grown up in the 1960s through 1980s in upwardly mobile middle-class Japanese families, many of us were given similar choices, and accepted the same definitions of happiness and accomplishment. In other words, we did share something close to Geertz's notion (1973) of "culture" as a system of meanings and worldviews. Indeed, while growing up in Japan I firmly believed that I was going to be a housewife and a mother. I carried a vague image of a husband who worked for a corporation or a government office, and understood that my chances of living overseas would come through the man I would eventually marry. The divergences between my life trajectory and those of my informants occurred only in young adulthood. When our paths crossed in a foreign city, and chance occurrences put us in the same room at the same time, we found our similarities and differences hard to reconcile. My concern was never about becoming one of them but of being reminded that I had no place in their world, because I had turned away from it by moving to America and choosing an academic career.

My "loafer" identity certainly had a pragmatic advantage in my fieldwork situation. It signified that I had a lot of free time and nothing important to do—which was essentially how these women perceived their own lives. Eventually my corporate-wife informants became convinced that it was no imposition to call me up at any time of the day and night, to gossip, to ask me out, or to ask favors of me, all of which dramatically increased my opportunities to "hang out" with them in different settings. More important, the negotiated identity of ethnographer as "loafer" led to a mutually eye-opening relationship, contesting and rewriting the formula of the anthropologist and her cultural "other." In subsequent encounters with these women our conversation often centered on our differences and our reflections on how those differences were produced. We were able to be playful with our differences. For instance, they would tell newcomers to the group that I claimed to "study them," yet what I really did was just hang out with them; or, in reverse, I seemed to be "playing," but actually I was cunningly studying their behavior. Such exchanges resulted in moments of profound reflection, unspoken yearning, and recognition of the possibilities for transformation.

Conclusion

I have outlined above the process of doing multisited ethnographic fieldwork with transnationally mobile groups of middle-class Japanese. In choosing my fieldsite, I consciously selected a particular social, rather than geographic, space located at the intersection of transnational capitalism and cultural identity, a space in which the "global" is localized and the "local" is globalized. In the process, I discovered that anthropology's traditional preoccupation with fieldwork in faraway places continues to have a powerful grip on how fieldwork practices are framed and on how professional credibility is attributed. The lack of resources available for multisited fieldwork in the United States, unexpected logistical complications, and questions about the validity of relatively novel ethnographic practices all combined to make my fieldsite an "awkward space."

However, this awkward space ultimately turned out to be an incredibly rich source of interaction, in which my informants and I negotiated our understandings of transient lives in an increasingly globalized world. George Marcus contends that multisited ethnography "in and of the world system" requires the ethnographer to situate herself within that system, instead of speaking "from above or 'nowhere' " (Marcus 1995:112). It certainly felt awkward to work against the traditional construction of the field. But, at the same time, I managed to locate myself in the most productive place for my work and my self to become part of my informants' knowledge of the world, while I learned from theirs.

CHAPTER 16

Multi-sited Methodologies

"Homework" in Australia, Fiji, and Kiribati

As a master's degree student at the Center for Pacific Islands Studies at the University of Hawai'i (UH), I was driven by one central purpose—to decolonize Banaban history.[1] This meant, among other things, letting Banaban voices speak (mine most loudly), and critiquing every piece of writing on Banaban history or culture produced by white scholars. I believed that the role of the "native" in the academy was to centralize cultural identity and to personalize and politicize our scholarship (cf. T. Teaiwa 1995; Trask 1999). My experiences as a doctoral student at The Australian National University (ANU) complicated that idea, committing me to a somewhat different approach to, and motive for, knowledge production.

This chapter is about the process and results of multisited "homework" undertaken in Fiji, Australia, and Kiribati between 1999 and 2002.[2] Kamala Visweswaran (1994) has described "homework" as a critique of the centrality that fieldwork holds for the discipline of anthropology. Clifford (1997b:85) suggests that Visweswaran's reflections, rather than standing in opposition to exoticist fieldwork, offer "a critical confrontation with the invisible processes of learning . . . that shape us as subjects . . . [placing an emphasis on the] discipline of unlearning as much as of learning." The result of my movements among multiple research sites was the displacement of the conventional single-site anthropological paradigm and the unlearning of anthropological *and* indigenous authority. As I detail below, homework, rather than fieldwork, thus became a more appropriate frame for my research project.

I was investigating the impact of phosphate mining on the indigenous people of Banaba in the Republic of Kiribati, or what Europeans called Ocean Island. This island was the home of my paternal great-grandfather,

Tenamo, and his mother, Kieuea. In order to secure unfettered access to the rich phosphate island, the British government, working with the British Phosphate Commission, relocated the entire Banaban population to Rabi Island in Fiji in 1945. Banaban identity—and by extension, rights to land on Banaba or Rabi—is identified by two main criteria: Banaban blood and participation in Banaban social and cultural life. It also assumes a proficiency in the Kiribati language (see Silverman 1971). Unlike my father, I have not spent a significant portion of time within Banaban communities, but my sisters and I recognize Banaba as our ancestral home.

My potential as "native anthropologist" (see Narayan 1993) made for awkward positioning both in the academy and "at home in the field." In the academic context I imagined myself between, or perhaps beyond, traditional anthropologists who maintained the appropriate distance between themselves and their "subjects," and other native anthropologists, many of whom were from Indonesia or Papua New Guinea, who spoke their own languages, and were, at least on the surface, comfortable with an objective approach to their research topics. The influence of my University of Hawai'i education compounded this lack of fit. The ANU provides an excellent research environment, but I sensed a general suspicion of personalized approaches to knowledge production and minimal attention to the politics of representation in both its anthropology departments.[3] This environment was very different from the highly politicized UH campus, where the indigenously run Center for Hawaiian Studies is a formidable presence.[4]

In the Banaban context I was what Dorinne Kondo (1990) called a conceptual anomaly—a Banaban woman with solid Banaban roots (my father was then the Chairman of the Rabi Council of Leaders), who nevertheless could not speak the language (most Banabans speak the Kiribati language with an accent) and who had access to overseas education. Aside from the obvious relevance to my ancestral homeland, "homework" became not so much a play on words or a tool to critique anthropological fieldwork traditions, but a deeply troubling experience of navigating contexts in which I was neither insider nor outsider. I was both, or somewhere in between, and my lack of proficiency or grounding in either anthropology or Banaban culture often made for a temporary sense of "homelessness."[5] I was constantly learning and unlearning what it meant to be a good Banaban and a good anthropologist, and I usually felt like I failed at both.[6] While homework provided one theoretical approach, I needed to find something else to further displace the authority and narrow subjectivities implied by the title "Banaban anthropologist."

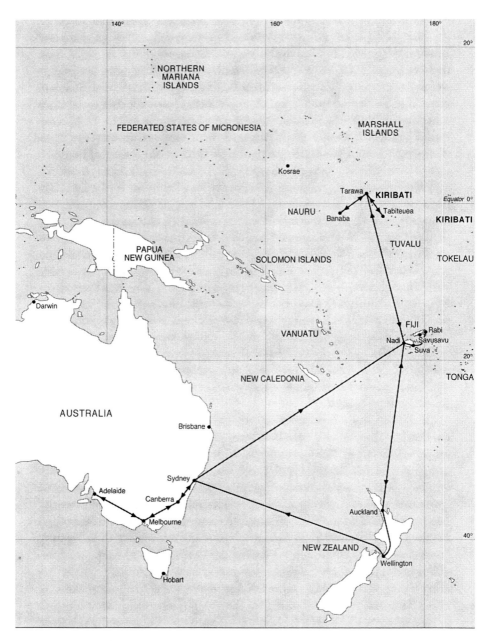

Figure 16.1 The research itinerary.

Melbourne and Canberra: Visualizing the Past

One day in early August 1999 I sat in a very quiet, very clean, white booth in the Lonsdale Street office of the Melbourne holdings of the National Archives of Australia (NAA). In front of me were the contents of file R140/1 Box 7 from the vast records of the British Phosphate Commission (BPC). I was looking at shipping records for the movement of phosphate rock from Banaba to Australia and New Zealand over a period of eighty years beginning in 1900. Memos, charts, and objective-looking figures covered the surface of my clean white desk.

Between 1900 and 1980, almost 20 million tons of phosphate were shipped from Banaba to Australia, New Zealand, England, Japan, and a few other locations in the Pacific and Europe. This material was extracted from a 2.5-square-mile island inhabited by about five hundred indigenous Banabans. My initial research proposal was to explore the impact of mining and the displacement of people on culture and politics. The Banabans were fond of using the phrase *e kawa te aba*, "pity the land / the people," to reflect upon both history and contemporary struggles on Rabi.[7] Banaban pity was a response to colonial exploitation, and to those nonindigenous peoples in Australia, New Zealand, and Britain whom Banabans perceived were growing rich off their phosphate. The initial focus of my thesis was on unequal relations between Banabans and "Europeans" (white people), or, in Kiribati, *I-Matang*.

This focus shifted dramatically when I was in the Melbourne offices of the NAA. What the diary entries, memos, charts, and figures in the archives revealed were the many lives, materials, and lands transformed by this massive mining industry. Banaba was a hub of the Pacific region, characterized by some of the most advanced mining and shipping technology in the region, and a well-provisioned town for the Australian, New Zealand, and British company employees. The typed, meticulously logged correspondence between these employees, BPC, and government offices in Melbourne, Sydney, Auckland, and London was largely concerned with removing the indigenous Banabans and securing land for mining. But it also provided an insight into the lives of the diverse group of white employees. This was the same archive used by Maslyn Williams and Barrie Macdonald (1985) to construct a celebratory history of the BPC, a history that marginalized most of the indigenous or Asian characters. The popular decolonization approach to such histories is to restore or write in the indigenous voice or experience. This was not exactly the approach I ended up taking.

In the latter part of that August I spent time in the East Burwood office of the NAA, where all of the company's photographs are kept.[8] I stared long and hard at the images of Gilbertese (now I-Kiribati) and Ellice Island (now Tuvaluan) workers on Banaba mining the rocks by hand, and at the pinnacle-ridden moonscape they left behind them. I noted the smart-looking white managers in snow-white suits and the dark-skinned "kanaka" and "coolie" (Chinese and Japanese) laborers working without protective head or footgear.[9] Next, I examined the never-ending images of ships with names like SS Ariake Maru, SS Port Denison, and SS Cromarty, and the prides of the BPC, the Triona, Triaster, Trienza, and Tri-Ellis.[10] All these ships radiated out from the island I had heard invoked by my own relatives in Fiji as the "homeland"; and all carried pieces of the island away with them.

With the permission of the NAA, and the help of professional photographer Mark Willie Chung, I rephotographed 380 of the BPC images. I returned from the archival trip to Melbourne with carefully indexed notes on both the documents and the photographs, research which set me up well for the historical section of my Ph.D. thesis. However, the very extensive but fragmented nature of both types of record, juxtaposed with my growing awareness of the movement of all kinds of bodies and materials that had been engaged in the mining industry, problematized my original goal to simply decolonize Banaban history. The trip to the Archives had made it impossible for me to ignore the complexity of the mining industry. My research was no longer just about Banabans or colonialism or an exploitative mining company. It was increasingly about the connections and differences between lands and peoples and the very specific, palpable oceanic spaces between them.

On my return from Melbourne I met with my supervisor, Professor Margaret Jolly. I spread the photographs I had copied from the archives across her office table—images of rocks, cantilevers, grab and skip mechanisms, hoppers, workers with no hard-hats and no shoes deep in the mine, of white women in flowery flowing dresses, of smiling children playing on the beach, of the moon rising past the reef at Home Bay, of numerous one-ton phosphate trucks, rows of Chinese and Japanese workers at dinner, white wooden mansions, bicycles, tea chests, and pianos.[11] Jolly reflected for a moment before saying, "You need to see Gary Kildea in the ethnographic film unit. Your project is visual!"[12]

Thanks to Margaret Jolly's intuitive directions I began to split my time between the anthropology department and the ethnographic film unit. I thus found myself divided between two rather different approaches to knowledge production, and the demands of simultaneously producing a thesis in text—constructing ideas in words—and on digital film—constructing ideas in images.

Figure 16.2 (*Top left*) Workers in an open mine on Banaba, early 1900s.

Figure 16.3 (*Top right*) Public notice on Banaba in Gilbertese, Tuvaluan (Ellice Islands), Japanese, and English, early 1900s.

Figure 16.4 (*Bottom*) "How the whites travel on Banaba," early 1900s.

The digital video camera that I used during fieldwork was the first of its kind bought for students in the ethnographic film unit. It was worth about $3,000AUS at the time, and I imagined every moment that I spent on a canoe or boat that it would fling itself into the ocean just to cause me extra anguish. On my departure from Canberra I signed a newly created release form saying that I, not the department, would pay for anything that happened to this camera. Over the next year it became an extension of my right arm.

Between Tabiteuea and Rabi: Reflections on Video

In March 2000, in the village of Tanaeang, on Tabiteuea *Meang* (north), in the southern part of Kiribati, I sat with three *uniwmane* (old men) and one male interpreter in a sleeping house with no walls. I was armed with one microphone, one digital video camera on a baby tripod, and a list of questions in both Kiribati and English. I asked: "What was it like to work in the phosphate mines on Banaba? Did anyone ever get sick or die? What kinds of interactions did the British colonials, Australian and New Zealand managers, Tuvaluan, Kiribati, Japanese, or Chinese workers have with each other? Were there any indigenous people on the island? Did you all get along?"

The three men, Temokou, Booti, and Enere, sat to my far right, front, and left, and as we talked I lifted and pointed the camera in each direction with one hand while juggling pen and microphone with the other. They mostly answered with short, brief statements. The bright light pouring in through all four sides of the wall-less *umwa ni matu* framed each man in the camera, turning them into black blobs in a white sea. I was so grateful that they had agreed to talk to me as a group that I left everything as it was. But I gazed longingly at the numerous pandanus mats folded neatly on one side of the raised floor and thought about how to turn one of them into a hanging wall to improve exposure.

In the meantime the men talked among themselves and with my interpreter, Temakau. They were mainly curious about who I was, where I came from, how old I was, and why I was not married. I had come to Tabiteuea to find out about Banaba and neglected the fact that it would very much matter to these people that my paternal grandparents, Takeua and Teaiwa, were Tabiteuean.[13] My efforts to gather information about Banaba were frequently confounded by what turned out to be my incredibly close relations to a large number of families across Tabiteuea *meang*. My duty was not to go around interviewing people but to be a guest in the

Figure 16.5   Author, Banaba, 2000. Photo: author

homes of close relatives. This was a role I grew to resent, as it seemed to interfere with my research agenda. For budgetary reasons I could spend only nine weeks in Kiribati, and I wanted to devote most of this to my Banaba topic.

People on most islands loved the video camera and used it as a source of entertainment. Adults and children alike would play to the camera eye and in between these amusements I filmed the ocean, the ground, the sky, the coconut tree, the cat snoozing, the airplane landing, the kids playing, the people dancing, the women washing clothes, and the men fishing. The most interesting footage I shot was obtained when I was completely unaware that I was studying or learning anything, when I held the camera steady and simply let things happen around me, sometimes following the action and sometimes letting it tumble in and out of the frame.

Video is a phenomenon that has reached even the most remote part of Kiribati. On Tabiteuea people would hire a portable generator and video monitor so I could use the digital camera as a playback machine and they could review my tapes. Dozens would gather in and around a sleeping house, to watch their own footage, footage from neighboring villages, or footage from distant islands. People in Kiribati especially wanted to see Rabi in Fiji, a place where many of their kin now reside.

Figure 16.6   A friend, Nei Aom, on the outrigger of a motor canoe between Tabiteuea north and south. Photo: author

Kiribati is a country of coral atolls where the land is no more than a few feet above sea level. The landscape is dominated by coconut trees, blinding white, sandy roads and beaches, and the blue ocean as far as the eye can see in *all* directions. "In-land" is a very short distance on any island in Kiribati. By contrast, Rabi is a volcanic island with a modest mountain and a much wider variety of plant and animal life. It is dominated by deep green flora, rich reddish-brown soil, and a view of the deep sea on one side and the large island of Vanua Levu on the other.

The videos I showed in Kiribati seemed to temporarily traverse these different locations divided by distances that most Banabans and I-Kiribati had never physically traveled. But while few travel between the islands, they remain deeply connected, economically, culturally, and genealogically. Throughout Kiribati compact discs, tapes, and videos are the new desired commodities. After I had finish showing my videos of Rabi, and everyone had marveled at just how different and similar those Rabi people were, my hosts would plug in a VCR and run the generator until the fuel ran out watching movies like *Delta Force Five, American Ninja,* and *Rambo.*[14]

I have relatives in many parts of Tabiteuea and the capital of Kiribati,

Figure 16.7   Author's cousin, Temanarara, fishing off the coast of Rabi Island. Photo: author

Tarawa. South Tarawa is the site of rapid urban migration and is densely populated. Some of my relatives live in tiny crowded houses with tin roofing, three-foot high corrugated-iron walls, and no water, toilet, or bath facilities. In these dwellings, I have seen Japanese video monitors, video decks, and stereo equipment.[15] There is also a Kiribati Film Unit in Bairiki, which promotes Kiribati culture, education, and health issues through its video productions.

On Rabi, where the electricity supply is limited and the economy dominated by subsistence activities, my uncle recently purchased a video deck and monitor. Until the video arrived leisure activities usually consisted of volleyball, card games, singing, dancing, and consuming *kava* (*piper methysticum*) or "grog" over a long nightly session that included much storytelling. In early 2003 a cyclone ravaged Rabi, destroying most of the houses in two of four villages and all the trees and food crops on the island. Thankfully no one was injured despite the cyclone's force, and a number of popular stories have emerged from the event. The most popular one is that while some members of our family had wisely taken shelter in my father's sturdy house, many stayed in my uncle's far less sturdy house to watch videos until the last second before the howling cyclone blew the roof away. Then everyone climbed through windows and ran for shelter.

These anecdotes hardly encompass the dynamics of life on Tabiteuea, Tarawa, or Rabi, but I share them to juxtapose very different islands connected by both the phosphate mining industry and my own genealogy and to highlight the growing dominance of video in these communities. In Kiribati and on Rabi I have seen the pages of books of all kinds used to roll tobacco, as toilet paper, and as fuel for fire: reading is not a natural pastime, even for school students. By contrast, video (in addition to sports, song, and dance) is an increasingly important form of entertainment and source of knowledge.

I have always been critical of writing as the primary medium of knowledge production in the social sciences and humanities. I believe that if the academy is to have a meaningful relationship with people in the rest of the world, urgent attention to audience and the forms of communication that those audiences best engage with, or are influenced by, is needed (cf. Appadurai 2000; Hereniko 1994, 2003; and Fernandez 2001). We have to learn how to *produce* knowledge in the same forms we encounter it, and to share the results with communities in effective ways (see Smith 1999). Otherwise we are merely being parasitic of indigenous knowledges. Thus I felt compelled not just to use the video camera as a recording device, as a substitute for a tape recorder, for example, but to eventually use it more creatively to make short films that Banabans and I-Kiribati themselves could engage with and participate in.

Discovering Montage and Feminist Ethnography

When I returned to Canberra with fifty hours of raw video footage and one little field notebook (measuring 6 by 4 inches) to add to my 380 photographs of Banaba and four newly acquired archival films of mining on Banaba in the 1930s and 1950s, the task of putting together a "whole" picture of Banaban history and culture, in "words" no less, was both daunting and ridiculous. My archival research had highlighted multiple lives, events, places, and moments in the history of phosphate mining in the Pacific, and my fieldwork, or homework, had personalized and brought to life communities shaped by that mining. All of these had been engaged in a highly visual mode, either through photographs, films, or digital video. This was not the kind of data I could simply "write up." In the rest of this essay, I will describe the process of sorting through such material; of how I came to acknowledge the experience as "homework," to present my research as "montage," [16] and to pay better attention to the relationships between multiple spaces, places, and peoples.

After returning from the field, every anthropology student at the ANU is required to give a "post-fieldwork paper." This, along with the "pre-fieldwork paper," marks the journey from student to "anthropologist." Under pressure to produce such a paper, I went to the library to do another kind of homework. The first thing I read that helped to shape my task was Donna Haraway"s "Situated Knowledges" (1988). In particular, her critique of "the god trick," the "seeing of everything from nowhere," and "a [distancing of] the knowing subject from everything and everybody in the interests of unfettered power" (581), gave me a means of positioning myself, my relatives, and all the places to which I had traveled within a specific *relational* configuration. I quickly got over anxieties about whole pictures and objective narrative strategies after accepting her version of "feminist objectivity," a call for accountable, limited, and situated knowledges (579). Haraway's piece also introduced me to the fact that the process of decolonization has been part of an ongoing agenda in feminist research for decades.

Next, I read Kirin Narayan's "How Native is a Native Anthropologist?" (1997), her collection on folk narrative, *Storytellers, Saints, and Scoundrels* (1989), and Dorrine Kondo's *Crafting Selves* (1990). Between Narayan and Kondo I reflected on experience and narrative as "theory," the use of the first person, and the multiple subjectivities that traveling anthropologists enact in between their "home" countries/fieldsites. While Kondo's and Narayan's subjectivities were mainly shaped along the two-sided Asian-American border, I came to realize that mine—between my African American mother and Tabiteuean and Banaban father, both of whom live in Suva, Fiji—straddled at least four islands and two continents. This "identity" map became a kind of template for organizing my research spatially as history and culture in and between connected places.

After I presented my "post-fieldwork paper" I began to focus on organizing my digital video footage into some kind of visual narrative. This involved the time-consuming process of logging and marking useful frames. The first thing I looked for in the videos was records of conversations that I could translate and transcribe to use as direct quotes in my text. On Tabiteuea, where I tried to do most of my interviews, the camera had dominated my research method. Similar to Visweswaran's (1994) experiences in Madras, my desire to capture the men's experiences on video eclipsed any possible attention to the cultural and gender dynamics of such a meeting in the first place. I did not even consider the possibility that the old men may have found the exercise of talking about their mining experiences as a group, to a young woman of both Tabiteuean and

Banaban descent who could not speak Kiribati and who had a fancy camera and a list of formal questions, slightly bizarre.

In between accounts of rocks falling on their fellow miners, of playing cricket against the Australian managers, of the wonder of living on an island with electricity and a film projector in the 1950s, they would ask each other or my interpreter the following kinds of questions: "How old is she?" "How many children does she have?" "How come she doesn't speak Kiribati?" "Why didn't her father teach her?" And they would make statements like: "She is too young to become a 'doctor' (but old enough to have five children)," and shake their heads in veiled admiration, confusion, and pity. I could not wait to escape such situations. I started to resent my father for not speaking to me in his native language. In this situation being both a so-called insider *and* outsider to the culture in question directly problematized the anthropological premise of getting to "know" another culture. Anthropologists, I-Kiribati, and Banabans all expected me to already *know* (something).

I have witnessed and participated in enough story-telling moments on Rabi and within Kiribati communities in Suva to know that the lack of spontaneity in the Tabiteuea situation was not a fault of the men but of my own assumptions about how to effectively capture information. The best stories are never planned. In her reflections on the failure of feminist ethnography, Visweswaran does much more than identify ethnographic failure as a reason to do better next time (1994:97). Instead she points to a fundamental problem of epistemology in both feminist and ethnographic representational strategies. "Failure," she suggests, calls into question the whole research agenda. Visweswaran writes,

> A failed account, I argue, occasions new kinds of positionings. Yet, a "failed" account resting on claims to totalizing explanation . . . gives way to partial accounts, which in turn "fail" for new reasons . . . If the response to a partial account is inevitably the demand for a fuller one, to refuse such a desire is immediately to jeopardize one's status as ethnographer. (1994:100)

In many ways I did view my fieldwork as a "failure." My visits in each place were short, I only recorded slices of each place and all on digital video, I did not become proficient in the Kiribati language, and I emerged still skeptical of the conventional anthropological paradigm. I was not compelled to become either a Banaba or Kiribati "authority" and take my place as a "Micronesianist" among the "Melanesianists" and "Polynesianists."

Visweswaran's chapter reminded me that the humanist project to know a culture on its own terms and render those terms responsibly is a power-laden exercise, but also that ethnography does not have to be a master narrative. What she interprets as "deconstructive ethnography," a deferral, a refusal to explain, where no shared audience is assumed, appeals greatly to me as it enacts useful strategies for a complex decolonization agenda (Visweswaran 1994:40–59, 78). By not spending much time in one place I was never deluded into thinking I could present a holistic picture of any place. My constant movements created a fragmented image that did not reveal authoritative accounts of people, place, or moments in history.

Once I had accepted that my thesis was not going to be a "total explanation" of a Pacific history or culture, I returned to the visual material. The video camera became a vehicle for resolving ethnographic "failure" by coming up with a new form for my Ph.D. thesis. When approached critically, the "excess of meaning" (Macdougall 1998:68) in a photograph or film frame problematizes the idea of a single and definite "truth." But the task must not stop at this relativistic assumption. If one's fieldwork material consists of numerous still and moving images across three islands, then one has to figure out how to edit or arrange it in ways that highlight the aesthetic, political, and cultural dimensions of lived human experiences in multiple and connected locations. Here, an attempt at "deconstructive ethnography" is fruitfully assisted by the technique of montage.

It was at this point that I discovered two important pieces by George Marcus. The first was "Ethnography in/of the World System" (1995), and the second, "The Modernist Sensibility in Recent Ethnographic Writing and the Cinematic Metaphor of Montage" (1994). Marcus' survey of modes for constructing multisited ethnography includes following the people, the thing, the metaphor, the plot, story, or allegory, the life or biography, or the conflict. As another alternative he suggests embedding the single site in a multisited context (1998:90–95). I had organized my research itinerary along most of these lines with the understanding that in a Banaban epistemology the people, the land, the conflict over phosphate, the lives of individual Banabans, and the dramas of everyday life were inextricably connected. "Good" research usually isolates one or two of these aspects to explore in depth; however, with a research itinerary that allowed me no more than several weeks in each site, this approach was impossible.

Marcus' reflections on montage and the experimental move in ethnographic writing helped me to find a way of dealing with the highly partial perspectives of each place that I had recorded on digital video. While this identification of the *current* experimental moment seemed to ignore much earlier experiments in anthropology by women like Zora Neale Hurston and Ella Deloria (see Behar & Gordon 1995), the identification and pairing of montage and ethnography was helpful for me. It allowed for a fracturing of ethnography—normally conducted over a longer period of time in a single setting—into smaller, shorter frames from multiple settings and moments in time. Authority over one setting or group of subjects was thus dissipated by a constant allusion to other settings and subjects. Marcus (1994:43–44) defined approaches to experimental ethnography as including the problematization of spatiality, temporality, and perspective or voice, the replacement of exegesis with the dialogic appropriation of narrative devices, the establishment of a connection between observer and observed, and the use of critical juxtapositions.

In cinema, critical juxtapositions are the guiding principles for montage. We see this approach today in everything from television advertising and music videos to Hollywood films. Meaning is created in the spaces *between* frames; associations are made possible between nice cars and beautiful, happy young people, for example, by superimposing or placing the two images side by side. I wanted to be able to use the same technique to associate images from, and by default histories of, Tabiteuea, Tarawa, Banaba, Rabi, Australia, and New Zealand. The result was a 100,000 word–thesis along with a ninety-minute DVD containing seven short films edited with Gary Kildea (K. Teaiwa 2002). All the islands and cities in my thesis were directly connected to my own history and that of my ancestors, thereby expanding my definition of "homeland."

For Kamala Visweswaran, homework means speaking from the place one really is located, not just a physical place but a subject position that accounts for power, class, race, sexuality, gender, and culture. "Speaking from a place where one is not, where location and locution are tightly bound by a distant imaginary, is, of course, the normative practice of anthropology" (Visweswaran 1994:104). For myself, "home" is both current location and lived connection, so to speak from one's location requires multisited locution; a location is not necessarily a singular point but rather a place between specific points. If one's identity includes "Pacific Islander" then it must be articulated with multiple and specific, connected Pacific places. In the pedagogical sense homework as a guiding principle also implies that knowledge is never fixed, that there is always a need to explore further, to accept the learning process as it unfolds and to never declare it at an end.

As a result of my homework journey I have a new understanding of the idea of home and a belief that individuals, peoples, lands, objects, histories, and cultures are productively engaged in the spaces and movements within *and* between them. So while Pacific Studies must promote an agenda that empowers Pacific peoples, it must also be an approach that conceives of Pacific peoples as specific, different, and connected individuals or groups. It has to conceive of Pacific peoples and places with respect to *each other* in the past and present as much as to colonialisms of all kinds. It has to move beyond connections limited to the cultural areas problematically named Micronesia, Melanesia, and Polynesia, for example, to connections and differences (or the production of connections and differences) between and within these areas.[17]

While I started my graduate studies with a narrow, oppositional definition of "decolonization," I emerged at the end of my Ph.D. with a broader, and yet more specific, understanding of this agenda. Learning to focus on the relationships between peoples and places through an attention to visual material in both the past and present was crucial to this understanding. A more effective decolonization has to displace the "us and them" binary, accept multiple methods for knowing the past and each other and multiple forms for knowledge production, and be articulated by multiple positioned subjects. Following Haraway's (1988) arguments for partiality and accountability, decolonization lies in resisting authority while staying accountable. Far from being what Visweswaran critiques as "transcendent transnationalism" (1994:111), an abandoning of the particular, this approach represents a challenge to unproductive nationalisms and a commitment to a liberating Pacific regionalism informed by our similarities and differences.

Notes

1. Pacific Islands Studies is an interdisciplinary program that promotes a regional approach to crosscutting island issues while working toward the empowerment of Pacific people. In some contexts, this takes the form of "decolonization"—unlearning colonial histories and critiquing disempowering representations of the Pacific. Throughout this essay I use the term "decolonize" specifically in the Pacific studies context, where (mainly) indigenous scholars reflect upon or critique colonial, neocolonial, and postcolonial power relations and representations (see Trask 1999; Smith 1999).

2. I also conducted some of the research for this project in New Zealand. See K. Teaiwa (2002) for discussion.

3. This was, perhaps, a consequence of the absence of indigenous Australian scholars.

4. One of my supervisors at UH, for example, was Haunani-Kay Trask, a dynamic Hawaiian activist famous for criticizing anthropologists (see Keesing 1989; Trask 1991; Linnekin 1991). Trask's influence surely contributed to my sense of awkwardness in the anthropological academy.

5. My lack of training or reading in anthropology was most awkward among students and faculty with strong backgrounds in the discipline. Anthropology

became, for me, a temporary location in which to learn and grow as I headed back toward Pacific studies, which I now teach at the University of Hawai'i.

6. At both the ANU and on Rabi and Banaba, I was expected to know certain things and act accordingly. For example, at a seminar on the Trobriand Islands I naively let slip that I did not know who Malinowski was. The chorus of gasps across the room was deafening. At the very least, as a good anthropologist I should have been aware of the Malinowskian tradition and located myself within that genealogy. In the Banaban context I was expected to situate myself within another kind of genealogy and act like a proper daughter, niece, cousin, and young unmarried woman.

7. *Te aba* refers to both the land and the people; the two are not distinct in Banaban epistemology though meaning is shaped by the context of use. For a solid, though dated, investigation into Banaban symbolic culture forged between the islands of Banaba and Rabi, see Silverman (1971).

8. The photographs of the British Phosphate Commission are located at the Victoria headquarters of the National Archives of Australia, Vision Drive, East Burwood, Melbourne in files R132/1, R140/1, R 10, R 32/4, ONX 15A, S6, S58, and R 125.

9. *Kanaka* was a widely used term for "native" derived from the Hawaiian word. It indexed not just native race but hard labor. The Melanesians who became part of the Queensland labor trade were also called *kanaka*. "Coolie" was a derogatory expression for Asians used throughout the British Empire.

10. The Tri-Ellis was named after New Zealander Albert Ellis, the man who discovered phosphate on Banaba in 1900 and spent the rest of his life securing lands for mining and protecting the agricultural interests of New Zealand.

11. All the archival photographs are from the BPC collection, courtesy of the National Archives of Australia, Burwood office, Melbourne.

12. Gary Kildea is a filmmaker, whose works include *Trobriand Cricket* (1976), *Celso and Cora* (1983), and *Man of Strings* (1999). He runs the ethnographic film unit attached to the Research School of Pacific and Asian Studies at the ANU, assists with various RSPAS film projects, and provides technical support for students.

13. Teaiwa was both Tabiteuean and Banaban, although he did not really discover his Banaban roots until he was recruited to work in the mines on the island. His Banaban relatives then recognized him, and he soon became part of the indigenous community.

14. Kiribati has a strictly regulated video industry managed by the Ministry of Women and Social Welfare and the Police Department. While living with my cousin Aren, a senior administrator in the ministry, I was able to observe what kinds of videos were entering the country. They were mostly action, comedy, fantasy, suspense, and science fiction, and all were in English.

15. Televisions and stereos enter Kiribati not so much through retail outlets but via the flow of goods supplied by the large number of I-Kiribati men who

work on ships overseas. These sailors, or *kaimoa*, facilitate the influx of everything from money and clothing to music, electronic goods, hand tools, AIDS, and venereal diseases.

16. I used montage in my thesis to describe the critical juxtaposition of frames, specific bodies, and places across time and space. It is a technique often used in film by which meaning emerges out of juxtaposition. See, for example, Eisenstein (nd) comparison of montage and mise-en-scène.

17. This is not an original idea. It has been variously detailed or engaged by Wendt (1976), Waddell, Hau'ofa & Naidu (1993), Hau'ofa (1993, 1998), Gupta & Ferguson (1997b), T. Teaiwa (1998, 2001a, 2001b, 2002), Diaz & Kauanui (2001), Subramani (2001), Clifford (1997a), and Jolly (2001).

REFERENCES

Abram, David. 1996. *The Spell of the Sensuous: Perception and Language in a More-Than-Human World*. New York: Vintage Books.

Abu-Lughod, L. 1990. "The Romance of Resistance: Tracing Transformations of Power Through Bedouin Women." *American Ethnologist* 17.1:41–55.

———. 1991. "Writing Against Culture." In Richard G. Fox, ed., *Recapturing Anthropology: Working in the Present*, 137–162. Santa Fe, NM: School of American Research Press.

Adams, Timothy D. 1990. *Telling Lies in Modern American Autobiography*. Chapel Hill: University of North Carolina Press.

Adler, P. 1990. "Ethnographic Research on Hidden Populations: Penetrating the Drug World." In Elizabeth Lambert, ed., *The Collection and Interpretation of Data from Hidden Populations*. NIDA Research Monograph Series 98. Rockville: NIDA.

Agar, Michael. 1980. *The Professional Stranger: An Informal Introduction to Ethnography*. New York: Academic Press.

Agency for Toxic Substances and Disease Registry. 2003. "Carbon Tetrachloride." http://www.atsdr.cdc.gov/tfacts30.html.

American Anthropological Association. 1997. *Survey of Anthropology Ph.D.s.* http://www.aaanet.org/surveys/97survey.html.

———. 1998. *Code of Ethics*. http://www.aaanet.org/committees/ethics/ethcode.htm.

Amit, V., ed. 2000a. *Constructing the Field: Ethnographic Fieldwork in the Contemporary World*. London: Routledge.

———. 2000b. "Introduction: Constructing the Field." In Amit 2000a:1–18.

Anderson, Gary L. 1989. "Critical Ethnography in Education: Origins, Current Status, and New Directions." *Review of Educational Research* 59.3:249–270.

Appadurai, Arjun. 1990. "Disjuncture and Difference in the Global Cultural Economy." *Public Culture* 2.2:1–24.

———. 1991. "Global Ethnoscapes: Notes and Queries." In Richard G. Fox, ed., *Recapturing Anthropology: Working in the Present*. Santa Fe, NM: School of American Research Press, 191–210.

———. 1996. *Modernity at Large: Cultural Dimensions of Globalization*. Minneapolis: University of Minnesota Press.

———. 2000. "Grassroots Globalization and the Research Imagination." *Public Culture* 12.1:1–19.

Appell, G. N. 1978. *Ethical Dilemmas in Anthropological Inquiry: A Case Book*. Waltham, MA: Crossroads Press.

Archivo Municipal de Tuxtla Gutiérrez, Expediente Zona Galáctica. Centro de Informacíon y Análisis de Chiapas (CIACH), Coordinación de Organismos No Gubermentales Por La Paz (CONPAZ), y Servicios Informativos Procesados. 1997. Para Entender Chiapas: Chiapas en Cifras. Mexico City: CIACH, CONPAZ, SIPRO.

Asad, Talal. 1986. "The Concept of Cultural Translation in British Social Anthropology." In Clifford and Marcus 1986:141–164.

Ashkenazi, M., and F. Markowitz. 1999. "Sexuality and Prevarication in the Praxis of Anthropology." In F. Markowitz and M. Ashkenazi, eds., *Sex, Sexuality, and the Anthropologist*, 1–21. Urbana: University of Illinois Press.

Atkinson, P., A. Coffey, S. Delamont, J. Lofland, and L. Lofland, eds. 2001. *Handbook of Ethnography*. California: Sage Publications.

Auge, M. 1995. *Non-Places: Introduction to an Anthropology of Supermodernity*. Trans. J. Howe. London: Verso.

Austin-Broos, D. 1998. "Falling Through the 'Savage Slot': Postcolonial Critique and the Ethnographic Task." *Australian Journal of Anthropology* 9:295–309.

Australian Bureau of Statistics. 1997. *Aspects of Literacy*. Canberra: ABS.

Backett, K. C. 1982. *Mothers and Fathers*. New York: St. Martin's.

Barlow, Cleve. 1991. *Tikanga Whakaaro: Key Concepts in Maori Culture*. Auckland: Oxford University Press.

Bauman, Z. 1992. *The Intimations of Postmodernity*. London: Routledge.

Beckerleg, S. 1995. "Heroin Inside-Out." *Anthropology in Action* 2.2:9–11.

———. Forthcoming. "How Cool Is Heroin Injection at the Kenya Coast?" *Drugs: Education, Prevention, and Policy*.

Behar, Ruth. 1994. "Dare We Say 'I'? Bringing the Personal Into Scholarship." *Chronicle of Higher Education* (pull-out section), June 29, 1994, section 2, B1–B2.

———. 1995. "Writing in My Father's Name: The Diary of *Translated Woman*'s First Year." In Behar and Gordon 1995:65–82.

———. 1996. *The Vulnerable Observed: Anthropology That Breaks Your Heart*. Boston: Beacon Press.

Behar, Ruth, and Deborah Gordon, eds. 1995. *Women Writing Culture*. Berkeley: University of California Press.

Beit-Hallahmi, Benjamin. 2001. " 'O Truant Muse': Collaborationism and Research Integrity." In Benjamin Zablocki and Tom Robbins, eds., *Misunderstanding Cults*. Toronto: University of Toronto Press.

Benmayor, R., and A. Skotnes. 1994. *Migration and Identity*. International Yearbook of Oral History and Life Stories vol. 3. Oxford: Oxford University Press.

Berreman, Gerald D. 1973. "The Social Responsibility of the Anthropologist." In T. Weaver, ed., *To See Ourselves: Anthropology and Modern Social Issues*, 8–9. Glenview, IL: Scott, Foresman, and Company.

———. 1991. "Ethics Versus 'Realism' in Anthropology." In C. Fluehr-Lobban, ed., *Ethics and the Profession of Anthropology*, 36–71. Philadelphia: University of Pennsylvania Press.

Best, Steven, and Douglas Kellner. 1991. *Postmodern Theory: Critical Interrogations*. London: Macmillan.

Biolsi, Thomas, and Larry Zimmerman, eds. 1997. *Indians and Anthropologists*. Tucson: University of Arizona Press.

Birckhead, Jim. 1976. *Toward the Creation of a Community of Saints*. Ph.D. dissertation, University of Alberta.

———. 1993. " 'Bizarre Snakehandlers': Popular Media and a Southern Stereotype." In Karl G. Heider, ed., *Images of the South: Constructing a Regional Culture on Film and Video*, 163–189. Athens: University of Georgia Press.

———. 1997. "Reading 'Snake Handling': Critical Reflections." In Stephen D. Glazier, ed., *Anthropology of Religion: A Handbook*, 19–84. Westport, CT: Greenwood.

———. 1999. "Brief Encounters: Doing 'Rapid Ethnography' in Aboriginal Australia." In Sandy Toussaint and Jim Taylor, eds., *Applied Anthropology in Australasia*, 195–228. Nedlands: University of Western Australia Press.

———. 2002. " 'There's Power in the Blood': Writing Serpent Handling as Everyday Life." In Spickard, Landres, and McGuire 2002:134–145.

Blain, Jenny. 2002. *Nine Worlds of Seid-Magic: Ecstasy and Neo-Shamanism in North European Paganism*. London: Routledge.

Blain, Jenny, Doug Ezzy, and Graham Harvey, eds. 2004. *Researching Religious Experiences: Academic Methodologies and Paganism*. New York: AltaMira.

Bloom, Leslie. 1997. " 'Locked in Uneasy Sisterhood': Reflections on Femininst Methodology and Research Relationships." *Anthropology and Education Quarterly* 28.1:111–122.

Bock, Philip K. 1988. *Rethinking Psychological Anthropology: Continuity and Change in the Study of Human Action*. Rev. ed. New York: Freeman.

Bond, Katherine C., David D. Celentano, Sukanya Phonsophakul, and Chayan Vaddhanaphuti. 1997. "Mobility and Migration: Female Commercial Sex Work and the HIV Epidemic in Northern Thailand." In Gilbert Herdt, ed., *Sexual Cultures and Migration in the Era of AIDS: Anthropological and Demographic Perspectives*, 185–215. Oxford: Clarendon Press.

Bons-Storm, Riet. 1984. *Kritisch Bezig Zijn met Pastoraat: Een Verkenning van de Interdisiplinaire Implicaties van de Practische Theologie*s. Gravenhage: Boekencentrum.

Bourdieu, Pierre, and Jean-Claude Passeron. 1977. *Reproduction: In Education, Society, and Culture*. California: Sage Publications.

Bourdieu, Pierre, and L. J. D. Wacquant. 1992. *An Invitation to Reflexive Sociology*. Cambridge: Polity Press.

Bourgois, Philippe. 1996. "Confronting Anthropology, Education, and Inner-City Apartheid." *American Anthropologist* 98.2:249–265.

———. 2002. "Understanding Inner-City Poverty: Resistance and Self-Destruction Under U.S. Apartheid." In Jeremy MacClancy, ed., *Exotic No More: Anthropology on the Front Lines*, 14–32. Chicago: University of Chicago Press.

Bourne, J. 1983. "Towards an Anti-Racist Feminism." *Race and Class* 25.1:1–22.

Bowles, Samuel, and Herbert Gintis. 1976. *Schooling in Capitalist America: Educational Reform and the Contradictions of Economic Life*. New York: Basic Books.

Bowman, M. 1995. "The Noble Savage and the Global Village: Cultural Evolution in New Age and Neo-Pagan Thought." *Journal of Contemporary Religion* 10.2:139–149.

Bradbury, Daniel. 1998. *Being There: The Necessity of Fieldwork*. Washington, D.C.: Smithsonian Institution Press.

Briggs, J. 1970. *Never in Anger: Portrait of an Eskimo Family*. Cambridge, MA: Harvard University Press.

Brookfield, F. M. 1999. *Waitangi and Indigenous Rights: Revolution, Law, and Legitimation*. Auckland: Auckland University Press.

Burbank, V. 1994. *Fighting Women: Anger and Aggression in Aboriginal Australia*. Berkeley: University of California Press.

Cassell, Joan. 1980. "Ethical Principles for Conducting Fieldwork." *American Anthropologist* 82:28-41.

Cassuto L. 1999. "Whose Field Is It, Anyway? Disability Studies in the Academy." *Chronicle of Higher Education* March 19, A60.

Chernela, Janet. 2001. "Piercing Distinctions: Making and Remaking the Social Contract in the North-West Amazon." In L. M. Rival and N. L. Whitehead, eds., *Beyond the Visible and the Material*, 177–195. Oxford: Oxford University Press.

Chödrön, Pema. 1997. *When Things Fall Apart: Heart Advice for Difficult Times*. Boston: Shambala.

Chrisman, N. J. 1976. "Secret Societies and the Ethics of Urban Fieldwork." In Rynkiewich and Spradley 1976, 135–147.

Clifford, James. 1983. "On Ethnographic Authority." *Representations* 1.2:118–146.

————. 1986. "Introduction: Partial Truths." In Clifford and Marcus 1986:1–26.

————. 1988. *The Predicament of Culture: Twentieth-Century Ethnography, Literature, and Art.* Cambridge, MA: Harvard University Press.

————. 1997a. *Routes: Travel and Translation in the Late Twentieth Century.* Cambridge, MA: Harvard University Press.

————. 1997b. "Spatial Practices: Fieldwork, Travel, and the Disciplining of Anthropology." In Gupta and Ferguson 1997a:185–222.

Clifford, James, and George Marcus. 1986. *Writing Culture: The Poetics and Politics of Ethnography.* Berkeley: University of California Press.

Coggeshall, John M. 1991. "Those Who Surrender Are Female: Prisoner Gender Identities as Cultural Mirror." In P. Frese and J. M. Coggeshall, eds., *Transcending Boundaries: Multi-Disciplinary Approaches to the Study of Gender,* 81–96. New York: Bergin and Garvey.

Cohen, A. 1985. *The Symbolic Construction of Community.* London: Routledge.

Cohen, L. 1998. *No Aging in India: Alzheimer's, the Bad Family, and Other Modern Things.* Berkeley: University of California Press.

Connell, Robert W. 1995. "Transformative Labour: Theorizing the Politics of Teachers' Work." In M.Ginsburg, ed., *The Politics of Educators' Work and Lives,* 91–114. New York: Garland.

Conway, Jill K. 1998. *When Memory Speaks: Reflections on Autobiography.* New York: Knopf.

Cook, Nerida, and Peter Jackson. 1999. "Introduction." In Peter A. Jackson and Nerida M. Cook, eds., *Genders and Sexualities in Modern Thailand,* 1–27. Chiang Mai: Silkworm Books.

Corker, M., and J. Davis. Forthcoming. "Shifting Selves, Shifting Meanings, Learning Culture: Towards a Reflexive Dialogics in Disability Research." In D. Kasnitz and R. Shuttleworth, eds., *Engaging Anthropology in Disability Studies.* Westport, CT: Greenwood Press.

Corsino, Louis. 1987. "Fieldworker Blues: Emotional Stress and Research Underinvolvement in Fieldwork settings." *Social Science Journal* 24.3:275–285.

Cox, James. 1998. *Rational Ancestors: Scientific Rationality and African Indigenous Religions.* Cardiff: Cardiff University Press.

Crick, Malcolm. 1993. "Introduction." In Crick and Geddes 1993:3–8.

Crick, M., and B. Geddes, eds. 1993. *Research Methods in the Field: Ten Anthropological Accounts.* Victoria: Deakin University Press.

Dabrowski, Kazimierz. 1967. *Personality-Shaping Through Positive Disintegration.* Boston: Little, Brown.

Damasio, Antonio. 1999. *The Feeling of What Happens: Body and Emotion in the Making of Consciousness.* New York: Harcourt Brace.

D'Andrade, R. 1995. "Moral Models in Anthropology." *Current Anthropology* 36.3:399–408.

Davidson, R. Theodore. 1983. *Chicano Prisoners: The Key to San Quentin*. Prospect Heights, IL: Waveland Press.

Davies, Scott. 1995. "Leaps of Faith: Shifting Currents in Critical Sociology of Education." *American Journal of Sociology* 100.6:1448–1478.

Davis, J. "Disability Studies as Ethnographic Research and Text: Research Strategies and Roles for Promoting Social Change." *Disability and Society* 15.2:191–206.

Deloria, Philip J. 1998. *Playing Indian*. New Haven: Yale University Press.

Deloria, Vine. 1997. "Anthros, Indians, and Planetary Reality." In Biolsi and Zimmerman 1997:209–221.

Devereux, George. 1967. *From Anxiety to Method in the Behavioural Sciences*. The Hague: Mouton.

Devine, John. 1996. *Maximum Security: The Culture of Violence in Inner-City Schools*. Chicago: University of Chicago Press.

Diaz, Vince, and J. Kehaulani Kauanui, eds. 2001. "Native Pacific Cultural Studies on the Edge." *Contemporary Pacific* 13.2:315–491.

Dubisch, Jill. 1995. "Lovers in the Field: Sex, Dominance, and the Female Anthropologist." In Kulick and Wilson 1995:29–50.

Dumbartung Aboriginal Corporation. 1995. *Bounuh Wongee/"Message Stick": A Report on* Mutant Message Down Under. Waterford: Dumbartung Aboriginal Corporation.

Dunlap, Eloise, Sylvie C. Tourigny, and Bruce D. Johnson. 2000. "Dead Tired and Bone Weary: Grandmothers as Caregivers in Drug Affected Inner City Households." *Race and Society* 3.2:143–163.

Eakin, Paul John. 1985. *Fictions in Autobiography: Studies in the Art of Self Invention*. Princeton: Princeton University Press.

Edgerton, Robert. 1968. *The Cloak of Competence: Stigma in the Lives of the Mentally Retarded*. Berkeley: University of California Press.

Edin, Kathryn. 2000. "What Do Low-Income Single Mothers Say About Marriage?" *Social Problems* 47.1:112–133.

Edwards, D. 1994. "Afghanistan, Ethnography, and the New World Order." *Cultural Anthropology* 9.3:345–360.

Eilberg-Schwartz, Howard. 1989. "Witches of the West: Neopaganism and Goddess Worship as Enlightenment Religion." *Journal of Feminist Studies in Religion* 5.1:77–95.

Eisenstein, Serge. N.d. *The Film Sense*. London: Faber and Faber.

Elbaz, Robert. 1987. *The Changing Nature of the Self: A Critical Study of the Autobiographic Discourse*. Iowa City: University of Iowa Press.

Emoff, R., and D. Henderson, eds. 2002. *Mementos, Artifacts, and Hallucinations from the Ethnographers' Tent*. New York: Routledge.

Erickson, K., and D. Stull. 1998. "Doing Team Ethnography: Warnings and Advice." *Qualitative Research Methods Series* 42. Sage University Paper. London: Sage.

Erlich, V. 1966. *Family in Transition: A Study of 300 Yugoslav Villages.* Princeton: Princeton University Press.

Ernst, T. 1990. "Mates, Wives, and Children: Concepts of Relatedness in Australian Culture." *Social Analysis* 27:110–118.

Evans, Mary. 1999. *Missing Persons: The Impossibility of Auto/biography.* London: Routledge.

Evans-Pritchard, E. E. 1976. "Some Reminiscences and Reflections on Fieldwork." Appendix IV in his *Witchcraft, Oracles, and Magic Among the Azande*, 240–254. Oxford: Clarendon Press.

Favret-Saada, J. 1980. *Deadly Words: Witchcraft in the Bocage.* Cambridge: Cambridge University Press.

Federal Court of Australia. 1998. "Guidelines for Expert Witnesses in Proceedings in the Federal Court of Australia." Memo. Sydney: Federal Court of Australia.

Feldman, A. 1991. *Formations of Violence: The Narrative of the Body and Political Terror in Northern Ireland.* Chicago: University of Chicago Press.

Fernandez, James W. 1990. "Tolerance in a Repugnant World, and Other Dilemmas in the Cultural Relativism of Melville J. Herskovits." *Ethos* 18.2:140–164.

Fernandez, Ramona. 2001. *Imagining Literacy: Rhizomes of Knowledge in American Culture and Literacy.* Austin: University of Texas Press.

Fetterman, David. 1983. "Guilty Knowledge, Dirty Hands, and Other Ethical Dilemmas: The Hazards of Contract Research." *Human Organization* 42:214–224.

Finnstrom, S. 2001. "In and Out of Culture: Fieldwork in War-Torn Uganda." *Critique of Anthropology* 21.3:247–258.

Fleisher, Mark. 1989. "Warehousing Violence." *Frontiers of Anthropology*, vol. 3. California: Sage Publications.

Flinn, J. 1998. "Introduction: The Family Dimension in Anthropological Fieldwork." In J. Flinn, L. Marshall, and J. Armstrong, eds., *Fieldwork and Families: Constructing New Models for Ethnographic Research*, 1–21. Honolulu: University of Hawaii Press.

Flood, Gavin. 1999. *Beyond Phenomenology.* London: Cassell.

Fog Olwig, K. 1997. "Cultural Sites: Sustaining a Home in a Deterritorialized World." In Fog Olwig and Hastrup 1997:17–38.

Fog Olwig, Karen, and Kirsten Hastrup, eds. 1997 *Siting Culture: The Shifting Anthropological Subject.* London: Routledge.

Fordham, Signithia. 1996. *Blacked Out: Dilemmas of Race, Identity, and Success at Capital High.* Chicago: University of Chicago Press.

Forsey, Martin. 2000. "The Anthropology of Education: Cultural Critique or Ethnographic Refusal?" *Anthropological Forum* 10.2:201–221.

Forsythe, D. 1993. "The Construction of Work in Artificial Intelligence." *Science, Technology, and Human Values* 18.4:460–479.

Fortier, Anne-Marie. 1996. "Troubles in the Field: The Use of Personal Experiences as Sources of Knowledge." *Critique of Anthropology* 16.3:303–323.

Foucault, Michel. 1980. *Power/Knowledge: Selected Interviews and Other Writings, 1972–1977.* Brighton: Harvester Press.

Frank, G. 2000. *Venus on Wheels: Two Decades of Dialogue on Disability, Biography, and Being Female in America.* Berkeley: University of California Press.

- Friedman Hansen, J. 1976. "The Anthropologist in the Field: Scientist, Friend, and Voyeur." In Rynkiewich and Spradley 1976:123–134.

Fry, C., and R. Dwyer. 2001. "For Love or Money? An Exploratory Study of Why Injecting Drug Users Participate in Research." *Addiction* 96:1319–1325.

Gallup, Alan. 1998. *The House with Golden Eyes.* Running Horse Books.

Ganguly-Scrase, Ruchira. 1993. "The Self as Research Instrument." In Crick and Geddes 1993:37–58.

Geertz, Clifford. 1966. "Religion as a Cultural System." In Michael Banton, ed., *Anthropological Approaches to the Study of Religion,* 1–46. New York: Praeger.

———. 1973a. *The Interpretation of Cultures.* New York: Basic Books.

———. 1973b. "Thick Description: Toward an Interpretive Theory of Culture." In Clifford 1973a:3–30.

Gelder, K., and J. Jacobs. 1998. *Uncanny Australia: Sacredness, Modernity, and Identity in a Postcolonial Nation.* Melbourne: Melbourne University Press.

Gerlach, Luther P., and Virginia H. Hine. 1970. *People, Power, Change: Movements of Social Transformation.* New York: Bobs-Merrill.

Gerrard, Nathan L. 1971. "Churches of the Stationary Poor in Southern Appalachia." In John D. Photiadis and Harry K. Schwarzweller, eds., *Change in Rural Appalachia: Implications for Action Programs,* 99–114. Philadelphia: University of Pennsylvania Press.

Giddens, A. 1992. *The Transformation of Intimacy: Sexuality, Love, and Eroticism in Modern Societies.* Stanford: Stanford University Press.

Gilbert, M. Jean, Nathaniel Tashima, and Claudia C. Fishman. 1991. "Ethics and Practicing Anthropologists' Dialogue with the Larger World: Considerations in the Formulation of Ethical Guidelines for Practicing Anthropologists." In C. Fluehr-Lobban, ed., *Ethics and the Profession of Anthropology,* 198–211. Philadelphia: University of Pennsylvania Press.

Gilmore, David. 1991. "Subjectivity and Subjugation: Fieldwork in the Stratified Community." *Human Organization* 50:215–224.

Goffman, Erving. 1959. *The Presentation of Self in Everyday Life.* Garden City, NY: Anchor.

———. 1961. *Asylums: Essays on the Social Situation of Mental Patients and Other Inmates.* Garden City, NY: Anchor.

———. 1963. *Stigma.* Englewood Cliffs, NJ: Prentice Hall.

Gold, G. 2001. "Searching for the Cure: Virtual Disability and Collective Action in an Electronic Support Group." In L. Rogers and B. Swadener, eds., *Semiotics and Dis/ability: Interrogating Categories of Difference*, 43–54. New York: State University of New York Press.

Golde, Peggy, ed. 1986. *Women in the Field: Anthropological Encounters*. 2nd ed. Berkeley: University of California Press.

Goldstein, P. J., B. J. Spunt, T. Miller, and P. Bellucci. 1990. "Ethnographic Field Stations." In Elizabeth Lambert, ed., *The Collection and Interpretation of Data from Hidden Populations*. NIDA Research Monograph Series 98. Rockville: NIDA.

Goodale, J. 1972. *Tiwi Wives: A Study of the Women of Melville Island, North Australia*. Seattle: University of Washington Press.

Goodman, Jesse. 1998. "Ideology and Critical Research." In J. Smyth and G. Shacklock, eds., *Being Reflexive in Critical Educational and Social Research*, 50–66. London: Falmer Press.

Gow, G. 2002. *Oromo in Exile: From the Horn of Africa to the Suburbs of Australia*. Carlton: Melbourne University Press.

Grace, Patricia. 1987. *Potiki*. London: Women's Press.

Greene, Graham. 1939. *The Lawless Roads*. London: Penguin.

Griffith, G. 1996. "Mixed Up Messages Down Under: The Marlo Morgan 'Hoax': A Textual Travesty of Aboriginal Culture." *Ulitarra* 9:73–85.

Grills, Scott, ed. 1998a. *Doing Ethnographic Research: Fieldwork Settings*. California: Sage Publications.

———. 1998b. "An Invitation to the Field: Fieldwork and the Pragmatist's Lesson." In Grills 1998a:3–18.

Grossman, M., and D. Cuthbert. 1998. "Forgetting Redfern: Aboriginality in the New Age." *Meanjin* 4:770–788.

Gupta, Akhil, and James Ferguson, eds. 1997a. *Anthropological Locations: Boundaries and Grounds of a Field Science*. Berkeley: University of California Press.

———. 1997b. "Discipline and Practice: 'The Field' as Site, Method, and Location in Anthropology." In Gupta and Ferguson 1997a:1–46.

Hakanson, D. 1998. *Oracle of the Dreamtime: Aboriginal Dreamings Offer Guidance for Today*. London: Connections Publishing.

Hamada, Tomoko. 1992. "Under the Silk Banner: The Japanese Company and Its Overseas Managers." In Takie Sugiyama Lebra, ed., *Japanese Social Organization*, 135–164. Honolulu: University of Hawaii Press.

Hammersley, M., and P. Atkinson. 1995. *Ethnography: Principles in Practice*. 2nd ed. London: Routledge.

Handelman, D. 1990. *Models and Mirrors: Towards an Anthropology of Public Events*. Cambridge: Cambridge University Press.

Hannerz, Ulf. 1996. *Transnational Connections*. New York: Routledge.

Haraway, Donna. 1988. "Situated Knowledges: The Science Question in Feminism and the Privilege of Partial Perspective." *Feminist Studies* 14.3:575–599.

————. 1991. *Simians, Cyborgs, and Women: The Reinvention of Nature.* New York: Routledge.

Harrell-Bond, B. 1976. "Studying Elites: Some Special Problems." In Rynkiewich and Spradley 1976:110–122.

Hart, C. W. M., A. R. Pilling, and J. Goodale. 1986. *The Tiwi of North Australia.* 2nd ed. New York: Holt, Rinehart, Winston.

Harvey, Graham. 1996. *The True Israel: Uses of the Names Jew, Hebrew, and Israel in Ancient Jewish and Early Christian Literature.* Leiden: Brill.

————. 1997. *Listening People, Speaking Earth: Contemporary Paganism.* London: Hurst

————. 1999. "Coming Home and Coming Out Pagan but Not Converting." In Christopher Lamb and Darrol Bryant, eds., *Religious Conversion: Contemporary Practices and Controversies,* 233–246. London: Cassell.

————, ed. 2000a. *Indigenous Religions: A Companion.* London: Cassell.

————. 2000b. "Art Works in Aotearo." In Harvey 2000a:155–172.

————, ed. 2003. *Shamanism: A Reader.* London: Routledge.

Hastrup, K. 1992. "Writing Ethnography: State of the Art." In Judith Okely and Helen Callaway, eds., *Anthropology and Autobiography,* 116–133. ASA Monograph 29. London: Routledge.

Hastrup, K., and K. Fog Olwig. 1997. "Introduction." In Fog Olwig and Hastrup 1997:1–14.

Hastrup, Kirsten, and Peter Hervik, eds. 1994a. *Social Experience and Anthropological Knowledge.* London: Routledge.

————. 1994b. "Introduction." In Hastrup and Hervik 1994a:1–12.

Hau'ofa, Epeli.1993. "Our Sea of Islands." *Contemporary Pacific* 5.2:148–160.

————. 1998. "The Ocean in Us." *Contemporary Pacific* 10.2:391–410.

Heelas, P. 1996. *The New Age Movement: The Celebration of Self and the Sacralization of Modernity.* Oxford: Blackwell.

Helliwell, C. 1996. "Space and Sociality in a Dayak Longhouse." In M. Jackson, ed., *Things as They Are,* 128–148. Indianapolis: Indiana University Press.

Henly, Julia R., and Sandra K. Danziger. 1996. "Confronting Welfare Stereotypes: Characteristics of General Assistance Recipients and Postassistance Employment." *Social Work Research* 20.4:210–237.

Henry, Jules. 1964. *Jungle People: A Kaingang Tribe of the Highlands of Brazil.* New York: Vintage Books.

Herdt, G. 1999. "Sexing Anthropology: Rethinking Participant Observation in Sexual Study." In D. Suggs and A. Miracle, eds., *Culture, Biology, and Sexuality.* Athens: University of Georgia Press.

Herskovits, Melville J. 1977. *Cultural Relativism: Perspectives in Cultural Pluralism.* New York: Random House.

Hinson, Glenn. 2000. *Fire in My Bones: Transcendence and the Holy Spirit in African American Gospel.* Philadelphia: University of Pennsylvania Press.

Hobbs, D., and T. May, eds.1993. *Interpreting the Field: Accounts of Ethnography*. Oxford: Oxford University Press.

Hogle, L., and G. Downey. 1999. "Introduction." *Anthropology of Work Review* 20.1:1–5.

Hooper-Greenhill, Eilean. 2000. *Museums and the Interpretation of Visual Culture*. London: Routledge.

Howell, N. 1990. *Surviving Fieldwork: A Report of the Advisory Panel for Health and Safety in Fieldwork*. Washington, D.C.: American Anthropological Association.

Hume, Lynne. 1985. "Making Lengwasa: A Women's Pig-Killing Ritual on Maewo (Aurora) Vanuatu." *Oceania* 55.4:272–287.

———. 1988. "Christianity Full Circle: Aboriginal Christianity on Yarrabah Reserve." In Tony Swain and Deborah Bird Rose, eds., *Aborigiinal Australians and Christian Missions*, 250–262. Adelaide: Australian Association for the Study of Religions.

———. 1997. *Witchcraft and Paganism in Australia*. Melbourne: Melbourne University Press.

———. 2002. *Ancestral Power: The Dreaming, Consciousness, and Aboriginal Australians*. Melbourne: Melbourne University Press.

Hutton, Ronald. 2003. Review of Harvey 2003. *Times Higher Education Supplement* 9 May, 25.

Imamura, Anne. 1987. *Urban Japanese Housewives*. Honolulu: University of Hawaii Press.

Instituto Nacional de Estadistica e Informacion. 1993. Tuxtla Gutiérrez, Estado de Chiapas: Cuaderno Estadistico Municipal. Tuxtla Gutiérrez: INEGI, Gobierno del Estado de Chiapas, H. Ayuntamiento Constitutional de Tuxtla Gutiérrez.

Iwao, Sumiko. 1993. *The Japanese Woman: Traditional Image and Changing Reality*. New York: Free Press.

Jackson, Anthony, ed. 1987. *Anthropology at Home*. ASA Monographs 25. London: Tavistock Publications.

Jackson, Michael. 1995. *At Home in the World*. Sydney: Harper Perennial.

Jacobs, J. B. 1977. *Stateville: The Penitentiary in Mass Society*. Chicago: University of Chicago Press.

James, A., J. Hockey, and A. Dawson. 1997. "Introduction: The Road from Santa Fe." In A. James, J. Hockey, and A.Dawson, eds., *After Writing Culture: Epistemology and Praxis in Contemporary Anthropology*, pp. 1–16. New York: Routledge.

Jolly, Margaret. 2001. "On the Edge? Deserts, Oceans, Islands." *Contemporary Pacific* 13.2:417–467.

Jolly, M., and T. Jamieson. 2001. "Anthropology: Reconfiguring a Janus Face in a Global Epoch." Final draft, for circulation at Australian Anthropological Society Conference, September 27–30, 2001.

Jules-Rosette, Benetta. 1978. "The Veil of Objectivity." *American Anthropologist* 80:549–570.

Kaplan Daniels, Arlene. 1983. "Self-Deception and Self-Discovery in Fieldwork." *Qualitatitve Sociology* 6.3:195–214.

Kasnitz, D., and R. Shuttleworth. 1999. "Engaging Anthropology in Disability Studies." Position Papers in Independent Living and Disability Policy 1.1: May.

———. 2001. "Anthropology and Disability Studies." In L. Rogers and B. Swadener, eds., *Semiotics and Dis/ability: Interrogating Categories of Difference*, 19–41. New York: State University of New York Press.

Keesing, Roger. 1989. "Creating the Past: Custom and Identity in the Contemporary Pacific." *Contemporary Pacific* 1:19–42.

Keyes, Charles. 1984. "Mother or Mistress but Never a Monk: Buddhist Notions of Female Gender in Rural Thailand." *American Ethnologist* 11.2:223–241.

Kidd, Rosalind. 1997. *The Way We Civilize: Aboriginal Affairs—The Untold Story*. St. Lucia: University of Queensland Press.

King, Arden R. 1987. "Anthropologist as Human: The Ultimate Paradox." *Anthropology and Humanism Quarterly* 12.2:47–51.

Kingshill, Konrad. 1991. *Ku Daeng Thirty Years Later: A Village Study in Northern Thailand, 1954–1984*. Dekalb: Northern Illinois University, Center for Southeast Asian Studies.

Kleinman, S., and M. Copp. 1993. "Emotions and Fieldwork." *Qualitative Research Methods* 28. California: Sage Publications.

Knauft, B.1996. *Genealogies for the Present in Cultural Anthropology*. New York: Routledge.

Kondo, Dorinne. 1990. *Crafting Selves: Power, Gender, and Discourses of Identity in a Japanese Workplace*. Chicago: University of Chicago Press.

Krieger, Susan. 1985. "Beyond 'Subjectivity': The Use of the Self in Social Science." *Qualitative Sociology* 8.4:309–324.

Kulick, Don. 1995. "Introduction: The Sexual Life of Anthropologists: Erotic Subjectivity and Ethnographic Work." In Kulick and Wilson 1995:1–28.

Kulick, Don, and Margaret Wilson, eds. 1995. *Taboo: Sex, Identity, and Erotic Subjectivity in Anthropological Fieldwork*. London: Routledge.

Kusserow, Adrie S. 1998. "Holy Ghost People (Scrabble Creek, West Virginia)." *Anthropology and Humanism* 23.2:209–210.

La Barre, Weston. 1962. *They Shall Take Up Serpents: Psychology of the Southern Snake-Handling Cult*. Minneapolis: University of Minnesota Press.

———. 1971. "Materials for a History of Studies of Crisis Cults: A Bibliographic Essay." *Current Anthropology* 12.1:3–44.

Langness, L. L., and Gelya Frank. 1981. *Lives: An Anthropological Approach to Biography*. Novato, CA: Chandler and Sharp.

Lareau, A., and J. Schultz, eds. 1996. *Journeys Through Ethnography: Realistic Accounts of Fieldwork*. Colorado: Westview Press.

Lasch, C. 1984. *The Minimal Self: Psychic Survival in Troubled Times*. New York: Norton.

Lattas, A. 1990. "Aborigines and Contemporary Australian Nationalism: Primordiality and the Cultural Politics of Otherness." *Social Analysis* 27:50–69.

Lavie, S., and T. Swedenburg, eds. 1996. *Displacement, Diaspora, and Geographies of Identity*. Durham, NC: Duke University Press.

Lawlor, R. 1991. *Voices of the First Day: Awakening in the Aboriginal Dreamtime*. Rochester: Inner Traditions International.

Lebra, Takie Sugiyama. 1984. *Japanese Women*. Honolulu: University of Hawaii Press.

Lee, Raymond, M. 1995. *Dangerous Fieldwork*. California: Sage Publications.

Leibowitz, Hubert A. 1989. *Fabricating Lives: Explorations in American Autobiography*. New York: Knopf.

Lemire, Elise. 2002. *"Miscegenation": Making Race in America*. Philadelphia: University of Pennsylvania Press.

Le Vine, S. 1981. "Dreams of the Informant About the Researcher: Some Difficulties Inherent in the Research Relationship." *Ethos* 9.4:276–293.

Levinson, Bradley, and Dorothy Holland. 1996. "The Cultural Production of the Educated Person: An Introduction." In B. Levinson, D. Foley, and D. Holland, eds., *The Cultural Production of the Educated Person: Critical Ethnographies of Schooling and Local Practice*, 1–54. New York: State University of New York Press.

Linnekin, Jocelyn. 1991. "Text Bites and the R Word: The Politics of Representing Scholarship." *Contemporary Pacific* 3:172–177.

Lockley, P. 1995. *Counselling Heroin and Other Drug Users*. London: Free Association Books.

Luhrmann, Tanya M. 1989. *Persuasions of the Witch's Craft: Ritual Magic in Contemporary England*. Oxford: Blackwell.

MacClancy, J. 1997. "Researching Culture in the Basqueland." In S. Nugent and C. Shore, eds., *Anthropology and Cultural Studies*. London: Pluto Press.

MacClancy, Jeremy. 2002. "Introduction: Taking People Seriously." In Jeremy MacClancy, ed., *Exotic No More: Anthropology on the Front Lines*, 1–14. Chicago: University of Chicago Press.

Macdougall, David. 1998. *Transcultural Cinema*. New Jersey: Princeton University Press.

Majors, Richard, and Janet Mancini Billson. 1992. *Cool Pose: The Dilemmas of Black Manhood in America*. New York: Simon and Schuster.

Malinowski, Bronislaw. 1967. *A Diary in the Strict Sense of the Term*. London: Routledge and Kegan Paul.

Malkki, Liisa. 1997. "News and Culture: Transitory Phenomena and the Fieldwork Tradition." In Gupta and Ferguson 1997a:86–101.

Marcus, George E. 1983. "Elite as a Concept, Theory, and Research Tradition."

In G. Marcus, ed., *Elites: Ethnographic Issues*, 7–27. Albuquerque: University of New Mexico Press.

———. 1994. "The Modernist Sensibility in Ethnographic Writing and the Cinematic Metaphor of Montage." In Lucien Taylor, ed. *Visualizing Theory*, 37–53. New York: Routledge.

———. 1995. "Ethnography in/of the World System: The Emergence of Multi-Sited Ethnography." *Annual Review of Anthropology* 24:95–117.

———. 1998a. *Ethnography Through Thick and Thin*. Princeton: Princeton University Press.

———. 1998b. "The Uses of Complicity in the Changing Mise-en-Scène of Anthropological Fieldwork." In *Ethnography Through Thick and Thin*. Princeton: Princeton University Press.

———. 1999a. "What Is At Stake—and Is Not—in the Idea and Practice of Multi-sited Ethnography." *Canberra Anthropology* 22.2:6–14.

———. 1999b. "Critical Anthropology Now: An Introduction." In G. Marcus, ed., *Critical Anthropology Now: Unexpected Contexts, Shifting Constituencies, Changing Agendas*, 3–28. New Mexico: School of American Research Press.

———. 2002. "Beyond Malinowski and After *Writing Culture*: On the Future of Cultural Anthropology and the Predicament of Ethnography." *Australian Journal of Anthropology* 13.2:191–199.

Marcus, George E., and Michael M. Fischer. 1986. *Anthropology as Cultural Critique: An Experimental Moment in the Human Sciences*. Chicago: University of Chicago Press.

Marcus, J. 1991. "The Journey Out to the Centre: The Cultural Appropriation of Ayers Rock." In A. Rutherford, ed., *Aboriginal Culture Today*, 254–274. Sydney: Dangaroo Press-Kunapipi.

Mataira, Peter. 2000. "Mana and Tapu: Sacred Knowledge, Sacred Boundaries." In Harvey 2000a:99–112.

———. 2001. "*Te Kaha o te Waiata*—The Power of Music: Maori Oral Traditions Illustrated by *E Tipu e Rea*." In Karen Ralls-MacLeod and Graham Harvey, eds., *Indigenous Religions: A Companion*, 22–34. London: Cassell.

Mattley, Christine. 1998. "(Dis)Courtesy Stigma: Fieldwork Among Phone Fantasy Workers." In J. Ferrell and M. Hamm, eds., *Ethnography at the Edge: Crime, Deviance, and Field Research*, 146–158. Boston: Northeastern University Press.

Mauss, Marcel. 1954 [1924]. *The Gift*. London: Cohen and West.

McCarthy Brown, Karen. 1991. *Mama Lola: A Vodou Priestess in Brooklyn*. Berkeley: University of California Press.

McCutcheon, Russell T. 1999. *The Insider/Outsider Problem in the Study of Religion*. London: Cassell.

McKay, George. 1996. *Senseless Acts of Beauty: Cultures of Resistance since the Sixties*. London: Verso.

————, ed. 1998. *DIY Culture: Party and Protest in Nineties Britain*. London: Verso.

McKegeney, N. 2001. "To Pay or Not To Pay: Respondents' Motivation for Participating in Research." *Addiction* 96:1237–1238.

McLaren, Peter. 1986. *Schooling as a Ritual Performance: Towards a Political Economy of Educational Symbols and Gestures*. London: Routledge.

Mead, George Herbert. 1934. *Mind, Self, and Society*. Chicago: University of Chicago Press.

Medicine, Beatrice. 2001. *Learning To Be an Anthropologist and Remaining "Native."* Urbana: University of Illinois Press.

Messerschmidt, Donald, ed. 1981. *Anthropologists at Home in North America*. Cambridge: Cambridge University Press.

Metcalf, P. 2001. "Global 'Disjuncture' and the 'Sites' of Anthropology." *Cultural Anthropology* 16.2:165–182.

Miller, Kevin, A. 1977. *Religious Revitalization: The Serpent-Handlers of Appalachia*. M.A. thesis, University of Cincinnati.

Mills, Mary Beth. 1999. *Thai Women in the Global Labor Force*. New Brunswick, NJ: Rutgers University Press.

Mitchell, D. 1999. "Response to Cassuto." Posted 3/15 at http://Chronicle.Com/Colloquy/99disability/06.Htm.

Moffat, Michael. 1992. "Ethnographic Writing About American Culture." *Annual Review of Anthropology* 21:205–229.

Moore, D. 1993. "Ethnography and Illicit Drug Use: Dispatches from an Anthropologist in the 'Field.' " *Addiction Research* 1.1:11–25.

Morgan, M. 1994. *Mutant Message Down Under*. New York: HarperCollins.

Mori, Rie, and Hibari Saike. 1997. *Chuuzaiin Fujin no Deepu na Sekai* (The profound world of expatriate wives). Tokyo: Media Factory.

Morris, Jackie. 1995. "Increasing Aboriginal Claimants' Control of the Native Title Claim Process." In Paul Burke, ed., *The Skills of Native Title Practice: Proceedings of a Workshop*, 1–2. Canberra: Australian Institute of Aboriginal and Torres Strait Islander Studies.

Morris, Rosalind. 2000. *In Place of Origins: Modernity and Its Mediums in Northern Thailand*. Durham, NC: Duke University Press.

Morton, J. 1997. "Essentially Black, Essentially Australian, Essentially Opposed: Australian Anthropology and Its Uses of Identity." In J. Wasserman, ed., *Pacific Answers to Western Hegemony: Cultural Practices of Identity Construction*, 355–385. Oxford: Berg.

Morton, John. 1999. "Anthropology at Home in Australia." *Australian Journal of Anthropology* 10.3:243–258.

Motoyama, Chisato. 1995. *Kouen Debyuu: Hahatachi no Okite* (Play park debut: the unspoken rules among the mothers). Tokyo: DHC.

Mouly, V. S., and J. K. Sankaran. 1995. *Organizational ethnography: An Illustrative Application in the Study of Indian R&D Settings*. California: Sage Publications.

Mulcock, Jane. 2001. "Ethnography in Awkward Spaces: An Anthropology of Cultural Borrowing." *Practicing Anthropology* 23.1:38–42.

———. 2002. *Searching for Our Indigenous Selves: Belonging and Spirituality in Anglo-Celtic Australia*. Ph.D. dissertation, The University of Western Australia.

Nader, Laura. 1974. "Up the Anthropologist—Perspectives from Studying Up." In D. Hymes, ed., *Reinventing Anthropology*, 284–311. New York: Vintage Books.

Narayan, Kirin. 1989. *Storytellers, Saints, and Scoundrels: Folk Narrative in Hindu Religious Teaching*. Philadelphia: University of Pennsylvania Press.

———. 1993. "How Native Is a 'Native' Anthropologist?" *American Anthropologist* 95.3:671–686.

———. 1997. "How Native Is a 'Native' Anthropologist?" In Louise Lamphere, Helena Ragoné, and Patricia Zavella, eds., *Situated Lives: Gender and Culture in Everyday Life*, 23–41. New York: Routledge.

Nash, Dennison. 1963. "The Ethnologist as Stranger: An Essay in the Sociology of Knowledge." *Southwestern Journal of Anthropology* 19:149–167.

Noone, R. 1972. *Rape of the Dream People*. London: Hutchinson.

Nordstrom, C., and A. Robben, eds. 1995. *Fieldwork Under Fire: Contemporary Studies of Violence and Survival*. Berkeley: University of California Press.

Norman, Karin. 2000. "Phoning the Field: Meanings of Place and Involvement in Fieldwork 'at home.' " In Amit 2000a:120–146.

Oakley, A. 1981. "Interviewing Women: A Contradiction in Terms." In H. Roberts, ed., *Doing Feminist Research*, 30–61. London: Routledge and Kegan Paul.

Oates, Joyce Carol. 2001. *Middle Age: A Romance*. London: Fourth Estate.

Okely, Judith. 1992. "Anthropology and Autobiography: Participatory Experience and Embodied Knowledge." In Okely and Callaway 1992:1–28.

———. 1996. *Own or Other Culture*. London: Routledge.

Okely, Judith, and Hellen Callaway, eds. 1992. *Anthropology and Autobiography*. London: Routledge.

Oliver, M. 1992. "Changing the Social Relations of Research Production." *Disability, Handicap, and Society* 7.2:101–114.

———. 1996. *Understanding Disability: From Theory to Practice*. New York: St. Martin's.

Ong, Aihwa. 1995. "Women Out of China: Traveling Tales and Traveling Theories in Post-Colonial Feminism." In Behar and Gordon 1995:350–372.

———. 1997. *Flexible Citizenship*. Durham, NC: Duke University Press.

Oral History Association. 1994. *Principles and Standards*. Washington, D.C.: Oral History Association.

Orange, Claudia. 1987. *The Treaty of Waitangi*. Wellington: Bridget Williams Books.

Ortner, Sherry B. 1995. "Resistance and the Problem of Ethnographic Refusal." *Comparative Studies in Society and History* 37:173–193.

Parkin, D. 1996. "Introduction: The Power of the Bizarre." In D. Parkin, L. Caplan, and H. Fisher, eds., *The Politics of Cultural Performance*. Providence: Bergham Books.

Passaro, Joanne. 1997. "You Can't Take the Subway to the Field!: 'Village' Epistemologies in the Global Village." In Gupta and Ferguson 1997a:147–162.

Pearl, J. 1987. "The Highest Paying Customers: America's Cities and the Cost of Prostitution Control." *Hastings Law Journal* (April):769–800.

Pels, P. 2000. "The Trickster's Dilemma: Ethics and Technologies of the Anthropological Self." In M. Strathern, ed., *Audit Cultures: Anthropological Studies in Accountability, Ethics, and the Academy*. London: Routledge.

Pfeil, F. 1995. *White Guys: Studies in Postmodern Domination and Difference*. London: Verso.

Phongpaichit, Pasuk. 1988. *From Peasant Girls to Bangkok Masseuses*. Geneva: International Labour Organization.

Pieke, F. N. 1995. "Witnessing the 1989 Chinese People's Movement." In Nordstrom and Robben 1995:62–79.

Pink, S. 2000. "Informants Who Come 'Home.' " In Amit 2000a:96–119.

Potter, Jack. 1976. *Thai Peasant Social Structure*. Chicago: University of Chicago Press.

Powdermaker, Hortense. 1966. *Stranger and Friend: The Way of an Anthropologist*. New York: Norton.

Power, R. 1995. "A Model for Qualitative Action Research Amongst Illicit Drug Users." *Addiction Research* 3.3:165–181.

———. 1996. "Rapid Assessment of the Drug-Injecting Situation at Hanoi and Ho Chi Minh City, Viet Nam." *Bulletin on Narcotics* 48.1 and 2:35–52.

———. 2001. "Reflections of Participant Observation in Drugs Research." *Addiction Research* 9.4:325–337.

Pratt, M. L. 1986. "Fieldwork in Common Places." In Clifford and Marcus 1986:27–50.

Prattis, Ian J. 1997. *Anthropology at the Edge: Essays on Culture, Symbol, and Consciousness*. New York: University Press of America.

Punch, Maurice. 1986. *The Politics and Ethics of Fieldwork*. Qualitative Research Methods 3. California: Sage Publications.

Rabinow, P. 1977. *Reflections on Fieldwork in Morocco*. Berkeley: University of California Press.

Radcliffe-Brown, A. R. 1929. "Notes on Totemism in Eastern Australia." *Journal Royal Anthropological Institute, London* 59:399–415.

Ralls-MacLeod, Karen, and Graham Harvey, eds. 2001. *Indigenous Religious Musics*. Aldershot: Ashgate.

Rambo Ronai, Carol. 1992. "The Reflexive Self Through Narrative: A Night in the Life of an Erotic Dancer/Researcher." In C. Ellis and M. Flaherty, eds.,

Investigating Subjectivity: Research on Lived Experience, 102–124. California: Sage Publications.

Rapport, N. 2000. "The Narrative as Fieldwork Technique." In Amit 2000a:71–95.

Reed-Danahay, Deborah. 1996. *Education and Identity in Rural France: The Politics of Schooling*. Oxford: Oxford University Press.

Reinharz, Shulamit. 1997. "Who Am I?: The Need for a Variety of Selves in the Field." In R. Hertz, ed., *Reflexivity and Voice*, 3–20. California: Sage Publications.

Rhodes, Lorna. 2001. "Toward an Anthropology of Prisons." *Annual Review of Anthropology* 30:65–83.

Ritchie, David. 1999. "Construction of Aboriginal Tradition for Public Purpose." In Sandy Toussaint and Jim Taylor, eds., *Applied Anthropology in Australasia*, 255–281. Nedlands: University of Western Australia Press.

Robinson, Gary. 1992. The Reconstruction of a Suicide. Unpublished manuscript, Kensington.

———. 1995. "Violence, Social Differentiation, and the Self." *Oceania* 65.4:323–346.

———. 1997. "Families, Generations, Self: Conflict, Loyalty, and Recognition in an Australian Aboriginal Society." *Ethos* 25.3:302–332.

Rose, Dan. 1990. *Living the Ethnographic Life*. California: Sage Publications.

Rosenberger, Nancy. 1994. "Indexing Hierarchy Through Japanese Gender Relations." In Jane Bachnik and Charles Quinn, eds., *Situated Meaning*, 88–112. Princeton: Princeton University Press.

Rynkiewich, M. A., and J. P. Spradley. 1976. *Ethics and Anthropology: Dilemmas in Fieldwork*. New York: Wiley.

Sachdev, P. 1989. "The Triangle of Fears: Fallacies and Facts." *Child Welfare* 68.5:491–503.

Sartre, Jean-Paul. 1953. *Being and Nothingness: An Essay on Phenomenology*. London: Routledge.

Scheer, J. 1994. "Culture and Disability: An Anthropological Point of View." In E. J. Trickett, R. J. Watts, and D. Berman, eds., *Human Diversity: Perspectives on People in Context*, 244–260. San Francisco: Josey-Bass Publications.

Schensul, J., and M. Le Compte, eds. 1999. *Ethnographer's Toolkit*. California: Altamira Press.

Scheper-Hughes, Nancy. 1992. *Death Without Weeping: The Violence of Everyday Life in Brazil*. Berkeley: University of California Press.

———. 1996. "Small Wars and Invisible Genocides." *Social Science in Medicine* 43.5:889–900.

Scott, James C. 1985. *Weapons of the Weak: Everyday Forms of Peasant Resistance*. New Haven: Yale University Press.

Shakespeare, T. 1996. "Rules of Engagement: Doing Disability Research." *Disability and Society* 11:115–119.

————. 1997. "Researching Disabled Sexuality." In C. Barnes and G. Mercer, eds., *Doing Disability Research*, 177–189. Leeds: Disability Press.

Shakespeare, T., K. Gillespie-Sells, and D. Davies. 1996. *The Sexual Politics of Disability: Untold Desires*. New York: Cassell.

Shuttleworth, R. P. 2000a. "The Search for Sexual Intimacy for Men with Cerebral Palsy." *Sexuality and Disability* 18.4:263–282.

————. 2000b. *The Pursuit of Sexual Intimacy for Men with Cerebral Palsy*. Ph.D. dissertation, University of California, San Francisco and Berkeley.

————. 2001. "Symbolic Contexts, Embodied Sensitivities, and the Lived Experience of Sexually Relevant, Interpersonal Encounters for a Man with Severe Cerebral Palsy." In L. Rogers and B. Swadener, eds., *Semiotics and Dis/ability: Interrogating Categories of Difference*, 75–95. New York: State University of New York Press.

————. In press. "Disability/Difference." In C. R. Ember and M. Ember, eds., *Encyclopedia of Medical Anthropology: Health and Illness in the World's Cultures*. Kluwer/Plenum.

————. Forthcoming. "Toward a Constructionist Approach to Disability and Sexuality and the Inclusion of Disabled People in the Sexual Rights Movement." In N. F. Teunis, ed., *Sexuality Inequalities: Case Studies from the Field*. New York: Routledge.

Silverman, Martin. 1971. *Disconcerting Issue: Meaning and Struggle in a Resettled Pacific Community*. Chicago: University of Chicago Press.

Simmel, Georg. 1950. *The Sociology of Georg Simmel*. Trans. Kurt H. Wolff. New York: Free Press.

Simon, David, and Edward Burns. 1997. *The Corner: A Year in the Life of an Inner City Neighborhood*. New York: Broadway Books.

Skrbiš, Z. 1999. *Long-Distance Nationalism: Diasporas, Homelands, and Identities*. Aldershot: Ashgate.

Smith, Linda Tuhiwai. 1999. *Decolonizing Methodologies: Research and Indigenous Peoples*. New York: Zed Books.

Sollis, David. 2002. *Queering Death: A Theological Analysis of the Reconnection of Desire and Immortality in the Shadow of AIDS*. Ph.D. dissertation, King Alfred's College, Winchester.

Sontag, Susan. 1961. "The Anthropologist as Hero." In E. Nelson Hayes and Tanya Hayes, eds., *Claude Levi-Strauss: The Anthropologist as Hero*, 184–196. Cambridge, MA: M.I.T. Press.

Spickard, James V., J. Shawn Landres, and Meredith B. McGuire, eds. 2002. *Personal Knowledge and Beyond: Reshaping the Ethnography of Religion*. New York: New York University Press.

Spradley, James. 1980. *Participant Observation*. Fort Worth: Harcourt Brace Jovanovich.

Spradley, James P., and David W. McCurdy. 1975. *Anthropology: The Cultural Perspective*. New York: Wiley.

Stacey, Judith. 1988. "Can There Be a Feminist Ethnography?" *Women's Studies International Forum* 11.1:21–27.

Steinberg, David Joel, ed. 1987. *In Search of Southeast Asia: A Modern History.* Honolulu: University of Hawaii Press.

Stewart, Alex. 1998. *The Ethnographer's Method.* Qualitative Research Methods 46. California: Sage Publications.

Stewart, Kathleen. 1996. *A Space on the Side of the Road: Cultural Poetics of an "Other" America.* Princeton: Princeton University Press.

Stivens, M. 1985. "The Private Life of the Extended Family: Family, Kinship, and Class in a Middle Class Suburb of Sydney." In L. Manderson, ed., *Australian Ways: Anthropological Studies of an Industrialised Society,* 15–32. Sydney: Allen and Unwin.

Stocking, G. 1992. *The Ethnographer's Magic, and Other Essays in the History of Anthropology.,* Madison: University of Wisconsin Press.

Stone, E., and M. Priestley. 1996. "Parasites, Pawns, and Partners: Disability Researchers and the Role of Non-Disabled Researchers." *British Journal of Sociology* 47:699–716.

Straight, Bilinda. 2002. "Introduction: Conflict at the Center of Ethnography." *Anthropology and Humanism* 27.1:3–9.

Strauss, S. 2000. "Locating Yoga: Ethnography and Transnational Practice." In Amit 2000a:162–194.

Subramani. 2001. "The Oceanic Imaginary." *Contemporary Pacific* 13.1:149–162.

Swain, T. 1992. "The Mother Earth Conspiracy: An Australian Episode." *Numen* 38.1:3–26.

Tannenbaum, Nicola. 1999. "Buddhism, Prostitution, and Sex: Limits on the Academic Discourse on Gender in Thailand." In Peter A. Jackson and Nerida M. Cook, eds., *Genders and Sexualities in Modern Thailand,* 243–260. Chiang Mai: Silkworm Books.

Tauroa, Hiwi, and Pat Tauroa. 1986. *Te Marae: A Guide to Customs and Protocol.* Auckland: Reed.

Tawhai, Te Pakaka. 1988. "Maori Religion." In Stewart Sutherland and Peter Clarke, eds., *The Study of Religion: Traditional and New Religion,* 96–105. London: Routledge.

Teaiwa, Katerina. 2002. *Visualizing Te Kainga, Dancing Te Kainga: History and Culture Between Rabi, Banaba, and Beyond.* Ph.D. dissertaion, The Australian National University.

Teaiwa, Teresia. 1995. "Scholarship from a Lazy Native." In Emma Greenwood, Klaus Neumann, and Andrew Sartori, eds., *Work in Flux.* Melbourne: University of Melbourne Press.

———. 1998. "Yaqona/Yagogqu: Routes and Roots of a Displaced Native." *UTS Review: Cultural Studies and New Writing* 4:92–106.

———. 2001a. "Lo(o)sing the Edge." *Contemporary Pacific* 13.2:343–358.

———. 2001b. *Militarism, Tourism, and the Native: Articulations in Oceania.* Ph.D. dissertation, University of California at Santa Cruz.

—. 2002. "Specifying Pacific Studies, for an Asia-Pacific Studies Agenda." Paper presented at *Remaking Asia Pacific Studies: Knowledge, Power and Pedagogy Conference*. Honolulu: School of Hawaiian, Asian and Pacific Islands Studies, University of Hawaii at Manoa.

Telfer, J. R. 2000. "Pursuing Partnerships: Experiences of Intercountry Adoption in an Australian Setting." In P. Selman, ed., *Intercountry Adoption: Developments, Trends, and Perspectives*. London: British Association of Adoption and Fostering.

Thomas, J. 1993. *Doing Critical Ethnography*. California: Sage Publications.

Thomas, Nicholas. 1991. *Entangled Objects: Exchange, Material Culture, and Colonialism in the Pacific*. Cambridge, MA: Harvard University Press.

Thompson, Charles D. 2001. *Maya Identities and the Violence of Place: Borders Bleed*. Aldershot: Ashgate.

Thompson, Paul. 1978. *The Voice of the Past: Oral History*. Oxford: Oxford University Press.

Toth, Jennifer. 1993. *The Mole People: Life in the Tunnels Beneath New York City*. Chicago: Chicago Review Press.

Tourigny, Sylvie C. 1988. *Death or Remission: Stress, Appraisal, and Coping Among Epithelial Ovarian Carcinoma Patients*. Ph.D. dissertation, University of Connecticut.

—. 1993. "Helping to Harm: The Dilemmas of Managing Politically Sensitive Data." *Western Michigan University Center for the Study of Ethics in Society* 6.5 and 6:1–55.

—. 1998. "Some New Dying Trick: African American Youths 'Choosing' HIV/AIDS." *Qualitative Health Research* 8.2:149–167.

—. 2001. "Some New Killing Trick: Welfare Reform and Drug Markets in a US Urban Ghetto." *Social Justice* 28.4:49–71.

Tourigny, Sylvie C., and Delores Jones-Brown. 2001a. "Introduction" *Social Justice* 28.4:1–3.

—. 2001b. "When All is Said and Done . . . : Conclusion." *Social* Justice 28.4:49–71.

Trask, Haunani-Kay. 1991. "Natives and Anthropologists: The Colonial Struggle." *Contemporary Pacific* 3:159–167.

—. 1999. *From a Native Daughter*. Honolulu: University of Hawaii Press.

Trouillot, Michel-Rolph. 1991. "Anthropology and the Savage Slot: The Poetics and Politics of Otherness." In Richard G. Fox, ed., *Recapturing Anthropology: Working in the Present*, 17–44. Santa Fe: School of American Research Press.

Turner, Aaron. 2000. "Embodied Ethnography: Doing Culture." *Social Anthropology* 8.1:51–60.

Turner, Jonathan H. 1978. *The Structure of Sociological Theory*. Rev. ed. Homewood, IL: Dorsey.

Turner, Victor. 1974. *Dramas, Fields, and Metaphors*. Ithaca, NY: Cornell University Press.

Van Esterik, Penny. 1999. "Repositioning Gender, Sexuality, and Power in

Thai Studies." In Peter A. Jackson and Nerida M. Cook, eds., *Genders and Sexualities in Modern Thailand*, 275–289. Chiang Mai: Silkworm Books.

Van Maanen, J. 1988. *Tales of the Field: On Writing Ethnography*. Chicago: University of Chicago Press.

———. 1995. "An End to Innocence: The Ethnography of Ethnography." In J. Van Maanen, ed., *Representation in Ethnography*, 1–35. California: Sage Publications.

Vernon, A. 2000. "Disabled People Doing Disability Research." Paper presented at the Annual Meeting of the Society for Disability Studies, July.

Visweswaran, Kamala. 1994. *Fictions of Feminist Ethnography*. Minneapolis: University of Minnesota Press.

Viveiros de Castro, Eduardo. 1999. "The Transformation of Objects Into Subjects in Amerindian Ontologies." Paper given at the 98th Annual Meeting of the American Anthropological Association, Chicago.

Vonnegut, Kurt, Jr. 1972. *Slaughterhouse Five*. New York: Dell Books.

Wadell, Eric, Epeli Hau'ofa, and Vijay Naidu. 1993. *Towards a New Oceania: Rediscovering Our Sea of Islands*. Suva: Beake House.

Wagner, Melinda Bollar. 1997. "The Study of Religion in American Society." In Stephen D. Glazier, ed., *Anthropology of Religion: A Handbook*, 85–101. Westport, CT: Greenwood.

Waldram, James. 1998. "Anthropology in Prison: Negotiating Consent and Accountability with a Captured Population." *Human Organization* 57.2:238–244.

Wallis, R. 1985. "Betwixt Therapy and Salvation: The Changing Face of the Human Potential Movement." In R. K. Jones, ed., *Sickness and Sectarianism: Exploratory Studies in Medical and Religious Sectarianism*. Hampshire: Gower.

Wallis, Robert. 2003. *Shamans/Neo-Shamans: Ecstasy, Alternative Archaeologies and Contemporary Pagans*. London: Routledge.

Warner, W. L. 1969. *A Black Civilization*. Gloucester, MA: Peter Smith.

Watson, C. W., ed. 1999. *Being There: Fieldwork in Anthropology*. London: Pluto Press.

Wax, Murray. 1982. "Research Reciprocity Rather Than Informed Consent in Fieldwork." In Joan Sieber, ed., *The Ethics of Social Research: Fieldwork, Regulations, and Publications*, 33–48. New York: Springer.

Weaver, Jace. 1998. "From I-Hermeneutics to We-Hermeneutics: Native Americans and the Post-Colonial." *Native American Religious Identity: Unforgotten Gods*, 1–25. New York: Orbis Books.

Weiner, J. 1995. "Anthropologists, Historians, and the Secret of Social Knowledge." *Anthropology Today* 11.5:3–7.

Weitzer, Ronald. 2000. "Why We Need More Research on Sex Work." In R. Weitzer, ed., *Sex for Sale: Prostitution, Pornography, and the Sex Industry*. New York: Routledge.

Welch, Christina. 2002. "Appropriating the Didjeridu and the Sweat Lodge: New Age Baddies and Indigenous Victims?" *Journal of Contemporary Religion* 17.1:21–38.

Wendt, Albert. 1976. "Towards a New Oceania." *Mana Review* 1:4–60.

———. 1999. "Tatauing the Postcolonial Body." In Vilsoni Hereniko and Rob Wilson, eds., *Inside Out: Literature, Cultural Politics, and Identity in the New Pacific*, 399–412. Lanham: Rowman and Littlefield.

Wengle, John L. 1984. "Anthropological Training and the Quest for Immortality." *Ethos* 12.3:223–244.

Whitty, Geoff, Sally Power, and David Halpin. 1998. *Devolution and Choice in Education: The School, the State, and the Market*. Canberra: ACER Press.

Wiebel, W. W. 1990. "Identifying and Gaining Access to Hidden Populations." In Elizabeth Lambert, ed., *The Collection and Interpretation of Data from Hidden Populations*. NIDA Research Monograph Series 98. Rockville: NIDA.

Williams, Maslyn, and Barrie Macdonald. 1985. *The Phosphateers: A History of the British Phosphate Commissioners and the Christmas Island Phosphate Commission*. Melbourne: Melbourne University Press.

Wilson, Bryan. 1970. *Religious Sects: A Sociological Study*. New York: McGraw-Hill.

Wilson, Peter J. 1974. *Oscar: An Inquiry Into the Nature of Sanity*. New York: Vintage Books.

Wolcott, Harry. 1973. *The Man in the Principal's Office: An Ethnography*. New York: Holt, Rinehart, and Winston.

Wolf, Diane, ed. 1996. *Feminist Dilemmas in Fieldwork*. Colorado: Westview Press.

Young, David E., and Jean-Guy Goulet, eds. *Being Changed by Cross-Cultural Encounters: The Anthropology of Extraordinary Experience*. Peterborough: Broadview Press.

Zinsser, William, ed. 1995. *Inventing the Truth: The Art and Craft of Memoir*. 2nd ed. Boston: Houghton-Mifflin.

CONTRIBUTORS

Michael V. Angrosino is Professor of Anthropology and Religious Studies at the University of South Florida. He is an applied anthropologist and oral historian specializing in mental health policy and service delivery, and in the influence of organized religious bodies on social policy. His most recent books include: *Opportunity House: Ethnographic Stories of Mental Retardation* (AltaMira, 1999); *Talking About Cultural Diversity* (AltaMira, 2001); *Doing Cultural Anthropology* (Waveland, 2002); and *The Culture of the Sacred* (Waveland, forthcoming 2004).

Susan Beckerleg is an applied anthropologist with over twenty years' experience in development issues, particularly international health, in East and West Africa, and the Middle East. Her interests include sexual health, illicit drug use, and the interface between traditional medicine and Western medicine. In 1995 she cofounded the Omari Project, a local Kenyan organization that aims to treat and prevent heroin use. She has worked with Gillian Lewando Hundt since 1994, first in Palestine and Israel and then in Kenya. She works freelance and is also an Associate Research Fellow of the Institute of Health at the University of Warwick.

Jim Birckhead is a Senior Lecturer in Anthropology and member of the Johnstone Centre (Research in Natural Resources and Society) at Charles Sturt University, Albury, N.S.W., Australia. His research interests include indigenous connection to "country," participatory approaches to conservation and development, anthropology of religion, and the cultural politics of "tradition" with respect to "Appalachia" and indigenous Australia. He is a coauthor of *Culture, Conservation, and Biodiversity* (Wiley, 1996).

John M. Coggeshall is a Professor of Anthropology at Clemson University (South Carolina). He has published on prison culture, U.S. regional folklife, vernacular architecture, sustainable tourism, and pedagogy. His current interests are in heritage tourism and regional folklife. Significant recent publications include " 'Ladies' Behind Bars: A Liminal Gender as Cultural Mirror," in *The Best of Anthropology Today* (Routledge, 2002); *Carolina Piedmont Country* (University

Press of Mississippi, 1996); and "A Culture of Servitude: The Impact of Tourism and Development on South Carolina's Coast" (with L. Faulkenberry, K. Backman, and S. Backman), *Human Organization* 59 (2000).

Val Colic-Peisker has researched Croatian postwar migration to Australia and recent refugee intakes from Bosnia and Croatia. She has published extensively in Croatian and English and is currently in the process of publishing two books on Croatians in Australia: *Migration, Values, and Identity* and *Croatian Stories*. Val is a postdoctoral research fellow at Murdoch University, Western Australia.

Ida Fadzillah is an Assistant Professor in Anthropology at Middle Tennessee State University. She conducted research on Northern Thai adolescent girls' "life strategy narratives" and is currently working on turning her dissertation into a book. Her article "The Amway Connection: How Transnational Ideas of Beauty and Money Affect Northern Thai Girls' Perceptions of their Future Options" is to appear in *Youth-Scapes: Popular Cultures, National Ideologies, Global Markets* (University of Pennsylvania Press, forthcoming).

Martin Forsey is an Associate Lecturer in Anthropology and Sociology at the University of Western Australia. His research interests include the anthropology and sociology of schooling, organizational culture and change, race and racism. He has recently become interested in the power of life history for revealing larger social patterns.

Graham Harvey is a Lecturer in Religious Studies at the Open University, UK. His publications include *The True Israel* (Brill, 1996), *Contemporary Paganism: Listening People* (New York University Press, 1997), *Indigenous Religions: A Companion* (Continuum, 2000), and *Shamanism: A Reader* (Routledge, 2003). His current research concerns the construction and performance of indigenous diaspora identities.

Lynne Hume is an anthropologist and Associate Professor in Studies in Religion at the University of Queensland, Brisbane, Australia. She has researched and published on Australian indigenous culture, contemporary Paganism, and new religious movements, and is currently working on a book on altered states of consciousness. Hume's recent publications include *Witchcraft and Paganism in Australia* (Melbourne University Press, 1997) and *Ancestral Power: The Dreaming, Consciousness, and Aboriginal Australians* (Melbourne University Press, 2002).

Patty Kelly is an Assistant Professor of Anthropology at John Jay College of Criminal Justice and a yoga teacher in New York City. She received her Ph.D. in anthropology from the City University of New York Graduate Center in 2002.

Sawa Kurotani is Assistant Professor of Anthropology at the University of Redlands, California. Her main research interests are globalization, Japanese national identity, and gender. She has also written on Japanese popular culture, consumption, food, urban folklore, social organization, and transnational businesses. Her first book is *A Long Vacation: Narratives of Home, Travel, and Self* (Duke University Press, forthcoming).

Gillian Lewando Hundt is Professor of Social Sciences in Health at the University of Warwick, where she directs the Institute of Health in the School of Health and Social Studies and leads a team of social scientists who teach in the Leicester Warwick Medical Schools. Her research experience in the Middle East, Kenya, and South Africa falls within applied medical anthropology and the sociology of health and illness. Her current research program is on Local Voices and Action on Global Health Issues with a focus on access, inequalities, gender, and ethnicity. She is experienced in the interface of anthropology and epidemiology.

Stewart Muir is completing a Ph.D. in the School of Social Sciences, La Trobe University. His dissertation research centers on the intersection of New Age and "alternative" spiritualities with representations of Aboriginal people and cultures. Since 1996 Stewart has also been employed as an Aboriginal Cultural Heritage Consultant.

Jane Mulcock is a Postdoctoral Fellow in Anthropology and Sociology at the University of Western Australia. Her Ph.D. research explored ideas of indigeneity and belonging among Australian Anglo-Celtic settler-descendants involved in the New Age movement. She is now researching and teaching in the area of environmental anthropology.

Gary Robinson began ethnographic fieldwork among the Tiwi of Bathurst and Melville Islands in 1985. Since then, he has continued his association with the Tiwi, conducting an evaluation of health services on the Islands and continuing to work with young people and their families. He currently directs a research center at Charles Darwin University in the Northern Territory.

Russell Shuttleworth is a medical anthropologist who focuses on disability issues. For the academic year 2002–2003, he was awarded an Ed Robert's Postdoctoral Fellowship in Disability Studies at the University of California, Berkeley. He worked for many years as a personal assistant for disabled men, and has published widely in the areas of disability studies, the anthropology of impairment-disability, and disability and sexuality studies.

Katerina Martina Teaiwa completed her Ph.D. in anthropology in 2003 at The Australian National University. She is now an Assistant Professor in the Center for Pacific Islands Studies at the University of Hawai'i at Manoa. Her research and teaching interests are women's studies, dance and the body in Oceania, cultural studies, globalization, and ethnographic film.

Jonathan Telfer was a fully qualified social worker and social anthropologist. While working full-time as a probation and parole officer, he studied part-time for a B.A. and a Ph.D. in the Department of Anthropology at the University of Adelaide.

Telfer's thesis on the anthropology of adoption practices was based on research in South Australia. At the time of his death in late September 2003, he had several papers either published or in press. His first book, *Duty of Care: A Brief History of Correctional Practices in South Australia* (The South Australian Institute of Justice Studies 2003), was published posthumously.

Sylvie Tourigny is a medical sociologist. She was Founding Director of Behavioural Studies and is currently a Senior Lecturer in Social Sciences and at the Queensland Alcohol and Drug Research and Education Centre, at the University of Queensland, Brisbane, Australia. Her work focuses on communities faced with complex converging public health problems, and the experiential consequences of marginalization. She has worked extensively with persons with HIV/AIDS, gang members and minority youth, welfare-defunded households under U.S. "welfare reform" policies, and persons involved in drug markets. She also has a keen interest in issues of leadership and professional ethics.

INDEX

CPSIA information can be obtained at www.ICGtesting.com
Printed in the USA
236307LV00001B/1/P

9 780231 130042